Decisively Digital

From Creating a Culture to Designing Strategy

Alexander Loth

WILEY

Copyright © 2021 by John Wiley & Sons, Inc. All rights reserved.

Published by John Wiley & Sons, Inc., Hoboken, New Jersey.

Published simultaneously in Canada.

No part of this publication may be reproduced, stored in a retrieval system or transmitted in any form or by any means, electronic, mechanical, photocopying, recording, scanning or otherwise, except as permitted under Sections 107 or 108 of the 1976 United States Copyright Act, without either the prior written permission of the Publisher, or authorization through payment of the appropriate per-copy fee to the Copyright Clearance Center, 222 Rosewood Drive, Danvers, MA 01923, (978) 750-8400, fax (978) 646-8600. Requests to the Publisher for permission should be addressed to the Permissions Department, John Wiley & Sons, Inc., 111 River Street, Hoboken, NJ 07030, (201) 748-6011, fax (201) 748-6008, or online at www.wiley.com/go/permissions.

Limit of Liability/Disclaimer of Warranty: While the publisher and author have used their best efforts in preparing this book, they make no representations or warranties with respect to the accuracy or completeness of the contents of this book and specifically disclaim any implied warranties of merchantability or fitness for a particular purpose. No warranty may be created or extended by sales representatives or written sales materials. The advice and strategies contained herein may not be suitable for your situation. You should consult with a professional where appropriate. Neither the publisher nor author shall be liable for any loss of profit or any other commercial damages, including but not limited to special, incidental, consequential, or other damages.

For general information on our other products and services please contact our Customer Care Department within the United States at (877) 762-2974, outside the United States at (317) 572-3993 or fax (317) 572-4002.

Wiley also publishes its books in a variety of electronic formats. Some content that appears in print may not be available in electronic formats. For more information about Wiley products, visit our web site at www.wiley.com.

Library of Congress Control Number: 2021936782

ISBN: 978-1-119-73728-5
ISBN: 978-1-119-73748-3 (ebk)
ISBN: 978-1-119-73729-2 (ebk)

Trademarks: WILEY and the Wiley logo are trademarks or registered trademarks of John Wiley & Sons, Inc. and/or its affiliates, in the United States and other countries, and may not be used without written permission. All other trademarks are the property of their respective owners. John Wiley & Sons, Inc. is not associated with any product or vendor mentioned in this book.

SKY10027170_052421

For Yue and Noah. And for my parents.

About the Author

Alexander Loth is a digital strategist with a background in computational nuclear research. For more than 12 years he has advised many large companies in their transformations as they become digital organizations. Since 2019 he has been with Microsoft as executive advisor.

Alexander has an MBA from the Frankfurt School of Finance & Management, where he is also a lecturer on the subject of the digital society. Prior to working for Microsoft, he worked for Tableau (now part of Salesforce), for Capgemini, for SAP, and at the European Organization for Nuclear Research (CERN).

Furthermore, Alexander studied at the China Europe International Business School (CEIBS) in Shanghai and was a postgraduate researcher at the University of the West of England's Department of Computer Science. His research focused on machine-learning algorithms for geodistributed petabyte-scale big-data processing.

A cofounder of fintech advisory Futura Analytics, Alexander has written and spoken extensively on topics such as digital transformation, artificial intelligence, blockchain, and business analytics. Alexander is the author of the book *Visual Analytics with Tableau*.

Acknowledgments

I would like to thank the many people who helped make this book a reality. They provided critical feedback on initial drafts, extremely useful input during many conversations, and general guidance throughout the whole project. They include the people at Wiley and my colleagues at Microsoft. I would like to specifically mention the following people:

Vladimir Alexeev, Bora Beran, Marcel Bickert, Sofie Blakstad, Sarah Burnett, Ian Choo, Edna Conway, Darren Cooper, Sophia Cullen, Achim Dettweiler, Sebastian Durnwalder, Martin Duschek, Duncan Elliott, Lee Feinberg, Elissa Fink, Pete Gaughan, Patrick Glauner, Mohamed Abdel Hadi, Henna A. Karna, Patrick Kirchgäßner, Daniel Kompe, Andreas Kopp, Kerstin Krämer, Mark Kromer, Barath Kumar Rajasekaran, Jens Lamparth, Celeste Luna, Christy Marble, Yilian Villanueva Martinez, Jim Minatel, Jordan Morrow, Ben Niu, Nico Peters, André Rabold, Florian Ramseger, Derek Roos, Philipp Sandner, Sven Sommerfeld, Kerem Tomak, Cameron Turner, Patrick Walsh, Louise Watson, Kim Wimpsett, Tatyana Yakushev, Qiang Yang, and Yue Zhou-Loth.

I especially thank my family for their patience and encouragement.

Thank you very much!

—Alexander Loth

Contents

X   CONTENTS

Foreword
by Bernard Marr

We are amidst a fourth industrial revolution that, like the previous three industrial revolutions, will transform many key aspects of business and society. While the previous industrial revolutions were driven by single technological shifts (steam power, electricity, and computers), over recent years, we have seen amazing advances in technologies such as artificial intelligence, big data analytics, cloud computing, virtual and augmented reality, the internet of things (IoT), 5G mobile networks, blockchains, intelligent robots, 3D printing, gene editing, and synthetic biology. Each of these trends could have triggered a new industrial revolution on its own, however, the simultaneous emergence of these technologies creates a perfect storm of unprecedented technology-driven innovation and transformation. The main consequence is that every single business, in every industry, has to become a technology business and a digital business. Any business that doesn't put technology and digitization at the center of their business strategy will simply be left behind.

The global coronavirus pandemic has only accelerated this transformation, as more business processes and customer interfaces needed to be digitized to enable organizations to carry on operating. It forced many organizations, even those that would not have focused on digital transformation, to prioritize it as a factor of survival. Over the past 12 months we have seen digital transformations that would have taken many years to complete under normal circumstances. As traditional channels to market got cut off as countries went into lockdown and as people required digital cloud-based working environments to carry on working from home, digital transformation was fast tracked. Today, we live in a digital-first environment that will never go back to what it was prior to the pandemic.

Therefore, every business needs to be decisively digital and create the culture and strategy to transform so it can thrive in the future. With this book, Alexander Loth has done an amazing job in creating a narrative that covers so many key aspects and challenges of this journey toward digitization. What's more, he has brought together some of the brightest voices and smartest thought leaders from leading organizations across many industries, to bring you unmissable insights and real-world examples to showcase how technology can improve your businesses and drive business results today and tomorrow.

This book is not only a joy to read, it is packed with invaluable advice for anyone who wants to lead an organization through the fourth industrial revolution. Enjoy!

—Bernard Marr, futurist, influencer and best-selling author of
Tech Trends in Practice and *The Intelligence Revolution*

Introduction

*D*ecisively Digital: From Creating a Culture to Designing Strat-egy is intended to be an overview of various state-of-the-art topics that are essential for organizations that want to transform and go digital. This book contains 24 interviews with executives, entrepreneurs, and researchers, as well as two real-life customer examples. My hope is that you will find useful ideas and inspiration for understanding the current trends and how to effectively establish a digital strategy that drives success in your organization, just as I have seen with the many organizations that I have had the privilege of working with over recent years.

The book should be of interest to different audiences:

- Chief information officers (CIOs), chief digital officers (CDOs), and any executive who crafts their organization's digital journey
- Professionals who want to understand how technology can improve their work
- Generally, anybody with interest in modern technology and a desire to understand how this blends into business

To follow the contents of this book, the reader requires neither a background in mathematics nor any programming experience.

Book Structure

This book is structured in six parts. Part I: Digital Strategy, provides a framework to identify requirements and define a strategy tailored to your individual organization.

Each of the remaining parts is dedicated to a specific strategic topic:

- Part II: Digital Culture and Modern Work
- Part III: Data Democracy and Analytics
- Part IV: Big Data Processing and Cloud Computing
- Part V: Artificial Intelligence
- Part VI: Process Automation, Blockchain, and the Internet of Things (IoT)

The strategic topic parts include interviews as well as real-life customer examples.

About the Interviews

All interviews in this book have some questions in common. The interviews start with personal questions to set the stage, and they conclude with questions for advice that you might immediately apply. Most questions are, however, tailored to catch the most relevant insights and ideas. These ideas serve as a toolkit for assembling your own digital strategy.

During the interviews, I also received counterquestions. I have answered the most common of them in the Appendix, "Reciprocity: Answering Some of My Own Questions."

Companion Website

All amendments, updates and recommended reading materials will be posted to www.decisivelydigital.org/.

> *Any sufficiently advanced technology is indistinguishable from magic.*
> —*Arthur C. Clarke*

Part I

Digital Strategy

Part I

Digital Strategy

Chapter 1

Introduction
to Digital Strategy

The digital age is here to stay. Unfortunately, many organizations do not take advantage of its possibilities. Every industry is facing transformational change right now. And for many organizations, how they defined success yesterday is not how they are defining it today. For example, while growth may have been the only goal in the past, other metrics, such as a sustainability score, have become essential nowadays.

Having endless possibilities (and new competitive challenges), organizations are asking themselves how their businesses must evolve to survive and thrive. The answer to this question is digital strategy!

A digital strategy will lead the way for your organization to become part of the digital age, also known as the Fourth Industrial Revolution. "The changes are so profound that, from the perspective of human history, there has never been a time of greater promise or potential peril," says Professor Klaus Schwab, founder and executive chairman of the World Economic Forum. "My concern, however, is that decision-makers are too often caught in traditional, linear (and nondisruptive) thinking or too absorbed by immediate concerns to think strategically about the forces of disruption and innovation shaping our future."[i]

Organizations that have already embarked on their transformation journey are seeing the advantages. Disney, for example, produced hand-drawn movies in the past, relying on a very costly distribution system. Today Disney has gone completely digital, from movie production to the screen, leveraging the entire value chain. Disney's new digital endpoint, the streaming service Disney+, is even outperforming its own forecasts.[ii]

With cloud-powered technologies, all organizations have access to AI-infused tools and modern work capabilities tailored to their needs. With scalability of implementation and speed of adoption, these organizations are seeing increased cost savings and more productive employees across all departments.

This is called *digital maturity* and is basically the sum of *digital capabilities* that are available in the organization. Every organization in every industry will increasingly need to level up their digital maturity to be successful and grow.

Strategic Topics

An organization's digital strategy is characterized by the application of new technologies to existing business activities and a focus on the enablement of new digital capabilities. These new digital capabilities can be clustered into five strategic topics (which form the structure of this book).

- **Modern Work (Part II)**: How does technology change the way we work and communicate, and how does this change interfere with culture and strategy?
- **Data Democracy and Analytics (Part III)**: How can every person achieve more by being enabled to access, understand, and communicate data?
- **Big Data Processing and Cloud Computing (Part IV)**: How do we retrieve, store, and process vast amounts of data?
- **Artificial Intelligence (AI) (Part V)**: How do intelligent agents take actions that maximize the chances of successfully achieving our business goals?

- **Process Automation, Blockchain, and the Internet of Things (IoT) (Part VI)**: How does direct integration of the physical world into computer-based systems result in efficiency improvements, economic benefits, and reduced human exertions?

Data is treated as a key strategic asset, and organizations are committed to realizing value from it. Therefore, data democracy and analytics and big data processing and cloud computing can be collectively referred to as *data strategy*.

Culture

Henry Ford said, "Culture eats strategy for breakfast." This statement has probably never been as relevant as it is today. Many employees started working from home because of the COVID-19 pandemic as this book was being written. Micromanagement, which is characterized by mistrust, became obsolete, giving rise to a new, digital culture of trustful cooperation. Crafting and fostering culture within an organization is essential. Culture supports the digital strategy, enabling and empowering all people in an organization during transformational change.

Organizations are best fitted to go through a transformation when employees are unified and working with shared values and ideas. They have a culture that keeps their team connected, and an organizational mindset rooted in flexibility and openness: openness to new ideas, technologies, and digital capabilities.

Organizations whose culture accepts the diversity of personalities, abilities, ideas, and those approaches that are requirements for driving an organization forward are those that do best with adopting new digital capabilities.

Culture is not mapped 1:1 to a single strategic topic. Culture spans multiple strategic topics, which also influence each other, as shown in Figure 1.1.

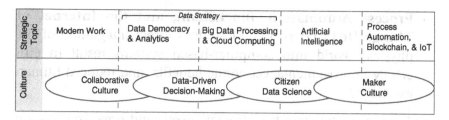

Figure 1.1 Strategic topics and culture

Collaborative Culture

Collaborative culture helps organizations maximize employee knowledge and capabilities. Ideas and information can spread more easily when employees communicate and collaborate freely across functional and departmental lines, which will have tremendous impact on the organization's performance. Amy Djeridi, group head of Workplace Products at AXA, explains: "Now that working together can be seamless, employees no longer struggle to make teamwork happen with time-consuming tools and technology. Today, we're focusing on the business stakes."[iii]

Adopting a collaborative culture breaks up knowledge silos. Employees collaborate on documents, spreadsheets, dashboards, and presentations, all while using chat and video call features. This enables employees to quickly exchange ideas and help each other to achieve more and achieve it much more quickly.

All kinds of information — from raw-data sources to polished presentations — are shared and searchable by everyone in the digital organization. This means employees seldom need to start from scratch but instead can leverage existing assets.

The collaborative culture is based on the strategic topics of modern work and data democracy and analytics and supports data-driven decision-making.

Data-Driven Decision-Making

Data-driven decision-making is the culture of making organizational decisions based on actual data rather than on observation or intuition alone. Data-driven decision-making involves collecting data based on measurable goals or key performance indicators (KPIs), analyzing patterns and facts from these insights, and using them to refine business strategies and activities that benefit the organization's goals.

The culture of data-driven decision-making is based on the strategic topics of data democracy and analytics and big data processing and cloud computing, and supports collaborative culture and the culture of citizen data science.

Citizen Data Science

While an academic education is necessary for data science, citizen data science is more a matter of attitude. In principle, every employee, even one without knowledge of statistics and programming, can become a citizen data scientist. Therefore, citizen data science should be viewed as a culture.

According to the analysts from Gartner, a citizen data scientist defines a citizen data scientist as a person who creates models that use advanced analytics and predictive and prescriptive capabilities, but whose primary job function is outside the field of statistics and analytics.[iv]

Citizen data scientists tell stories about a company based on company data by translating this data into a language that everyone can understand. Most of all, citizen data scientists need to be curious. They have to be able to recognize potentially useful information in a large amount of data and to highlight and translate key findings for other employees and departments.

The culture of citizen data science is based on the strategic topics of big data processing and cloud computing and artificial intelligence, and supports data-driven decision-making and the maker culture.

Maker Culture

The maker culture encourages employees to think about what kind of apps, processes, or algorithms they could build for their organization. While it once required software development skills, building apps today can be done within minutes and without writing a single line of code. This creativity is not limited to apps; it also includes process automation and algorithms that can be easily reused in the entire organization.

The maker culture is based on the strategic topics of artificial intelligence, process automation, blockchain, and Internet of Things (IoT), and it supports citizen data science.

Impact

Every organization has a set of core competencies and unique assets. The digital strategy needs to identify specific differentiators that can unlock impact beyond the original core competencies and leverage the unique assets.

Core competencies can manifest in different ways depending on the industry. Unique assets might be physical assets like retail stores, proximity to customers, or intellectual property. While some of these impacts are specific to core competencies and unique assets, some impacts are more generic and can be triggered by fostering a certain culture. Here are some examples:

- **Attracting new employees**, enabled by the collaborative culture
- **Knowledge generation and exchange**, enabled by the collaborative culture and the culture of data-driven decision-making
- **Understanding customer behavior**, enabled by the culture of data-driven decision-making and the culture of citizen data science
- **Improving products and customer service**, enabled by the culture of citizen data science and the maker culture
- **Reducing time to market**, enabled by the maker culture

There are, of course, also certain impacts that cannot directly map to the culture but are conditioned by a strategic topic directly. Here are some noteworthy examples:

- **Reducing total cost of ownership (TCO)**, enabled by big data processing and cloud computing

- **Scalability**, enabled by big data processing and cloud computing
- **Agility**, enabled by process automation, blockchain, and IoT

Furthermore, it is possible that impact initiated by a certain culture helps to improve another culture within the organization, for example, by using the insights from remote work data to understand the way the team works (data-driven decision-making) and to modify future tasks and processes for better collaboration (collaborative culture).

Digital Capabilities

Enabling impacts requires continually developing a wide range of digital capabilities. Let's stick with the previously mentioned examples and take a look at which digital capabilities would be required to pursue them.

Attracting New Employees
- **Unified communications:** Using chat and video call beside traditional channels, such as email and phone
- **Collaboration tools:** Working together on notes, documents, spreadsheets, and so on
- **Remote work:** Working from everywhere with secure access to all company resources

Knowledge Generation and Exchange
- **Self-service business intelligence:** Asking your own questions without tying up your traditional business intelligence (BI) team
- **Visual analytics:** Seeing and understanding patterns with interactive visual interfaces[v]
- **Data literacy:** Communicating insights for a human-information discourse

Understanding Customer Behavior
- **Stream processing:** Streaming customer feedback and needs in real time

- **Governed data discovery/mining:** Acquiring new or enriching existing data sources that the organization can rely on
- **Social media ingestion:** Improving customer retention by leveraging social media data

Improving Products and Customer Service

- **Machine learning:** Providing the ability to automatically learn and improve from experience without being explicitly programmed
- **Chat bots and recommender systems:** Providing information to users according to their preferences via a chat interface
- **Human-in-the-loop:** Leveraging the power of human intelligence to improve machine learning–based models

Reducing Time to Market

- **Low-code/no-code:** Allowing citizen developers to drag and drop application components, connect them, and create platform-agnostic apps
- **Application design (UI/UX):** Creating products that provide a meaningful user interface (UI) and a relevant user experience (UX)
- **Cybersecurity:** Protecting computer systems from the damage or theft of data, as well as from service disruption

Reducing Total Cost of Ownership (TCO)

- **Serverless architecture:** Eliminating the need for server software and hardware management
- **Data center transformation:** Migrating the on-premise IT infrastructure to a cloud hyper-scale environment
- **DevOps:** Shortening the development life cycle and providing continuous feature delivery

Completing Your Digital Strategy Big Picture

Once you've identified the impacts that you want to generate and the corresponding digital capabilities, it is time to complete your digital strategy big picture, as shown in Figure 1.2.

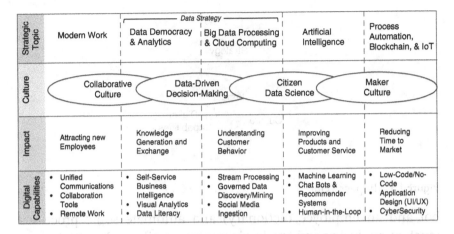

		Data Strategy			
Strategic Topic	Modern Work	Data Democracy & Analytics	Big Data Processing & Cloud Computing	Artificial Intelligence	Process Automation, Blockchain, & IoT
Culture	Collaborative Culture	Data-Driven Decision-Making	Citizen Data Science		Maker Culture
Impact	Attracting new Employees	Knowledge Generation and Exchange	Understanding Customer Behavior	Improving Products and Customer Service	Reducing Time to Market
Digital Capabilities	• Unified Communications • Collaboration Tools • Remote Work	• Self-Service Business Intelligence • Visual Analytics • Data Literacy	• Stream Processing • Governed Data Discovery/Mining • Social Media Ingestion	• Machine Learning • Chat Bots & Recommender Systems • Human-in-the-Loop	• Low-Code/No-Code • Application Design (UI/UX) • CyberSecurity

Figure 1.2 Digital strategy big picture

This digital strategy big picture serves as reference while you adopt a strategic topic, foster culture, generate impact, and implement digital capabilities. The template is available online.[vi]

While the first rows, strategic topic and culture, should be fairly static, the impact and digital capabilities vary depending on your industry and your current level of digital maturity and organizational readiness.

Impact Venn

Your digital strategy will not generate impact if you don't foster culture or acquire digital capabilities, as illustrated in Figure 1.3. As you will probably not start on a greenfield, it is important to identify and fill the missing pieces to generate impact.

For example, an organization wants to create apps and automate processes faster and therefore sets up a low-code/no-code platform. However, the platform is seldom used because the organization lacks the maker culture. Once the employees are nurtured with workshops, hackathons, and casual training days, many employees gain new ideas and have an intrinsic motivation to pursue them. Soon after, the employees develop many apps (such as an HR chat

Figure 1.3 Impact Venn

bot and an employee dictionary) and automate some processes (such as analyzing and tagging incoming email attachments).

Digital Maturity and Organizational Readiness

Acquiring more digital capabilities will increase the organization's level of *digital maturity*. Providing digital capabilities is just the first step into transforming into a digital business. Helping employees to adopt these new digital capabilities is crucial for any digital strategy.

The level of adoption is called *organizational readiness*. While some digital capabilities will be adopted more quickly (like unified communications), some digital capabilities require some more training or skilling initiatives (like low-code/no-code). The level of adoption depends on how the organization nurtures the skills of the employees who then drive the innovation process and manifest it into your business processes. This is how you truly enhance your digital capabilities.

These are further aspects to consider that can drive organizational readiness:

- Are our employees well connected?
- Do we need a center of excellence or user groups?
- Does everyone have the resources needed to do their job?
- How are people being trained to work in new ways?

Digital maturity and organizational readiness can be tracked as KPIs for your entire digital strategy — or for each strategic topic. Measuring digital maturity and organizational readiness by strategic topic delivers a good indicator that helps you to define or adjust your digital strategy.

Figure 1.4 shows an example of both values plotted by strategic topic. In this graph we see that the organization has plenty of digital capabilities for big data processing and cloud computing, but the employees are not yet trained accordingly. On the other side, the employees are ready for modern work, but the organization has not yet adopted the required digital capabilities.

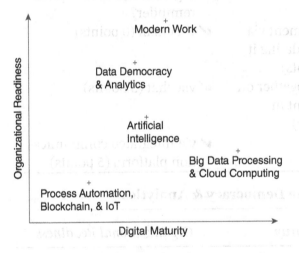

Figure 1.4 Graph showing digital maturity and organizational readiness by strategic topic

Digital Maturity Assessment

A digital maturity assessment, shown in Figure 1.5, can help you to understand which digital capabilities are already available in your organization and if the organization is ready to use these capabilities. These questions are quite generic and should be seen as a rough blueprint that you can enhance and fine-tune for specific audiences within your organization.

The questions for this assessment are grouped by strategic topic and have two sections each.

- **Digital Maturity**: The digital capabilities that are available in the organization
- **Organizational Readiness**: The digital capabilities that are adopted by the employees

Modern Work

Digital Maturity	*Organizational Readiness*
How do you work together on the same document?	How do colleagues in your organization send a quick reminder?
✔ Sending the document via email and consolidating it afterwards (0 points)	✔ via email (0 points)
✔ Working online together on the same document in real time (5 points)	✔ via chat (3 points)
	✔ via integrated communication platform (5 points)

Data Democracy & Analytics

Digital Maturity	*Organizational Readiness*
What do you do when you need another type of aggregation in your report/dashboard? ✔ Nothing (0 points) ✔ Ask the BI department and wait some days (1 point) ✔ Copy data from the PDF report and perform some magic in Excel within hours (3 points) ✔ Use a self-service BI tool to modify this dashboard within minutes (5 points)	Do employees have access to analytics tools and data sources to ask questions of their own business data? E.g., an accounts-receivable specialist analyzing his own collection effectiveness rate or analyzing average days outstanding for invoices in a certain region ✔ No (0 points) ✔ Limited on certain teams/ roles (3 points) ✔ Available for everyone (5 points)

Big Data Processing & Cloud Computing

Digital Maturity	*Organizational Readiness*
Where is your organization's data stored? ✔ Somewhere on a network share (0 points) ✔ On a relational database on premises (1 point) ✔ On a multi-node data warehouse on premises (3 points) ✔ On a cloud-based data lake (5 points)	How does your organization apply the term big data? ✔ Excel files that are larger than 50 mb (0 points) ✔ We don't use the term big data (1 point) ✔ Large data sets stored in the cloud or on a server (3 points) ✔ Data of high volume, high velocity, and high variety (5 points)

Artificial Intelligence (AI)

Digital Maturity	*Organizational Readiness*
How does your organization apply artificial intelligence? ✔ That's not happening (0 points) ✔ We locally run some Python scripts that we found on GitHub (1 point) ✔ We assembled our own data science environment (3 points) ✔ We use cloud-based pre-trained models and add customizations if needed (5 points)	How does your organization think about chatbots? ✔ Useless functionality (0 points) ✔ Limited as customer-facing support channel (3 points) ✔ Feature that also boosts the productivity within the organization (5 points)

Process Automation, Blockchain, & IoT	
Digital Maturity	*Organizational Readiness*
How does your organization automate (small) processes?	How does your organization enhance existing processes?
✔ We don't do that (0 points)	✔ We'd better not touch it (0 points)
✔ We have some legacy VBA/Java/etc. code (1 point)	✔ A change request needs to be filled out and signed on paper (1 point)
✔ We use a low-code solution that everyone understands (5 points)	✔ A change request needs to be sent by email (2 points)
	✔ Everyone can use drag & drop to easily modify an existing process (5 points)
Sum: ____	Sum: ____

Figure 1.5 A digital maturity assessment

Based on your results you can further explore specific (or all) strategic topics with the interviews and customer examples in the following chapters.

Endnotes

i   Schwab, Klaus, *The Fourth Industrial Revolution.* Geneva: World Economic Forum, 2016.

ii "Disney Strikes Streaming-TV Gold," *The Economist*, November 12, 2020 (www.economist.com/business/2020/11/14/disney-strikes-streaming-tv-gold).

iii Microsoft, "AXA Ensures Innovation in Digital Customer Service and Empowers Employees with Microsoft 365," November 13, 2019 (customers.microsoft.com/de-DE/story/765562-axa-insurance-m365-casestudy).

iv Tapadinhas, Joao, and Idoine, Carlie, "Citizen Data Science Augments Data Discovery and Simplifies Data Science," December 9, 2016 (www.gartner.com/en/documents/3534848).

v   Loth, Alexander, *Visual Analytics with Tableau*. Hoboken, NJ: John Wiley & Sons, 2019.

vi The Digital Strategy Big Picture Template is available online within the Supplementary Material section on the Decisively Digital companion website: www.decisivelydigital.org/supplementary-material/.

vii "Gartner's Big Data Definition Consists of Three Parts, Not to Be Confused with Three 'V's," Forbes, www.forbes.com/sites/gartnergroup/2013/03/27/gartners-big-data-definition-consists-of-three-parts-not-to-be-confused-with-three-vs/

Part II

Digital Culture and Modern Work

Chapter 2
Elissa Fink: How to Charge a Brand with Culture

Elissa Fink, former CMO, Tableau Software
Source: Erin Rinabarger

Recently retired as CMO for Tableau,[i] Elissa Fink led all market-ing strategy and execution for 11 years, from pre-IPO startup with ~$5 million annual revenue to public enterprise with $1 billion+ in revenue. She knows growth, scale, and building disruptive brands. Prior to Tableau, Elissa served in marketing, product management, and product engineering executive positions. Now semiretired, Elissa advises tech companies, serves on multiple boards, and teaches at the University of Washington.

In this interview with Elissa we are going to explore how to charge a brand with culture and how this also helps in hiring people.

Alexander: As CMO you were creating a culture that is unique for a B2B software company. How did you discover Tableau? How did you become Tableau's CMO?

Elissa: I discovered Tableau as I was browsing the web — my very first exposure was when I was looking for Excel add-ins to help me force Excel to be an analytical tool. In fact, I was a Tableau customer before I even joined the company!

But Tableau became front and center to me when I wanted to relocate to be closer to my extended family. I read a LinkedIn job description, and the way that the company described itself intrigued me. I had downloaded the product, and I knew this product was going to change the world. So I really wanted to be part of this company.

When I interviewed with Christian Chabot[ii] on the phone, I asked him what the mission of the company was. He said it was to help people see and understand their data. And then he stopped. Silence. No long-winded blather about stakeholders, just a mission with a clear purpose. That was it. I knew this was the right company for me.

Alexander: That is indeed an amazing journey. How far in advance did you plan? Did you have a vision for the first six months, first year, or even five years?

Elissa: Because I saw from the start how the product was just going to change things and revolutionize the industry and the way people use data, I always had a long-term sense of where we were going to go. Being a small startup, you do have to think deeply and think long term, but act quickly in the short term and constantly be taking small steps that prepare you for the long term.

Sometimes you're so excited about the big that you start building for the big before you're ready for it and you don't focus enough on what's needed in the current so you can get to the long term. But on the other hand, you don't want to be acting so reactively in the short term that you're not ready for the future. So it's a real balancing act.

Community in particular is a great example of that. I knew the community was going to be a critical linchpin even before I joined the company. We have always been mindful of making sure that our community, even when it was small, really felt part of something and they were connected to each other.

Alexander: *Very interesting approach. How much did you have to adjust your vision over time? How much did you have to align your vision with the C-level team? How much freedom did you get?*

Elissa: Our founders are so amazing. CEO Christian Chabot and chief development officer (and inventor) Chris Stolte[iii] are both brilliant Stanford graduates. Pat Hanrahan[iv] is an Oscar-winning professor — and won the Alan Turing Award (which is basically an Oscar for computer scientists). These brilliant guys invented the product.

I was worried because I didn't come from that kind of pedigree at all. I was really concerned I might not hold up, but they were so respectful and incredibly open. It was something that just really struck me. These guys started a company, a culture, a movement where you didn't have to be a genius; you just had to have something to contribute. The fact is that the founders were humble and smart (in fact, I coined the term "humblesmart" to describe Tableau people). At the same time it meant they really wanted people to bring their "A games." They wanted to give opportunities to people of all kinds who could contribute.

So even if you were not from some hot company or didn't fit the typical hot startup profile, their attitude was: You can add to this. You could be part of this. We want your opinion. We want your thoughts. We want your contribution.

Alexander: *Not so long ago, data analytics, dashboards, and reports were considered boring work done by experts. Many questions* *could only be solved with heavy SQL knowledge. The visual output of course was not fancy and not interactive. How did you manage to create a culture where working with data was cool and inspiring? Which role did this culture play in shaping Tableau's brand?*

Elissa: Using data makes you smarter and makes you more curious. I was an English major in college, so I didn't think of myself as a numbers person at all. Then I realized I really liked data, but I knew nothing. I became a bad Excel user, breaking all these rules, not knowing what I was doing. But with Tableau, it was different. With Tableau, people could start thinking of themselves in a different way.

But to your point, one of the most important things we had to do was get people to give it a shot — to get people to experience it. You have to be convincing that you're worth the time or effort to try. That's hard, especially when you have no brand or no image.

Because we did convince a few people along the way, they could convince more people. So enabling them and getting them to share their experiences rather than us talking was critical. That was the huge thing: people connecting with other people who might join the family, become customers, and be part of the community.

We spent a lot of time and energy on cultivating customers who could come forward and show what they accomplished and what they did. And in a lot of ways, that was the beauty of Tableau Public.[v] Because that was a public forum that allowed people to showcase what they accomplished with Tableau. It was a passion project a lot of times and that, I think, did a lot to help us make it easy for people to convince other people.

Alexander: People also meet and share their ideas at Tableau Conference.[vi] This is also an opportunity for people who know each other via Tableau Public and Twitter to catch up face to face. Besides the Tableau Conference, what role did social media play? How were you building a social media community that is so active and well connected?

Elissa: When I joined back in 2007, it existed, but not widely. I thought, "We don't have a lot of money, so we've just got to leverage every angle." But I also saw that it gave a lot of people a voice — that they could start or participate in a conversation on any topic locally or globally with anyone. It's crazy to think back to what it was like when you first came upon Twitter or Facebook.

Social was something we cared about pretty early on, and it also is a great way to carry your brand and your voice, because it's somewhat casual and very temporal. You could have a little more fun with it, which of course was a huge part of our brand.

But you also have to be respectful and responsive. When people complained or needed help, you had to help.

Alexander: How did the culture and brand evolve over time from pre-IPO startup to public enterprise with $1 billion+ in revenue? How did you feel the change?

Elissa: When we started, we were very personal — we were much about the rogue data analyst or the casual data enthusiast. Data to the people, we'd say. Our brand was very much about individuals embracing their inner geek and sort of breaking the rules. Or, getting around the old ways of how people use data. But then as we got bigger and more accepted, we also realized so much more the importance of IT, of governance, and the possibilities of large numbers of people sharing and using data. I think we became as much about democratizing data for one person as democratizing data for groups of people and then making sure that we adhered to and helped with the organization of that in a governed way.

Through this, we never wanted to lose the soul of Tableau that data geeks identified with. But it had to be expressed in a way that was, as we grew, and our customers grew in number, congruent with their vision and their ideas of how to use data within their organizations. I think we got more sophisticated and smarter about that.

Alexander: Besides the customer-facing brand, Tableau also had a unique culture among its employees. Customers describe Tableau employees as freakishly friendly. How important is this for the company's culture and brand?

Elissa: The employees are super important. We couldn't have done it without all those employees. They are who most customers interact with and so it's just so important that they feel that passion. They are just so fundamental to representing Tableau, expressing

Tableau, and carrying the Tableau brand. But it's a circular thing. Employees impact that brand, modernize it, and keep it going.

Alexander: And how did you achieve this? How to hire the right people? Would you say this is because cool people hire cool people?

Elissa: We definitely had a huge number of employees come through referrals. So yes, cool people hire cool people, but in Tableau's case it was maybe more that data geeks hire data geeks. I look at the management team and the executive team, and most of them were referrals. (For the record, I wasn't. Sometimes you need to break out of your own circles.) I think when you are hiring, you are looking for passion, and you are looking for attitude. If they don't have passion for data and they don't have the attitude of work hard, work smart, and always be learning, then I don't care about [the] CV because [they're] not going to work here.

I think the company did a really good job of having the referral network and then really understanding how to hire for passion and attitude.

People went through the wringer on interviews. But the thing about a great culture is not only does it attract the right people, sometimes it helps people understand when they need to move on or move out.

That's why we would put cultural aspects in performance assessments. And it wasn't just checkbox. You had to assess if the employee was living our cultural values. Tableau put a lot of energy into all those hiring and onboarding aspects to ensure the right people were on the bus and had the tools to be successful.

Alexander: Onboarding is a very good topic. Tableau's onboarding process is well known in the software business for featuring a two-week bootcamp organized by Nate Vogel[vii] and his team. Bootcamp happened almost every month, and cofounder Christian Chabot used to welcome every new hire. How much does such an extensive onboarding shape the culture within the company?

Elissa: I think it was huge. People came from all over the world for two solid weeks. That was not common at the time. And it just spoke volumes: you chose us, and we chose you, and this is an investment for both sides.

This is a relationship we're investing in from the ground up because we believe in you and you believe in us. So, we want you to be as smart as possible as fast as possible.

And then, of course, the payback. It's hard to measure directly, but you can so see it as people were just more efficient and more effective sooner. And so, from a business perspective, it was smart because people could get efficient and effective a lot faster than not doing it.

Alexander: *I was at your farewell party right after Tableau Conference 2018 in New Orleans. All our colleagues were very sad and touched. How much do you miss your Tableau colleagues and your Tableau identity?*

Elissa: That was a night I'll never forget — thank you for being there. I do miss Tableau — the people, customers, and fellow employees, mostly — very much and I'm just so proud of it. I'm so proud to have been a part of it, what we invented and what we accomplished together. There were so many interesting people who had so much to give and had such interesting lives. I felt like I had done everything I could, and it was time for me to just get out of the way in a lot of respects.

Alexander: *You are now semiretired. How did you adjust? Which things did you learn?*

Elissa: It took me a while to adjust to a different pace and realize my schedule was my own. I would wake up on a Monday and look at my calendar. I'd be like — holy smokes, I don't have 30+ meetings on my calendar this week. I'm not in wall-to-wall meetings from 8 a.m. to 7 p.m. That was my life as a CMO.

I've learned a lot as well, some of which I wish I knew before I retired. A big lesson has been to take time for reflecting — for activities like learning, thinking, getting advice, considering new ideas, reading, really listening. In a fast-growing company like Tableau, the pace is relentless, and you're constantly trying to squeeze more into your day. So I often sacrificed reflecting time to get more doing time. That's not always an exchange worth making. I would have been better at my job if I had taken more time for reflecting.

Now, I'm advising companies, serving on a few boards, doing some teaching at the University of Washington, mentoring or being a sounding board, and most importantly spending more time being truly available to my family.

Alexander: So many companies do not have such a strong and positive culture. Which advice can you give other companies that are at a very early stage?

Elissa: My advice would be three things, all related to taking deliberate action. First, reflect on what your culture is already beginning to be. What culture are you already building? Does it reflect the values you want to cultivate?

Second, culture comes a lot from the personality of the people, especially the early people. So ask yourself — am I surrounded by people I want to build this culture with? Are they displaying the kinds of behaviors we want institutionalized? If not, maybe you need to make some people changes now. It will be a lot easier in the long run.

Third, culture shapes behavior but behavior shapes culture as well. It's kind of like smiling; sure, you smile when you're happy, but sometimes the act of smiling can bring happiness to you. So not only should your culture already be shaping your accepted norms of behavior, but also are you consciously choosing to behave in ways that represent the kind of culture you want?

Alexander: What is your advice for established companies that want to refresh their culture?

Elissa: Refreshing your culture is not something you do a one-day workshop on, list some attributes you wish for, publish an email about that, and then think it's going to refresh. It's going to take deliberate evolution over a long period that starts with the truth about who you are. It's an overused word these days, but authenticity is critical.

I think a great example of a refreshed culture is Microsoft. It's an amazing company, but for a long time, it had a pretty tough culture. But Satya Nadella, an insider who became CEO, has transformed the culture over a multiyear journey.

Culture is reflected in your hiring. Deliberately hire for the culture you want.

So a lot of culture refreshing can be similar to early-stage culture building as discussed before. One way to think about it is through the people you're bringing in, especially the role models at the top.

Second to that is encouraging and recognizing the behaviors and norms you do want and honor them as examples to be emulated. Show people why those cultural behaviors are good.

And finally — maybe most importantly — pay attention to the folklore or cultural stories that get told and repeated. Social scientists tell us stories played at least two important functions for our ancient ancestors: to help people remember important information before we had written language and to help establish what's considered acceptable behavior in terms of social cooperation.

You need leadership with courage.

Alexander: *That's great advice. I guess it also takes plenty of courage to perform a huge cultural shift as Satya Nadella did within Microsoft. Don't you think so?*

Elissa: I'm glad you brought up courage. It's such an important part of everything we've been talking about. Because if you don't have the courage to be yourself, if you don't have the courage to change, if you don't have the courage to try again after failure, if you don't have the courage to make the first move, well, a whole lot of stuff is just never going to happen. You need leadership with courage.

Alexander: *Besides Tableau, what are your favorite apps, tools, or software you can't live without?*

Elissa: I use this app called Done. It's a to-do app where you can set goals in order to get in the habit of doing certain things. I love it because it just kind of keeps me focused on the five or six things I want to do regularly to make sure that I'm building the habit.

I love reading so I'm a huge Kindle fan, but I also love the *New York Times* and the *Washington Post*. I am a big Evernote user. Actually, I love Flipboard, because it gives me a perspective of lots of different media sources. I also love Spotify, Slack, Waze, Dropbox, and all kinds of word games.

And I still of course love Tableau. I love using it in my class to teach it to show my students that you need to be analytical. But I also use it to analyze the data coming out of my class: Who's paying attention? Who is participating?

Alexander: What is your smartest productivity hack or work-related shortcut?

Elissa: Whatever problem you have, somebody else has had it, so don't think "I'm in this on my own." Anytime there's a problem, I always think I'm sure that I can't be the first person who has had this problem. Someone else solved it. They got out of it. They survived. You can too. And maybe you can even solve it better.

Alexander: What is the best advice you have ever received?

Elissa: One of my brothers and Christian Chabot gave me great advice. Let's start with my brother. When I was getting out of college, I told him I thought I wanted to do a certain job, but it's too competitive. He replied: "Elissa, there's always room for the best. Don't give up on your dreams because you think you can't compete. If you're the best, there's always room for you."

Related to that, he said in the same conversation: "You can become the best if you're willing to work hard and you're willing to learn and work smart."

The third one is from Christian. He said when you're hiring, hire people who have their best years ahead of them. In other words, hire people who are excited about the future and want to change and learn and make the most of today and their future opportunities.

Alexander: How should a business evolve to survive and thrive in an increasingly digital world?

Elissa: As you know, the COVID-19 pandemic forced us all to be increasingly digital at an accelerated pace. Businesses needed to evolve in several ways.

First is about hiring your people. Being more digital and more remote has meant that the talent pool for every position has greatly expanded — you know now that you don't have to have every employee in the office every day, that we can work remotely at scale. So take advantage of the expanded talent pool and hire the best people you can find, wherever they are (within reason).

That being said, we're all going to have to get much better at establishing deep and trusting relationships without necessarily experiencing in-person touchpoints. That's hard to do, from the interview or first meeting to the daily working relationship. That means reading people well, sending clear signals, and delivering on the things we say we're going to do.

We're also going to have to find ways to make teams work efficiently together at scale in digital environments. I've noticed in my teaching that I can't cover as much material in a virtual class as I did in an in-person class. But there are practices and techniques that can shorten the time to efficiency.

And finally, when it comes to sellers and buyers, I'll make a pitch for my discipline. In an increasingly digital world, marketing is going to own more and more of the customer journey because marketing teams can generally execute digital experiences well. So seeing sales, customer success, and marketing come into greater alignment and integrate better is going to result in more customers acquired, happier customers, and more turnover.

Key Takeaways

- Social media is a great way to carry your brand and your voice, because it's casual and temporal. You could have a little more fun with it, which can be a huge part of your brand.
- Culture comes from the personalities of the employees. You need to be surrounded by people you want to build this culture with.
- Refreshing culture is not done in a one-day workshop. It's going to take deliberate evolution over a long period that starts with the truth about who you are.

Endnotes

i   Tableau is a product-driven software company focusing on data visualization. The company was founded in 2003 and is headquartered in Seattle, Washington. On August 1, 2019, Salesforce acquired Tableau.

ii Christian Chabot is a cofounder and the former CEO of Tableau Software.

iii Chris Stolte is a cofounder and the former chief development officer of Tableau Software.

iv Pat Hanrahan is a cofounder and the former chief scientist of Tableau Software.

v Tableau Public is a free online service where everyone can share their visualizations.

vi Tableau Conference is an annual conference for Tableau users.

vii Nate Vogel is the VP of worldwide sales and partner readiness at Tableau Software.

Chapter 3
Patrick Kirchgäßner: Making Invaluable Pools of Information Accessible and Searchable

Patrick Kirchgäßner, senior product manager, Highspot
Source: Patrick Kirchgäßner

In his current role, Patrick is building an analytics platform that includes self-serve reports, powerful data visualizations, and raw data exports for the business customers of Highspot's sales enablement solution. He has led ecommerce businesses and is developing a real estate lead acquisition platform leveraging chatbots and social ads. In prior roles, Patrick has built consumer apps in the multimedia and entertainment space, where he had to rely on data to drive product improvements.

Alexander: You are senior product manager at Highspot. What is your mission?

Patrick: Highspot is an enablement solution focused on improving the performance of customer-facing teams. I'm spending my time building the analytics engine that gives our customers the data to create better content and improve rep behavior.

Alexander: How should business models evolve to survive and thrive in an increasingly digital world?

Patrick: More so than ever, 2020 has shown us that businesses that can adapt and evolve quickly are resilient to unforeseen or sooner-than-expected change in the environments that surround them. To be successful in the digital world, businesses need to understand the metrics that make them tick, leverage data to understand changes in their environment early, and be ready to course-correct quickly.

Alexander: How can technology shift the roles and responsibilities of the workforce?

Patrick: Technology in many ways makes much of our work more measurable and thereby more predictable. While it helps businesses to be more efficient, it can make individuals feel uncomfortable or left behind. To successfully adopt technology, it is important to bring the workforce along as the technology gets introduced — so they can use it to their advantage rather than being afraid of it. With information having become a ubiquitous commodity, the ability to leverage it with technology has become an invaluable skill.

Alexander: Which technology or digital capabilities are essential for a digital strategy?

Patrick: Even in the digital world, there is a workforce behind products, solutions, and services that are built and provided. Enabling that workforce to do their best work is going to yield the best business impact. Efficient communication tools and the ability to work from anywhere and at any time are top-of-mind capabilities, independent of industry or market segment. A close second is business KPIs — prioritized by the impact of improving them. What would move the needle the most? A 20 percent change in lead-acquisition cost, customer satisfaction, COGS, employee retention? Implementing the tools to measure those indicators reliably and transparently is the basis for driving continuous improvement around them.

> *Efficient communication tools and the ability to work from anywhere and at any time are top-of-mind capabilities, independent of industry or market segment.*

Alexander: Today, many companies use email as their main communication channel. Are there better approaches?

Patrick: Companies often encourage the use of email instead of distracting, spontaneous phone conversations, but chat tools like Slack or Microsoft Teams are able to bridge that gap much better. They enable real-time conversations where needed but allow members to adjust notifications to what fits their working style to avoid distractions. By implementing channels, companies can make many formerly private conversations public to their teams and co-workers. Doing so enables new team members to learn along the way and experienced team members to save time, and instead of building tribal knowledge, companies create invaluable pools of information that are accessible and searchable for years to come.

Alexander: If a company offers multiple ways to communicate (email, chat, phone), which channel should be used for which purpose? Do you have examples or best practices?

Patrick: Email is a great tool for long-form, asynchronous communication. It works well for bidirectional exchanges with single individuals or exceedingly small groups. It also works great as a broadcasting tool for unidirectional one-to-many use cases.

Chat is great for exchanging bits of information, getting questions answered quickly, and looping additional people into conversations. It works great for distributed teams, across time zones and even languages. Once a conversation turns complex enough to require multiple paragraphs of text, a phone or video conversation can often be the more efficient tool — ideally scheduled in advance so participants have time to prepare or invite other subject-matter experts.

Alexander: How about collaboration? Which approach could a distributed team use to work together on a whitepaper or a sales deck?

Patrick: Platforms like Microsoft Office 365 or Google G Suite offer great collaboration tools for all kinds of documents and are integrated with chat solutions such as Microsoft Teams or Slack.

Alexander: How could a company skill up their employees fast without leaving anyone behind?

Patrick: By having access to well-crafted training through a learning management system, employees can learn at their own pace. By selecting solutions that are leading in user experience and similar to consumer services, companies can shorten the time to productivity and increase employee satisfaction.

Alexander: What will happen to companies that do not level up in digital maturity and organizational readiness?

Patrick: The workforce of today and tomorrow expects to be able to work from anywhere and at any time. Not offering and working with state-of-the-art technology is not only a competitive disadvantage but also a disadvantage in attracting the best talent in the labor market.

Alexander: Do you see a chance in low-code environments for employees to design business processes without software development skills?

Patrick: By moving enterprise software from what used to be custom on-prem solutions to globally available cloud solutions, data and services have become a lot more unified and accessible. With that, marketplaces for plugins and extensions for thousands of enterprise scenarios have become available for every solution. Automations that required a team of highly specialized engineers only a few years ago can now be created in drag-and-drop interfaces in a matter of minutes.

Alexander: Ten years from now, how do you think our workplace will look?

Patrick: In tech, one of the key trends we have witnessed over the past 10 years is that more and more of companies' tech stacks got commoditized. Where companies had to entertain data centers and have teams of engineers available around the clock to maintain infrastructure, we now have smaller DevOps teams that can provision services with infinite scaling capabilities at the click of a button. The result is that most of the workforce are working on creating customer value, at the core of companies' DNAs. I imagine this trend will expand to other, nontech sectors of the market through more outsourcing and usage of highly reusable platform concepts.

Alexander: Why do data visualizations have such a strong impact on our decisions?

Patrick: The old adage "a picture is worth a thousand words" still holds true for modern-day businesses. Data visualizations can be made up from millions of individual data points but still convey an insight while just glancing at them. They can provide insights into past performance and real-time trends, are used to forecast future KPI development, and often are the language that subject matter experts use to drive conversations with higher-level executives, such as a company's leadership team.

Alexander: Why is data storytelling the essential data science skill that everyone needs?

Patrick: A few years ago, the act of just collecting data is what put many companies ahead of the curve. Today, it is hard to imagine not having data available. It turns out that just having data, often very raw data, is only a fraction of the equation. Being able to interpret data and understand it in the very context of a business and derive insights and suggest actions based upon it are important skills that enable us to extract true value out of data.

Alexander: How can everyone learn to communicate better with data?

Patrick: Without data, conversations are often driven by personal experiences and expectation bias and are generally subjective. With objective data in the room, conversations become a lot less emotional and a lot more focused on the subject matter. The key to communicating with data is to have data. Whenever we introduce a new process or change an existing one, we should ask ourselves how we can measure objectively whether the change had an impact. Oftentimes, we will find ourselves in situations where we don't have the perfect tools at hand to measure what we would like to. Surveys and other techniques can help us to bridge technology gaps and at least get us to a point where we have *some* data.

Alexander: Companies usually have plenty of legacy dashboards, the messages of which cannot be seen at first glance. What would a workshop to improve visual data communication look like?

Patrick: Dashboards lose their value if people lose trust in the data that is presented on them. Having a strong data framework in place that defines key KPIs and the very measures that go into them helps deliver a consistent message. At scale, this often means that companies have to come up with their own internal data dictionaries.

Alexander: What basic guidelines and patterns should always be considered for an expressive visual dashboard?

Patrick: The key goal of dashboards is to deliver insights at a glance. In order for that to be true, the data on dashboards should be visible at all times — which means that they need to be responsive to or optimized for the presentation layers they are used on without requiring users to scroll or click them. To turn a data point into an insight, [a dashboard] also needs to provide guidance to its relative context. It is unclear whether 5 of something is good or bad. Five of something on a colored scale from 1 to 25 turns that data point into an insight.

Alexander: Who should you trust with helping you monitor the changes you are making and testing your dashboard prototype to see if it meets expectations?

Patrick: Three stakeholders come to mind: the owner or creator of the data, the consumer of the data, and — depending on the sensitivity of data — a legal or data-security role that confirms that the data presented respects privacy regulations and conforms with legal requirements.

Alexander: Why should companies set up an Analytics Center of Excellence as part of their digital strategy? What are some strategies for setting this up?

Patrick: To do data analysis right, companies need resources that are skilled to do the job and have the priority and time on their hands to do so. Most of the time, neither of the two is true for people, and teams try to do data analysis on top of what feels like their actual job. Successfully implementing an analytics strategy requires deep understanding of the processes and metrics that drive business outcomes. A good approach to get to the scope of work for an Analytics Center of Excellence is to start with interviewing future consumers of data and business stakeholders to be able to build a data framework for the company.

Alexander: What are your personal top three dos and don'ts for an engaging visualization?

Patrick: Keep the visualization simple and easy to grasp, provide guidance or links to a drill-down, and provide as much context for the data as possible — such as a target KPI or a cohort comparison.

Alexander: Thank you, Patrick. What quick-win advice would you give that is easy for many companies to apply within their digital strategies?

Patrick: Focus on simplicity and transparency.

Alexander: What are your favorite apps, tools, or software that you can't live without?

Patrick: Snowflake, Tableau, DBeaver, MongoDB, Slack, Trello.

Alexander: Do you have a smart productivity hack or work-related shortcut?

Patrick: Respectfully decline meeting invites.

Alexander: What is the best advice you have ever received?

Patrick: We often think about personas and audiences when we build products. The best advice I have received is to actively think about that for most anything we do. In the business world, it helps me tailor the message about something I am seeking approval for to the very target audience I'm speaking to. In the data world, it helps me select the right granularity of data that informs but does not overwhelm.

Key Takeaways

- Chat tools bridge the gap between emails and distractive phone calls. Once conversations turn complex, a video conversation can be a more efficient channel.
- Employees can learn at their own pace if they have access to well-crafted training through a learning management system.
- Companies have to come up with their own internal data dictionaries for delivering a consistent message.

Chapter 4
Edna Conway: Protecting the Modern Workplace from Cyber Threats and Compliance Risks

Edna Conway, VP, chief security and risk officer for Azure, Microsoft
Source: Edna Conway

Edna Conway forecasts the future of business and creates clear strategies to deliver new and secure operating models for a digital economy. She is a sought-after industry influencer, bringing rich perspective forged from more than 30 years of broad and deep leadership success creating new organizations and delivering cybersecurity, compliance, and risk management across a $143 billion technology company. Conway is a builder of new capabilities that achieve lasting and pervasive operational improvement.

Alexander: *You are Azure's VP, chief security and risk officer at Microsoft. What is your mission?*

Edna: It is an interesting mission because it is a role that didn't previously exist. As a result, I had the great privilege to craft its scope and mission to deliver optimum impact. My team's focus is ensuring that Azure is the most trusted cloud platform on the planet. This mission drives every aspect of what we do.

The core of this mission is ensuring customer trust — trust in the Azure platform itself and trust in us as a partner in their success. Earning that trust requires two digital capabilities: security and resilience.

A comprehensive approach to security fully addresses these concerns:

- Physical security
- Logical and operational security
- Behavioral security
- Information security
- Intellectual property protection
- Privacy

An approach to risk management and resilience must focus on continuing operations in a world-class manner. For my mission that includes the following:

- Business continuity and disaster recovery
- Anti-bribery and anti-corruption protocols
- Human rights and labor rights

- Health and safety
- Environmental sustainability
- Trade and export controls

Alexander: *How should business models evolve to survive and thrive in an increasingly digital world?*

Edna: The global pandemic has accelerated the pace of the digital transformation journey that so many governments and enterprises were already on. In fact, that transformation became an immediate necessity. It also has uncovered the opportunity we have before us to rethink the efficiency and productivity of our business models.

As we evolve our business models to thrive in the increasingly digital economy, we must consider two fundamentals. First, understand what can and should be automated. Second, undertake a core versus context analysis. Digitize using internal core competencies with your own capabilities and talent. Leverage third-party services and solutions (for example, XaaS[i]) to optimize the implementation of your digital strategy and drive efficiency.

> *To thrive in the digital world, we must optimize to leverage human talent to meet the needs of customers. After all, digital capacity has a singular purpose: to serve people, not the other way around.*

Working through these fundamentals will allow you to begin to free your internal talent to address strategy, transformation, and the roadmap for the next generation of your business. To thrive in the digital world, we must optimize to leverage human talent to meet the needs of customers. After all, digital capacity has a single purpose: to serve people, not the other way around.

Alexander: *How can technology shift the roles and responsibilities of the workforce?*

Edna: We need to remind ourselves that technology can often give us insight into performance, trends, and anomalies. That insight can empower us to make changes before the full negative impact of an anomaly takes place. Conversely, such insight can provide us with a view to a positive change that we may not have otherwise been able to appreciate without the "help" of technology.

Imagine, for example, a sensor on a manufacturing line that provides real-time feedback. A digitally connected sensor can offer data that can be analyzed in a cloud-based IoT service, affording the manufacturer an opportunity to take action to adjust anomalies or capitalize upon an otherwise undetectable process improvement. Absent that assist from technology, our operational effectiveness may not be as swiftly optimized.

This digital insight allows enterprises to achieve and maintain their critical commitment to customers — trust.

Alexander: *Which technology or digital capabilities are essential for a digital strategy?*

Edna: To answer that we must first appreciate that we have entered a platform economy. In fact, platforms are pervasive in industry and our personal lives, from connected factories leveraging a single platform for visibility to operations to our own individual use of on-demand personal transportation platforms.

Given that reality, we must apply a layered approach to our digital strategies. There are two technologies that form the foundational layer of any digital strategy: cloud and mobile. These two are must-haves.

Of course, no conversation about digital strategy would be complete without addressing the use of artificial intelligence and machine learning. These capabilities can only be deployed on a foundation of mobile data capture, data storage, and data sharing within a cloud platform.

As a start, I suggest applying your digital strategy to your data storage needs. Then you can move on to address the variety of compute capacity needs for your business.

Alexander: *What ingredients are required to establish a digital culture?*

Edna: As I list those ingredients, let me first note that I believe culture is about people, *not* technology, so my answers are offered with that perspective.

The first ingredient is fostering open minds that are comfortable with technology.

The second ingredient is appreciating the criticality of including those who may not be comfortable with technology. After all, if you have a group of citizens or a group of co-workers who are not digitally savvy, you are not optimizing the use of their skills and also risking reducing the resilience of your enterprise.

The third ingredient is relentless curiosity: continuously exploring how operations currently work, what can make them more efficient, and how value can be added. This rigorous approach will create a culture that builds digital thinking into strategy and operations.

Alexander: What approaches will managers need to take to advance an enterprise's digital culture?

Edna: Similar to what I shared about the ingredients for establishing a digital culture, managers must focus on people.

First, managers should ensure that those whom they have the privilege of leading have a strong digital foundation. That foundation must include methods to assess and further develop digital skills and techniques to evaluate where and how a digital solution could enhance the business.

Second, managers must embrace regular reevaluation of their operational plans. That reevaluation should include asking yourself and your team these questions:

- Is there already an existing tool that we could leverage to free time for critical thinking rather than task implementation?
- Does another team already have a digitized process that can be applied to this team's work and goals?
- Can we, and how would we automate operational tasks?
- What are the platforms and tools we *are* using or *could* use to collaborate digitally and serve as the repository(ies) of our work product?

Applying this approach to managing routine operations and new initiatives allows a manager to make digital thinking part of the team's DNA.

Alexander: *What are the most important digital capabilities for protecting users' identities and data?*

Edna: I would focus on the following four digital capabilities to protect identity and data:

- Role-based access control
- Digital identity management
- Encryption
- Network and function segmentation

And, as always, educate users on how to identify and evade efforts to gain credentials and information.

Alexander: *A recent study found that unmanaged devices are 71 percent more likely to have malware.[ii] What's the most effective way to combat this?*

Edna: Today's reality is that the workforces of both private enterprises and the public sector use their own devices. No one entity can manage all the devices in the modern economy. You can, however, manage the way those devices

- access your core infrastructure;
- access, duplicate, edit, or extract your information; or
- implement workflow tasks.

Deploying identity management (for example, multifactor authentication) and monitoring who is creating, accessing, changing, and operating from what device will serve you well.

Alexander: *Threats are changing. How do we have to adapt?*

Edna: There are three key points that we need to consider when we want to adapt to new threats:

- Slow down: You are at risk of making a mistake when you are in a rush.
- Be vigilant: Stay aware of the changing threat landscape and attack vectors and leverage a revisit of your security practices as you learn.
- Conduct pre-deployment testing: Running in sandboxes prior to full operational deployment supports a diligence process based

on staged implementation. Only when verification is achieved should a full deployment proceed.

Alexander: What will happen to companies that don't level up in digital maturity and organizational readiness?

Edna: They won't be in business. Leveling up in digital maturity and organizational readiness is not optional — it is an intrinsic necessity in today's digital age.

Alexander: Do you see a chance in low-code environments for employees to design business processes without software development skills?

Edna: I think that employees can design business processes at any point in time without software development skills. However, processes need to be implemented. Doing so in a digital age may not require software development skills if the implementation plan was designed with developers at the table who could ensure that process users can implement digitally. At some point someone who knows how to code needs to have been part of the team — period!

Alexander: Ten years from now, how do you think our workplace will look?

Edna: People will be wherever they want to be. Ten years from now, there will still be meetings at headquarters because people are creatures who require being with one another and developing rapport. We will never stop shaking hands, hugging, and understanding the feedback we get from being physically with one another.

I also believe that efficiencies will be added by the use of digitally controlled machinery and vehicles. These are adding more to our human capabilities every day.

Alexander: Thank you, Edna. What quick-win advice would you give that is easy for many companies to apply within their digital strategies?

Edna:

- Deploy a flexible enterprise resource planning (ERP) system.
- Lock down identity management deployed in conjunction with a role-based access plan.
- As for your data: segment, segment, and segment.

Alexander: Do you have a smart productivity hack or work-related shortcut?

Edna: Pick up the phone and talk to someone.

Alexander: What is the best advice you have ever received?

Edna: The best advice I ever received was from my mother: never judge a book by its cover. This advice is even more relevant in today's digital world.

Key Takeaways

- Going digital demands that you assess what *should* be automated, not just what *can* be automated.
- To build and retain trust, focus on two key digital capabilities: security and resilience.
- In 10 years, people will be wherever they want to be, but we will never stop shaking hands, hugging, and seeking the feedback we can only gain from being physically together.

Endnotes

i   XaaS (X as a Service) refers to something being presented to a customer as a service, typically in the context of cloud computing. XaaS provides endpoints for customers that are usually API driven but can also be controlled via a web browser or within applications. Typical examples are software as a service (SaaS) such as Office 365, infrastructure as a service (IaaS) such as Hyper-V, and platform as a service (PaaS) such as Azure.

ii "2020 Global IoT/ICS Risk Report," CyberX, https://cyberx-labs .com/resources/risk-report-2020.

Chapter 5
Florian Ramseger: The Future of the Digital Society

Florian Ramseger, economist, data scientist, and futurist

Source: Florian Ramseger

Florian is an economist turned data scientist with wide-ranging work experience in different countries and in different fields — the private sector, the public sector, and NGOs and international organizations. In his current role as senior product specialist he helps Salesforce customers from different industries implement their data projects. Prior to Salesforce, he was with the International Red Cross, the World Economic Forum, and the WU Vienna business school. Florian has a BSc in economics and geography from University College London and an MSc in economics and economic history from the London School of Economics. Currently based in Frankfurt, Germany, he has spoken and written about how the digital transformation affects organizations and societies, based on his experience with implementing IT projects of various shapes and sizes and drawing on his background as a trained economist.

Alexander: We have talked about the digital transformation of society on several occasions; how do you think about digitalization and how does it change our lives?

Florian: The digital transformation over the last few decades can be broken down into three stages, and each stage comes with its own benefits. When a process has become "digitalized" we notice it, either because the input form is now digital or because the end product is presented in a digital format. Capturing and presenting information in digital form started some 40 years ago with the widespread adoption of the personal computer.

The decreasing costs of all sorts of sensors and the rise of the Internet of Things, as well as advances in machine vision, voice recognition, and natural language processing, mean that we digitize increasingly more analog content. The value associated with this first stage of the digital transformation, sometimes referred to as *digitization*, was traditionally seen in the savings in physical or human resources, but nowadays digital content is also the building block for the other transformations that we are seeing.

With the advent of network computing, the Internet, and later smartphones, we moved to the second stage of the digital transformation, which allows more people to access the digitized information. The value here lies in how information flows faster from A to B.

This can eliminate small inconveniences in life, such as having to call for a taxi, by using a service like Uber instead, or it can help with providing lifesaving real-time information, as in the case of natural catastrophe warning apps. It also means that information can be fed back in real time, as when Google Maps uses the travel speed of smartphones to estimate traffic flow on streets. 5G and the proliferation of blockchain technology will further accelerate this stage.

Another reason that digital information can make our lives better, and this is the third stage, is that we can generate additional insights from the stored and shared information. This has been around for a while in the form of business intelligence (BI) — basically ever since we had databases. But several factors, including the rise of cloud computing and the general increase in computing power, have led to the impressive developments in the field of artificial intelligence (AI) that we have seen over recent years. With quantum computing, which is on the horizon to become widely available, this stage will explode.

While these different technologies emerged more or less sequentially, which is why I call them stages (see Figure 5.1), we are now in a situation where technological advances are happening at each level. Further, as already mentioned, innovation in AI and in different network technologies leads to ever more content becoming digitized, which in turn can be accessed and mined for new information, meaning that we see self-reinforcing loops between the different building blocks. This explains the rapid acceleration of the digital transformation that we are currently witnessing.

Alexander: *What role does Big Data play in this transformation, or is that just a buzzword?*

Florian: Big Data is a real paradigm shift. Whereas in the past we had to rely on small samples to make inferences about the wider population, in the statistical sense of the word, in many cases we now have data points about every single unit in the population. This could be individual shoppers who frequent an online store. Or it could be the fuel consumption of the vehicles in the fleet of a delivery company. This brings with it two advantages.

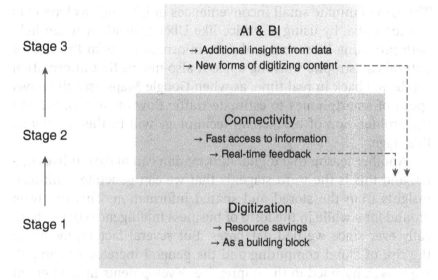

Figure 5.1 The three stages of the digital transformation

First, we have more data to play with when we want to make predictions, so data scientists can throw in everything but the kitchen sink to find interesting patterns. The sky is the limit for what businesses can do with big data. I have a device under my mattress that can provide me information about my sleep quality as well as my risk for sleep apnea. Although it costs less than EUR 100, it can approximate the results one would get in a sleep lab using an algorithm that was probably trained on a large set of medical data.

This device also illustrates the second advantage to Big Data, namely, that individual units can be identified, and tailor-made action can be taken. We are all familiar with applications of this in our daily lives, such as when we get personalized movie recommendations from Netflix. But there is still huge potential for society on many other fronts. In the future, just as my sleep analyzer does, many of our devices will notify us when our personal data deviates from the norm. Researchers are already working on smart toilets that can automatically analyze your urine!

Alexander: Do you see every country and industry moving through these stages as you described them?

Florian: A lot of what I described is not that new: machine learning, Big Data, Internet-connected devices, and so on have been around for a number of years already. However, there are huge differences in the adoption of these technologies across countries and industries, but also within them.

I went to a regional newspaper in Germany to give a software training. They had neither laptops nor guest WiFi. Instead, we had to use a training room in the basement that reminded me of the computer lab in my high school 30 years earlier. On the other hand, when I visited the data journalism team of the newspaper *Die Zeit*, I felt like I was on the Google campus. They had top-notch equipment, and they were hosting data science meetups in a room complete with beanbags and a beer-filled fridge. They are producing cutting-edge data journalism.

No matter what the starting point is, we are now seeing a wider adoption of digital technologies, because these technologies are becoming commoditized, meaning they become more accessible and easier to implement.

Especially here in Europe, concerns about data privacy have held us back in many regards. Perhaps we have good reasons to be skeptical; we Germans are all too aware how authoritarian regimes can use information about their citizens for total surveillance. Nonetheless, public acceptance of technology that relies on private data is slowly increasing. I am actually amazed that Germany put out a coronavirus warning app that lets you know when you were in the vicinity of someone who later tested positive for COVID-19.

Alexander: So where do you see this going in the future? In what fields do you see the biggest changes?

Florian: All sectors and industries will be affected, because most business processes involve moving information around.

The most obvious ones are sectors such as banking that already have gone through the first stage of the transformation — bank account records are already nothing but 0s and 1s. With the advent of so-called robo-advisor apps and other fintech innovations, we now see second- and third-stage technologies being used to democ-ratize investment products that in the past were accessible only to the rich, who could afford their own private wealth managers.

But healthcare is where I see the biggest potential for society, both in medical research and in clinical practice.

Diagnosing a patient is, after all, just a pattern recognition task: a doctor considers your symptoms, lab results, MRI images, and so on, and compares them to what illnesses they have learned about and encountered in their careers so far. But medical professionals, like all humans, are affected by different behavioral biases, such as recency bias, which can lead to unfortunate cases of misdiagnosis. Further, consider the fact that, in the EU alone, 30 million people are estimated to suffer from one of more than 6,000 different rare diseases — and those are just the ones that we know about. No doc-tor could possibly learn about all these diseases in medical school.

So, one could imagine that computers might be able to assist doctors in diagnosing patients by comparing their health records to the different patterns of diseases in a database. Already today, there are studies showing that computers can be better than humans at spotting potential tumors in mammograms.

With machine learning, researchers are currently studying how innovative types of medical data, including, for example, the gut biome composition, relate to different illnesses, meaning that we will have more noninvasive tests that can catch diseases early, before they cause any symptoms.

Also, in a future where anonymized digital patient records of whole populations are available to scientists, they will be able to slice and dice the data in many ways to find more relevant insights for different subgroups of the population. Because they are typically limited in size, traditional clinical trials often gloss over differences between different age groups, ethnic groups, or groups of people with different comorbidities.

There is the potential for different digitally facilitated services to help us reduce congestion in cities. In the US, Uber offers a service called Uber Pool. Their algorithms find efficient routes for several passengers to share a ride, instead of each taking a separate car. That's brilliant. We need more approaches to society's problems like this!

Alexander: So, there are many developments on the horizon that will make our lives better!

Florian: Yes, but the digital transformation also comes with its problems. Any new technology can be used for both good and bad. For example, authoritarian governments can use facial recognition technology to implement Orwellian surveillance in public spaces.

Even in more democratic societies, the Cambridge Analytica scandal opened our eyes to how our personal data can be abused for political manipulation. Machine learning algorithms have been shown to pick up racist or otherwise discriminatory patterns from the training data that their makers feed them.

Cloud and Big Data technologies require big servers to run on, which use large amounts of energy. If not sourced from renewable sources, these contribute to air pollution and global warming. You might have seen the line "Consider the environment before printing this email," but maybe we should also add a warning about the environmental effects of reading your mail online!

As an economist, I am also deeply concerned about the gig economy and the potential for it to create a precariat of unseen scale. Jobs with platforms like Uber, Deliveroo, and Amazon deliveries can be stepping stones for people who are able to use that income to invest in their future, but these same jobs can also create dependencies that expose workers to the pricing algorithms of these companies and leave them without any safety nets. This is why our politicians need to build the right social and economic fabric for these technologies to become a force for good for society as a whole.

Alexander: You already alluded to the changing world of newspapers and other media organizations. Given that you have had a number of clients from that sector, how do you see the digital transformation play out in that sector?

Florian: Newsrooms have been hit by several disruptions simultaneously, and I fear for quality journalism, which is in rapid decline, perhaps with the exception of the top-tier newsrooms. That is a real threat to our democratic societies, for which the so-called Fourth Estate is absolutely vital, with investigative journalism helping to hold our elected leaders accountable.

The first disruption was the loss of revenue from classified ads that followed the rise of dedicated websites such as eBay, Craigslist, Gumtree, and others (stage-one replacements of an analog product). Local newspapers were particularly hard hit by this.

Second, big tech and social media companies have become the de facto newsstands of our times, because they distribute individual news articles either directly, as in the case of Apple News or Google News, or by controlling what gets shared on their platforms, in the case of Twitter and Facebook (stage-two technologies). The result was that subscriptions and newsstand sales plummeted.

Even more worrying, industry insiders have told me that the tech giants can tell newspapers exactly what type of content and in what form they want to distribute, not to mention the power of the social media distribution algorithms that decide who gets to see what. In a way, then, they are becoming the de facto editors too.

Third, the only revenue stream left to news organizations was online ads. Yet again, big tech companies are driving this business model. Google Ads is deeply embedded in most news websites because they have all the information from tracking people across the web to serve the reader "relevant" ads — including ads for toasters, weeks after you just bought a new toaster (a stage-three technology).

The issue here is that the ads only get seen when people open the links they see in their news apps or social media feeds. Thus, a lot of what is published is often sensationalized, no matter how trite the story, so as to get you to click the headline.

Alexander: *Do you mean clickbait?*

Florian: In a way, yes. Engineers at social media companies can tell you that it is difficult to use natural language processing algorithms to filter out fabricated news stories on their platforms, because they are so similar to real news. Partly that is because many people who distribute false news actually believe them to be real. But the opposite is also happening: real news is using a lot of the same tactics to lure people to their sites. Quality journalism gets drowned out in a world of false and trivial content.

What is worse, in the US, there is a trend where we see political organizations, especially on the far right, buying up failing local newsrooms to spread their messages of hate and division. This is really troubling for our societies.

Now, I don't like the blanket news bashing that we hear in pub conversations or in press conferences of certain politicians, so I want to make it clear that there are still fantastic newsrooms out there, such as the *Financial Times*, the *Wall Street Journal*, and *Die Zeit* here in Germany, among others. By pivoting toward digital subscriptions and away from advertisement, they are able to withstand some of these negative influences. In Switzerland there is a great project, called *Republik*, which is a newsroom that is entirely reader-financed. But these examples are unfortunately becoming the exception and not the norm.

Alexander: *You mentioned how some companies pick up on new opportunities and others miss out on them. How then should business models evolve to survive and thrive in an increasingly digital world?*

Florian: Many companies use different types of digital technologies to automate and streamline their business processes, but I think you have to look at it not only from an optimization perspective, but also from the perspective of what new value you can deliver to your customers.

B2C businesses in particular have to think about how they can use digital technologies to play in the "experience economy," as Joseph Pine and James Gilmore call it.[i] Brands like Apple, Starbucks, and Tesla understand they don't just sell phones, drinks, and cars, but that through the various interactions with the customers they create experiences, long-lasting feelings, and, if done right, a sentiment of belonging to a tribe.

It depends of course on the industry, but many businesses can still do better at providing information about their offerings on the web — a simple stage-one technology. Others could think about stage-two strategies, such as interacting with their customers via an app or creating an online marketplace. An example of a stage-three strategy could be to think about what information you can gain from your data that could be valuable for your customers in real time. This could justify a switch to a subscription model, as we see happening in so many markets.

I rolled my eyes when I read the other day that a meal-delivery startup described itself as a "tech company" because they have all that data about their customers. But there might be some truth in it. From my inputs in their app, they know that I like spicy curries and that I don't eat raw fish. If they use that information to set up a just-in-time supply chain for fresh produce but also let me see

> *"What would your business model be if you were founded as a tech company?" This is especially true if you are a brick-and-mortar company. Because if you don't ask that question, someone else will and will roll up your market.*

where my order is at any point in time and maybe also provide me with additional content, for example in the form of tailor-made recipes, then they are actually closer to a tech company than a traditional grocery store.

Most businesses need to ask themselves, "What would your business model be if you were founded as a tech company?" This is especially true if you are a brick-and-mortar company, because if you don't ask that question, someone else will and will roll up your market. In other words, companies have to watch out that they don't get stuck in what Clayton Christensen called the innovator's dilemma.[ii]

Alexander: *What are some of the mistakes you see that lead to this dilemma?*

Florian: Many businesses and organizations realize that there is value in digitalization. But they often just replicate analog processes in digital form, often with the goal of saving physical resources or reducing labor costs. In other words, they are stuck in what I earlier described as stage one of the digital transformation. The companies that are leapfrogging the competition are the ones that don't necessarily try to replicate the analog world, but use the digital building blocks from all three stages to create something completely new — including that customer experience that I just mentioned.

Audi, for example, doesn't give out paper brochures anymore, as most customers peruse Audi's website instead. However, the website doesn't provide that much additional value over a paper brochure. True, you can play around with different configurations, but if you want to buy a new car, you still must haggle with a car dealer over the price.

Contrast that with the experience of buying a Tesla. You can reserve a car and pay by credit card right there and then, just like when you buy a pair of Nike shoes from Zappos. And you never get any buyer's remorse that comes from being pressured by a car salesman.

It starts with the shopping experience, but it doesn't stop there. From the way you contact customer support to providing software updates over the air to unlocking the car with the phone, every rock of the traditional car experience has been turned over to see how it can be improved. Tesla was not successful in breaking into a market dominated by traditional firms because they made cleaner vehicles. Instead, Tesla built the first car for people who think of themselves as digital natives.

Alexander: What will happen to companies that don't level up in digital maturity and organizational readiness?

Florian: As one of my colleagues at Salesforce puts it, it's "digital or disappear." The best examples are taxi businesses in many countries. Only a couple of years ago you would have thought that, because they are part of the service economy, they are immune to threats by technological innovation. With the rise of the so-called ride-sharing apps, we now know that that was wrong.

But it is a mistake to think that that is only because Uber and Lyft are cheaper. Instead, these challengers successfully built their business models on stage-two and stage-three technologies. They created added value by letting the customer order and pay for a ride with a single click on the app. Compare that with my experience, late at night after a trans-Atlantic flight, having to find a taxi driver at Frankfurt airport who was willing to accept credit card payment. It is mind-boggling that in this day and age many of them still insist on cash payment.

Don't forget the value that the Uber customer gets from having a real-time map showing the suggested route. Anyone who has ever been taken on the scenic route by a taxi driver wanting to squeeze the customer for an extra dollar appreciates this real-time information.

The fate of the taxi industry was not inevitable. The shakeup could have been avoided in two ways. First, taxi businesses every-where should have emulated London black cabs, with their clean, spacious, and safe cars and their courteous, knowledgeable, and honest drivers.

Second, they should have done earlier what some taxi compa-nies eventually did: they got together and introduced a taxi app.

Alexander: *And how can companies increase their digital matu-rity? Which technologies or digital capabilities are essential for a digi-tal strategy?*

Florian: It depends of course on the industry, but it is no secret that machine learning and other forms of artificial intelligence are today's game changers.

I like to say that AI helps organizations "outsource decision-making to computers," thereby allowing them to automate more of their existing business processes and create new offerings that were unthinkable only a few years ago.

The classic example of process optimization is banks that use algorithms to automatically approve loan applications that meet certain criteria. Some of the more innovative use cases that we have already talked about, whether self-driving cars, ride-sharing services, or smart toilets, demonstrate the potential this technology has for new products in all sorts of fields.

Alexander: *But will every decision eventually be outsourced to computers?*

Florian: No. While the realm of what AI can be used for will increase drastically over the next few years, there are still plenty of business decisions to be made every day that can't be automated, either because we don't have enough historical data or because we don't feel comfortable surrendering that decision.

This is where the often-cited data-driven decision-making comes in; I actually prefer to call it data-informed decision-making, because at the end of the day it is still the human who will make the decision. You want the human to be able to do so, after having consulted the available data. For that you need technologies that allow everyone in the organization to have access to the organization's data and to make sense of it — business intelligence (BI) tools.

Alexander: *What other technologies are interesting besides AI and BI?*

Florian: Cloud computing will continue to change things. Here in Europe especially, I see companies catching up in this space. Both in terms of the physical servers that their own app offerings live on, but perhaps even more so in terms of software as a service (SaaS) applications. It started with tools like Workday, which allows you to manage employee leave applications, but nowadays there is an off-the-shelf SaaS tool for almost any type of business process.

Cloud offerings like Amazon Web Services, Microsoft Azure, and Google BigQuery also allow companies to build their own applications and help power a lot of the AI and BI processes that we just talked about.

Besides these broad-scale technologies there are innovations that might be more specific to certain business processes or industries. Blockchain will enable fast verification of all sorts of transactions. Lamborghini, for instance, uses blockchain technology to certify the authenticity of their vintage cars. Buyers can follow the history of the car and all its spare parts and thus be assured about what they are purchasing.

But you could imagine applications that are useful not only for the super-rich. Anyone who has ever bought or built a property knows that it takes weeks to clear many bureaucratic hurdles. What if building permits could be issued via blockchain technology? What if a contract could be notarized with the push of a button?

Fast, reliable business transactions will be like grease to our modern business machinery. At the same time, by making transactions transparent, it could mean the end for another type of "grease," namely, bribery, kickbacks, and other corrupt practices that endanger the trust of our societies.

Alexander: How can technology shift the roles and responsibilities of the workforce? You mentioned the commoditization of modern digital technologies before.

Florian: First, we already talked about how everything that can be automated will eventually be automated, whether it is capturing or presenting information (what we called stage one), transmitting information (stage two), or making inferences from that information (stage three). Therefore, fewer of those tasks will be done by humans.

Instead, your employees will generate new ideas, create new content, and make decisions that can't be based on historical data. The role of the knowledge worker will continue to become more important. In many organizations it is, for example, common for someone to take notes during a meeting and share them with the rest of the team afterward. AI-based transcription services can now automate that task for you. That means that that person who used to have their head buried in the notepad now can join the discussion and contribute new ideas.

Second, and this is where the commoditization of digital technologies comes in, everyone will in some ways become involved in setting up new automated processes, whether that is by working with ready-made SaaS offerings or by creating customized services with so-called low-code platforms.

We are even seeing first products that commoditize machine learning so that anyone can deploy AI technology on their data.

The integration of separate services also will become more prominent as B2B companies offer more holistic offerings, such as the Salesforce Customer 360 platform. Offerings such as those by MuleSoft allow you to string together your different data sources and the individual steps of business processes.

At a simpler level, the online tool IFTTT, which stands for "If This Then That," lets anyone connect their popular business apps with one another, including Outlook, Google Sheets, Asana, and many more. For example, you can easily connect your SurveyMonkey form to Slack so that you can be notified when a new survey response has come in.

In other words, many things that traditionally were done by IT can now be done by the subject-matter experts themselves. Therefore, the role of IT changes too. It is more about managing and enabling, as opposed to creating new systems.

Alexander: *How can companies today prepare their employees to achieve organizational readiness for the digital future?*

Florian: Everyone should have a basic understanding of how machine learning works. I don't mean that everyone should know how to code, but they should be able to explain the concept to their grandmothers so that they can evaluate the potential of using AI-powered applications in different business processes.

Given how AI changes our everyday lives, I would recommend that everyone take the free online course "Elements of AI" that was created by the University of Helsinki.

I would also make sure that all my employees have some basic data literacy skills to be able to take part in the conversations. Once, when explaining some research findings in a meeting, I had a participant ask halfway through, "Why are we looking at all this data in the first place, when statistics is all lies anyway?" I had to take a long detour to explain the fundamentals of what we were doing.

Alexander: *What can managers do to develop and foster the company's digital culture?*

Such a culture would be one of collaborative problem solving, innovation, and constant introspection. Now, there are many factors that influence a company's culture, but here are a few things that any manager can practice.

First, encourage employees to point out problems and inefficiencies. I know an organization where every day a certain boring and time-consuming task is performed, involving the manual transfer of content from one system into another. For over 10 years, complaints by employees fell on deaf ears. Some employees were admonished for their lack of enthusiasm. Not surprisingly, attrition is high on that team. A simple upgrade of the system that would automate the bulk of the process could have saved many labor hours and, more importantly, the morale of the team.

Managers should ask themselves whether they can apply the Japanese manufacturing principle of the Ando cord. In car factories this is a safety cord that any employee is allowed to pull to stop a production line if they think there is a problem. The tool in itself is secondary. It is the culture that it fosters — one where anyone's input is taken seriously, no matter their pay grade. If you want to use the digital transformation to grow your business, you need every input that you can get.

Second, because it is not enough to just optimize, you will want to keep some creative heads around too. People who can come up with innovative ideas that will help you leapfrog ahead, rather than just change incrementally. That means you need to learn to put up with their quirks and antics. In an effort to treat everyone the same, creative people are often pushed out of organizations, and teams become too homogenous in their thinking.

Third, empower your IT and subject-matter experts to come up with solutions together. When I worked at a business school, we asked the IT department to set up a form where students who wanted to change courses could put their names on a waiting list. Since IT didn't have time to help, we secretly proceeded to set up a form using an off-the-shelf SaaS tool instead. This sort of self-service culture should be fostered, not forbidden. But you still want IT to vet and manage the different solutions; you can't have everyone rebel against IT, fun as it was for us back then.

Alexander: *Returning to the socioeconomic consequences of the digital transformation, 10 years ago you predicted that cloud applications like Google Docs and Microsoft Office 365 would change the way we work. You argued that knowledge workers could be more geographically mobile and less dependent on corporate employers, because they could own the tools of their trade — their laptops. Has this become a reality, and where do you see this trend going in the next 10 years?*

Florian: Business applications in the cloud have absolutely made remote collaboration so much easier. I have worked with many geographically distributed teams and with tools like Google Docs, Slack, and WebEx, by and large, collaboration was as good as, if not better than, it was in in-person teams.

What hasn't happened yet is that all knowledge workers became freelancers, partly because of IT security concerns that prevent people from bringing their own devices to collaborate. The bigger issue, though, is that in many countries being a full-time employee is a requirement of becoming part of the social safety net. The US, where health insurance premiums and retirement fund contributions are paid by employers, is an extreme example.

All that said, the number of freelancers seems to be going up. In the US, 35 percent of the workforce has done freelance work in 2019, with 28 percent of the workforce doing it full-time — that is up from 17 percent in 2014.[iii]

Alexander: Can a universal basic income (UBI) help here?

Florian: If implemented well, it could make it a lot easier for people to transition back and forth between employment, freelance work, educational breaks, and, yes, even time for self-discovery.

But it is not enough to simply give people EUR 1,000 a month. It is about changing the mindset that being part of the social net requires you to be an employee. It is about making sure that healthcare and retirement plans are continuous as you transition between different life stages — or even from one employer to the next — and that people who are stuck and can't find work get the necessary help.

The old model for the social safety net in Western societies, where transfer payments such as pensions and unemployment benefits are conditional on having held a "proper" job, worked for the industrial age, but the digital age might require a new framework.

Our politicians would love to see more tech startups in Europe. We need to provide people the flexibility required for modern work and life if we want the next Google to come from here.

Alexander: Whether it is to finance a UBI or to pay for unemployment benefits, some people have suggested that we tax machines to compensate those who lose their jobs as a result of the digital transformation. What do you think about that?

Florian: Taxing machines and technology would be the wrong approach. All long-term economic growth ultimately comes from the fact that machines make us more productive and that we can have ever more specialized division of labor. We can afford the things that make our lives better and easier, because technology enables specialists to produce them for us, and the market allows us to trade them in exchange for our own services in the domains that we are good at.

Alexander: *Today, many knowledge workers spend time analyzing data, creating slides, and writing emails. In the next 10 years, what do you think our work will look like?*

Florian: It will be more data analysis, fewer emails, and about the same amount of time creating slides.

The more data analysis part is probably obvious. We will be inundated in data, whether we like it or not. The different steps of the analysis process will be more and more automated and commoditized so that even people with very limited experience in data analysis will be exposed to it.

The fewer emails part is perhaps wishful thinking, but I am hopeful that other forms of digital communication will replace it. Tools like Slack, Chatter, Quip, and Teams are great if used correctly.

Their greatest value is that they allow us to organize conversations around topics or projects, whereas emails are organized by who sends what to whom (and who is left off the recipient list). The benefit of that cannot be overstated, as it creates true transparency and free knowledge transfers within organizations. This only works, however, if people are intentional about this. I have seen it happen that a social collaboration tool was implemented and then employees used it to directly message their colleagues, just like they would with email.

One thing I can see happening is that we will use data dashboards more often in meetings rather than slide decks with static charts. Charts and figures are often the cues for further questions. My colleague Andy Cotgreave likes to say that the quality-control method of asking "five whys," as pioneered by Sakichi Toyoda at Toyota, is what one should use when using data to answer questions: don't stop until you have asked "why?" five times.[iv] Being able to interact with data during meetings allows one to go down such routes of interrogation.

Alexander: Do you think that the automation of processes and the commoditization of digital tools will mean that we will have much less work to do? Would it be an option to reduce work time, let's say to three days per week, to avoid a loss of jobs?

Florian: Individual tasks can take up less time when new digital tools are introduced, but it is a fallacy to think that the overall amount of work will decrease as a result. There is no fixed stock of work that needs to be done. Instead, when new tools help us increase our productivity, we, as a society, tend to produce more. Hence the effect on economic growth I mentioned earlier. Also, don't forget people have to build these tools.

There are two caveats to this answer, though. First, individual jobs will fall away. Companies used to have typists who would type up the letters that their bosses dictated for them on a voice recorder. With the advent of the personal computer, workers can now write their own letters, and as a result many typists lost their jobs. This process will repeat itself continually as new technologies are adopted to automate tasks. Therefore, our education and welfare systems are crucial. They can ensure that people have the right skills for the right jobs and that they can transfer from those jobs that have become obsolete into those that society requires.

Second, we might still see a change in work time in certain professions. The traditional five-day workweek with eight-hour days made sense in the industrial age, where everyone had to be at the conveyor belt at the same time for the production process to work.

With the rise in knowledge work, that requirement is going away in many places. It makes more sense to ask what the best work schedule for a knowledge worker would be for them to achieve peak performance. For some it might be a three-day work week; for others it might be a different arrangement.

Perhaps we even must reframe it from "work time" to "time when you are contactable" and from asking people to sell you their time to selling you their productive output. You see, when you get your best work ideas in the shower, the concept of a workweek goes out the window!

Alexander: Earlier you mentioned self-driving cars and digital patient records. In many countries, efforts to further drive these innovations are hampered by local regulations. What role does the government play here?

Florian: If we, as a society, are to benefit from all the new technologies that are becoming available, regulation needs to not only catch up but actually spearhead the development, especially when it comes to crucial infrastructure investments.

In terms of self-driving cars, a lot of the public discourse centers around the question of who is liable when something goes wrong. That is an important question, but it shouldn't dominate the discussion and hamper any progress. This is a technology that already can save lives and will do so even more in the future. So, any day that goes by that we don't make progress on this front means more people will unnecessarily die or get injured in road accidents.

When people rightly point out that the computer vision used in self-driving cars sometimes struggles with bad road markings, that shouldn't be a warning about how bad self-driving cars still are. Instead, we should go out and make sure lane markers are painted properly. That is a paltry cost compared to the huge benefit we would derive from it.

You could go further: Why do cars have to learn how to "see" lanes and stop signs and so on in the first place? Why haven't we thought about using technology so that the infrastructure can communicate with cars more directly? It is not that far-fetched when you think about the fact that trains receive signals from the tracks that they need to stop automatically when there is a red light, or that airplanes receive radio signals from the runway to indicate the perfect glide path. Incidentally, trains and planes are also much safer, generally speaking, than cars.

It is a similar story with digital patient records. I see, of course, the sensitive nature of digitizing this kind of data, but it is a tractable problem that can be solved, and, again, the opportunity cost of sitting on the problem is bigger than doing something about it. Countries like Canada, Denmark, and Estonia have shown that it can be implemented safely for the benefit of society. Other countries can learn from them.

Alexander: *Thank you, Florian. What quick-win advice would you give that is easy for many companies to apply within their digital strategies?*

Florian: Find out what the key strengths of your employees are! We have talked a lot about new digital tools, but who are the right people to operate these tools? There are two mistakes that are being made in this context.

The first is to think that just because the tool is simple to operate, anyone can now do so. I have seen this with the commoditization of survey tools that make it easy for anyone to create survey forms. It actually takes quite a bit of knowledge to set up a survey that will yield reliable results! That doesn't mean you have to hire people with the right skills for every task at hand. But you have to ask who might be able to learn the basics of good survey design.

There are of course many tools that don't require any specialized skills. Still, it would be a mistake not to think about who should be operating them. With modern content management systems, for example, it is easy to update the content of a website. But should the person who wrote a blog post for the organization's website also be the one to enter the text into the system? Perhaps not, because there is a huge opportunity cost of asking a talented writer to fiddle around with the website, both in terms of their time but more importantly in terms of whether they find enjoyment and fulfillment in their work.

Knowledge workers can be divided into two groups: the more creative ones who are good at abstraction and the more detailed-oriented ones who are good at implementing. So find out what your employees' superpowers are. There are different ways to go about it, but I particularly like the *Strengths Finder* test by Gallup.

Alexander: *What are your favorite apps, tools, or software that you can't live without?*

Florian: I'm a little biased, because I work for the company that makes it, but I am a huge fan of Tableau Prep, which is a tool for cleaning, restructuring, and integrating different data sources. It allows you to see the changes that you are making to a data table before you run the script. I am a curious creature and like to dig into all sorts of different data sets, so this tool has become a real game changer for me.

Another app that I recently discovered is Notion. I use it for my to-do lists, to keep web snippings, and to jot down ideas. But it has many other functionalities, including Kanban bords, and calendars, timelines, and it can be used by teams too. It is like a Swiss Army knife for organizing content and tasks.

Alexander: *Do you have a smart productivity hack or work-related shortcut?*

Florian: This is going to sound funny, given the topic of this book, but there are two hacks that I use, and they both involve protecting myself from digital content!

The first is that I have blocked Twitter, Facebook, and most news sites on my work laptop. In his book *Indistractable*, author Nir Eyal explains how these sites are designed to keep you on them for as long as possible, for example, by suggesting ever more content for you to check out. So I try my best to avoid tripping into one of these time sinks. Nowadays, I get my daily news update mostly by listening to the radio, and I try to stay in touch with friends mostly by phone and text message.

The second hack is that I try to avoid looking at any type of device after 10 p.m. The blue light emitted by screens suppresses the rise in melatonin that is required for us to feel sleepy at night. From the book *Why We Sleep* by Matthew Walker, I learned that most people who claim they can get by with less than seven hours of shut-eye are lying and are hurting not only their productivity but also their long-term health.

Alexander: *What is the best advice you have ever received?*

Florian: When I worked for the World Economic Forum (WEF), I was involved in several projects creating digital offerings for the WEF community, including what was essentially a social collaboration platform for the world's foremost leaders and thinkers. A colleague there introduced me to the P-O-S-T framework for thinking through new project ideas like these:

- People: Define your audience.
- Objective: Define what you want to do for your audience.
- Strategy: How will you achieve that objective?
- Technology: What technology do you need to implement the strategy?

This is extremely useful, because when we get excited about a new technology, the temptation is to try it immediately, without having really thought through whether it makes sense in the given context. With the *T* being the last step in the suggested process, the P-O-S-T framework is a nice forcing function to counter this inclination.

Key Takeaways

- Companies that don't use cutting-edge digital technologies to create value for their customers will lose out in the "experience economy."
- Technologies like AI will become ubiquitous as they become commoditized, but managers will need to learn how to harness the creativity of their knowledge workers alongside the machines.
- If the requisite regulatory frameworks can be put in place, the digital transformation will help to address major societal issues, including healthcare, traffic, pollution, and corruption.

Endnotes

i   Pine II, Joseph B., and Gilmore, James H., "Welcome to the Experience Economy," *Harvard Business Review*, 76, no. 2 (July/August 1998): 97–105.

ii Christensen, Clayton M., *The Innovator's Dilemma: When New Technologies Cause Great Firms to Fail*, Boston, MA: Harvard Business School Press, 1997.

iii Pofeldt, Elaine, "Full-time Freelancing Lures More Americans," *Forbes*, October 5, 2019 (https://www.forbes.com/sites/elainepofeldt/2019/10/05/full-time-freelancing-lures-more-americans).

iv Cotgreave, Andy, "Find Hidden Insights in Your Data: Ask Why and Why Again," *InfoWorld*, September 16, 2016 (https://www.infoworld.com/article/3120513/find-hidden-insights-in-your-data-ask-why-and-why-again.html).

Chapter 6
Corporate Social Network to Drive Collaborative Culture as Key Enabler for Modern Work

This real-life example is based on an engagement at a pharmaceutical company.

The pharma company's communication and collaboration were limited to emails. Teams were working in silos, using various consumer tools such as WhatsApp to connect and to share information. Without a central platform for collaborating and sharing knowledge, employees had a difficult time finding the information they needed. They had to send documents and spreadsheets as attachments to work on them together.

Drupal, an open source content management system (CMS), was used as knowledge storage, but it was poorly maintained and the information was usually out of date. A platform for video calls was used only for external purposes, as its limited usability and the lack of integration were not attractive to the employees.

Best-of-Breed vs. Best-of-Suite

In choosing solutions for improved communication and collaboration, the pharma company followed the best-of-breed approach. A best-of-breed approach means that the organization must invest time in each individual product's upgrade cycle for integration and testing. Some components even lack a proper integration, which makes workarounds (with scripts or additional integration tools) necessary. In a best-of-suite solution, this is typically not required, as the suite's components usually follow the same release cycle and are already well integrated.

If companies can cover this investment, best-of-breed is a very flexible approach that might cover niche use cases better. This was, however, not the case for this pharma company. Therefore, the pharma company's (chief information officer) CIO decided to migrate to the best-of-suite approach as part of their digital strategy.

Instead of implementing products from seven different vendors, they choose Microsoft, which has a broad and integrated portfolio. The Microsoft 365[i] (M365) suite fully meets their needs for communication and collaboration tools.

Corporate Social Network

In a brainstorming session with the C-level staff, the idea of a corporate social network came up. While the chief marketing officer (CMO) immediately liked the idea of "a LinkedIn only for our company," other executives were more reserved. The main concern was that employees could get too confused about which channel to use for which information.

A workshop highlighted the main use cases of a corporate social network:

- Building community at scale across organizations
- Using communication and collaboration to share and leverage the knowledge that people within an organization possess
- Ensuring that leaders and employees get engaged at scale

The platform is a distinct way to connect larger communities of workers with long-tail information to share, rather than smaller focused groups, which are more likely to use chat for immediate communication. This allows conversations with longer half-lives that are not serviced through a chat mechanism alone. Whereas a chat within a team is almost not that useful 48 hours later, conversations on a corporate social network may be useful months or even years later.

Employees are gravitating toward a corporate social network for top-down scenarios, from leaders to employees to broad communities, whereas chat drives bottom-up adoption, connecting individuals and teams. Both approaches contribute to the company's collaborative culture.

Following the Collaboration Framework

The Collaboration Framework provides guidance based on urgency and target audience (see Figure 6.1). The products in this Collaboration Framework follow the pharma company's decision to adopt the best-of-suite approach with M365. The framework would also be applicable for the best-of-breed approach with products of various vendors.

The pharma company decided to follow and adopt the Collaboration Framework. This framework implies the following:

- Urgent communication is handled via chat (Teams).
- Non-urgent communication is done via email (Outlook), informing about events, news, etc.
- Individuals store information on a file-hosting service (OneDrive) or in notetaking software (OneNote); both allow sharing with others.
- Teams and departments are organized within a collaborative software platform (Teams); some also use a task management tool (Planner).

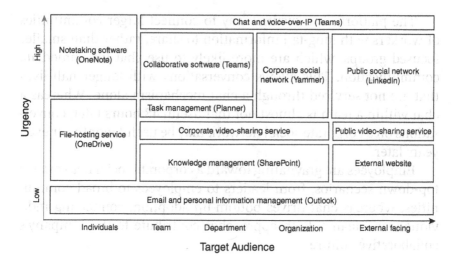

Figure 6.1 Example of a collaboration framework based on Microsoft 365 products

- Persistent information is stored in a knowledge management platform (SharePoint) instead of the former intranet solution.
- Company-wide information and employee-driven initiatives are shared on a corporate social network (Yammer).

Driving Adoption

Hands-on workshops were executed to drive adoption. After the workshops, most employees understood the basics of what they could do with the platform. Once they start using it, their knowledge began to expand quickly. A regular newsletter sent via email encouraged the use of the other channels. This newsletter also featured best practices to further enhance the chat and meeting culture of the company.[ii]

Later the company deployed a bot called Icebreaker[iii] to further boost social interaction. Icebreaker helped the teams to build cohesion by pairing two random team members each week to meet. The bot makes scheduling easy by automatically suggesting free times that work for both members.

One year later nearly every employee was using the chat and notetaking software, while 85 percent of the employees were regularly engaged on the corporate social network. The bot helped to strengthen personal connections and build a tightly knit community. This strategic shift increased the company's productivity by 18 percent.

Key Takeaways

- A best-of-suite approach requires less investment in integration and maintenance compared to the more flexible best-of-breed approach.
- A corporate social network connects larger communities of workers with long-tail information to share, while smaller, more focused groups are more likely to use chat for immediate communication.
- Hands-on workshops and regular newsletters can help to drive adoption of the Collaboration Framework.

Endnotes

i   Microsoft 365 (M365) is a superset of Office 365 with Windows 10 Enterprise licenses and security and device management products.

ii "5 Productivity Hacks to improve your Meeting Culture," a generic example of how a newsletter can help to shape the meeting culture: https://www.linkedin.com/pulse/5-productivity-hacks-improve-your-meeting-culture-alexander-loth/.

iii Icebreaker bot on GitHub: https://github.com/OfficeDev/microsoft-teams-apps-icebreaker/wiki.

Part III

Data Democracy and Analytics

Chapter 7
Yilian Villanueva Martinez: Visual Analytics as Strategic Asset

Yilian Villanueva Martinez, VP of Tableau Services, Lovelytics
Source: Yilian Villanueva Martinez

Yilian Villanueva is the VP of Tableau Services at Lovelytics. Traditional as it may sound, her day to day goes everywhere from taking sales calls to putting out fires at client sites, as well as leading the occasional webinar on visual analytics and mentoring and coaching Lovelytics' newer recruits. Originally from Havana, Cuba, Yilian graduated as a telecommunications engineer from Havana Polytechnic University, where she taught physics upon graduation. After this, she worked for Tableau as a product consultant before moving to Deloitte to explore the consulting world, landing at Lovelytics later for a role that combines the best of the previous two. She runs on pure-grade Cuban coffee, probably because she is not a morning person.

Alexander: You are VP of Tableau Services at Lovelytics. What is your mission?

Yilian: My mission is to bring data democratization to companies to help people truly see and understand their data and make informed decisions in order to grow.

Alexander: How should business models evolve to survive and thrive in an increasingly digital world?

Yilian: Business models should evolve to be tech-oriented, to be constantly innovating, and to use data to drive the decision-making process. Driving the decision-making process with data will be the main asset to interpret the business and to find new sources of revenue. Looking at today's most successful companies, there is one thing they have in common — they are customer-centric. Understanding and anticipating customers' needs will be key for any business to be successful. For example, every day more companies shift to SaaS and subscription models. This allows them to engage and keep up with their customers and their specific needs and provide new services based on those needs, which guarantees retained (happy) customers and growing accounts. Providing solutions that are flexible and easily scalable and removing high up-front costs will open the business to a wider audience and will increase the customer base.

Alexander: How can technology shift the roles and responsibilities of the workforce?

Yilian: Fear of technology overtaking jobs is something we have been hearing about for a while. To your point, technology's impact will instead be reflected as a shift in the roles and responsibilities in the workforce. For instance, moving to SaaS platforms and not having to maintain in-house infrastructure allows network specialists to focus on automating processes, improving performance, and reducing lag times. Democratizing data and using machine learning and natural language processing allows the business user to dive deeper and to find meaning in the data, identify outliers to help improve processes, and make the right decisions for the business. I believe technology is there to remove repetitive, time-consuming work, and to open the door for human creativity, productivity, and innovation.

Alexander: Which technologies or digital capabilities are essential for a digital strategy?

Yilian: A digital strategy needs visual analytics supported by a robust data analytics tool in order to stand a chance at pointing the business in the right direction. For a really long time, our strategies have relied on static reports built by analysts from static data that may be a month old to make decisions that are consequently based on yesterday's news. Having real-time insights presented in a visual, easy-to-understand manner, with the ability to dive deeper and the flexibility to ask questions about current data, can take your digital strategy to the next level. Put machine-learning algorithms on top of this, and you're now able to predict how things will look in the future. This allows you to drive the decision-making process in a proactive manner, instead of solely reacting to what you had in the past. Add natural-language processing, and you'll bring self-service visual analytics to the table, enabling everyone to understand and explore the data, tech background or not, and

> *A digital strategy needs visual analytics supported by a robust data analytics tool in order to stand a chance at pointing the business in the right direction.*

giving a 360-degree view to the business user who is no longer limited to what the analyst provides.

Alexander: Why do data visualizations have such a strong impact on our decisions?

Yilian: Data visualizations act like translators between the raw data and humans, making it easier to understand the message and meaning behind the hundreds of millions of rows. When we look at a visualization, there are pre-attentive attributes that our brains are trained to understand without even thinking about it, which tell us at a glance that something is good or bad, better or worse than before. A color gradient that indicates the density of a metric, position of marks, length, or trends — all these visual cues make it easy to spot outliers and data behaviors, telling you more in a few seconds than what a crosstab could ever convey.

Alexander: Why is data storytelling the essential data science skill that everyone needs?

Yilian: Think of data storytelling as an equal to communication skills. You could have great thoughts, but if you're unable to articulate them eloquently, you won't get them across to others. Any data scientist can get the answers they need from a data set, but it will be harder for others to make sense of it. However, if you build engaging data visualizations and put them together to tell a story with a natural flow that's easy for anyone to understand and interact with, you allow everyone else, including people who don't have a technical background, to find meaning in the data. Storytelling makes data accessible, not boring and hard as it has historically been, but something you can have fun with. It opens up the way for curiosity, and for a data-based culture at all levels.

Alexander: How can everyone learn to communicate better with data?

Yilian: Two words: data literacy. The same way we learn to read and write at school, we need to learn how to read, understand, and communicate data. It's not practical to just sit through webinars: people should get their hands dirty and dive into the data with the tools they have available. There are some good ones out there you can use for free, like Tableau Public. A good exercise to get started would be to take some of your own data from social media plat-forms, streaming services, and activity-tracking apps, and use it to investigate your own patterns. The value of doing this is that you will always have questions to ask, since the data is about you. You might be surprised with what you find! I analyzed my Spotify data and found out that I listen to Shakira a bit too much.

Alexander: Companies usually have plenty of legacy dashboards, the messages of which cannot be seen at first glance. What would a workshop to improve visual data communication look like?

Yilian: This use case is quite common. A workshop to improve the visual display of data should be based on human-centered design. I usually break it down into five steps. First, find out what audience these dashboards are trying to reach. This will define the type of dashboard you will be building. Second, you need to under-stand which are the key performance indicators (KPIs) in the data. These will most likely be displayed as summary metrics in your dashboard. The next step is to gather the business questions the dashboards should answer. Think of these directly linked to story-telling with data, as the questions will allow you to guide the end user through the story they tell when put together.

Step four is getting an understanding of the visual preferences of the end users, so you can use them as recommendations when building the visualizations. This one is particularly tricky, because legacy reports and visuals don't always align with visual best prac-tices, and people like to stick to what they know. I try to understand why they may prefer one visual over another and offer alternative options where I see fit. At this stage it's good to pause and explain why one visual is harder to understand while others are more pre-attentive. The last step is to take all this information and build the dashboard and then have the end users test it and provide feedback to fine-tune it to their preferences.

This will be an iterative process, as I'm sure you'd expect. Also, something I didn't include here is wireframing, as an optional task before building the dashboards. Wireframing sometimes helps you have a clear idea of what you will create, and you can use it to share with the audience to get their input before getting started.

Personally, I find that my design creativity spikes when I'm hands on building the visuals, so I tend to skip the wireframing piece. You should make the process your own and run it however it feels right for you, as long as you're keeping the end user as the main point and focus of your approach.

Alexander: What basic guidelines and patterns should always be considered for a visual expressive dashboard?

Yilian: Simplicity is key when building a visually engaging dashboard. My main rules are using a reasonable number of colors and keeping colors consistent across visuals. Use different colors to represent discrete metrics like categories, while using shades of a color to display continuous metrics, or a diverging color scale to represent positives and negatives. Add action-oriented titles for views and filters so that the end user knows what they are supposed to do to interact with the dashboard. Use tooltips to show details, as opposed to adding too much detail in the dashboard at once. Reduce the number of views per dashboard. Avoid scrollbars, size the dashboard to easily fit the screen of the device it is meant to be consumed in. I try to think how I would react to the dashboard if it would be my first time seeing it. It helps me spot areas for improvement.

Alexander: Who should you trust with helping you monitor the changes you're making and testing your dashboard prototype to see if it meets expectations?

Yilian: I usually go to that co-worker who is detail-oriented and not technical. Kyle, you know who you are! :) Another good person to get feedback from would be someone unrelated to the field, like a friend or family member (as long as it's not sensitive data, of course). Have them take a shot at understanding the dashboard and interacting with it on their own, and then listen to their questions — these will point out the areas that need improvement! If they are able to get it, you'll know you've built a great dashboard.

Alexander: What are your personal top three dos and don'ts for an engaging visualization?

Yilian: I'm going to start with my don'ts. Personally, I don't use pie charts ever. I know some people like them, but I don't quite believe in their power to display data efficiently or beautifully. I don't use one color in the same dashboard to represent two different metrics. Sometimes, for the sake of minimizing the number of colors in a dashboard or following company guidelines, we use the same color throughout, making it confusing for the person consuming the dashboard. Lastly, I don't add too many filters. When you build a view, thinking of usability and performance, reducing the number of filters is key. I have seen dashboards with twenty filters or more — this just ends up being confusing for the person interacting with the views, let alone slow.

Something I do, jumping into my dos now, is to try to move the filtering options to the views within the dashboard. For instance, if there is a view displaying categories, I would allow the end user to click the categories there as opposed to giving them a drop-down filter. It's more intuitive, it helps with performance, and it saves some dashboard real estate.

My second do is to clean the tooltips and include views with details in them where it makes sense. Tooltips are a great way to display data and details without cluttering a dashboard. Third and last, I use the correct visualization type for the data I'm trying to display:

- A scatter plot if I'm comparing two metrics
- A line chart if I'm looking at data over time
- A bar chart if I'm looking at a comparison of a metric between different groups
- A tree map if I'm trying to represent parts of a total (great alternative to pie charts)

These are only a few examples, but you get the idea.

Alexander: *Thank you, Yilian. What quick-win advice would you give that is easy for many companies to apply within their digital strategies?*

Yilian: You're most welcome! The best advice I could give anyone is to invest in self-service analytics. This will be a key part of your digital strategy, as it will help point your business in the right direction and pay back by empowering people to be smarter.

Alexander: What are your favorite apps, tools, or software that you can't live without?

Yilian: In apps, Tableau is leading the way. I use it at work, at home, pretty much for everything, from allocating my team's projects to tracking my spending and investments. Spotify as well — I listen to music when I'm working, studying, doing chores. It helps me focus and be more productive (nothing like some Metallica tunes to keep me in the zone). There's also Peloton, which I use for spinning, running, and yoga trainings, as I prefer to work out at home or run outside as opposed to going to the gym. In tools I'd have to list my MacBook Pro. She's (yes, it's a she) always fast and efficient and has followed me all around the world to client sites, conferences, and vacations.

Alexander: Do you have a smart productivity hack or work-related shortcut?

Yilian: I do! Blocking time on my calendar for the things I need to get done is what keeps me productive all day. There are always small tasks, like responding to an email, that easily get pushed back in the day as others take priority, and I end up postponing or forgetting them. By having allocated a specific time to take care of those, I'm more likely to handle them sooner and more efficiently.

Alexander: What is the best advice you have ever received?

Yilian: To keep an open mind, and to be flexible to changes. I remember thinking I wanted to be a network engineer at the beginning of my career, and I was quite set on that. When my uncle, Ramon Martinez, who was a Tableau Zen Master at the time, started talking to me about data back in 2014, I thought the subject wasn't interesting. He still encouraged me to go see him present on visual best practices at an analytics event and to give it a shot. Turns out I love data and can't imagine liking doing anything else this much.

Key Takeaways

- Data visualizations act like translators between the raw data and humans, making it easier to understand the message and meaning behind the hundreds of millions of rows.
- Simplicity is key when building a visually engaging dashboard, using a reasonable number of colors, and keeping colors consistent across visuals.
- Think of data storytelling as an equal to communication skills. It makes data accessible, not boring as it has historically been seen, but something you can have fun with. It opens up the way for curiosity and for a data-based culture at all levels.

Chapter 8
Jordan Morrow: Bringing Data Literacy to the World

Jordan Morrow, global head of data literacy, Qlik
Source: Jordan Morrow

Jordan is known as the "Godfather of Data Literacy," helping pioneer and build the field of data literacy as one of the first to bring data literacy to the world. In his career, Jordan helps individuals and organizations realize their data and analytical potential by bringing to light and enhancing skills and strategies in data literacy, and data and analytics in general. When not immersed in data and analytics, Jordan can be found with his large family or trail running the mountains as an avid ultramarathon runner.

Alexander: *You are global head of data literacy at Qlik. What is your mission?*

Jordan: I feel like my answer has changed over time. In the beginning, my ideas and thoughts were all around helping to train and empower people with skills in analytics. So I set out to build analytical courses with a product-agnostic approach. That was very big for me in the beginning and still is. Data literacy is not about a product, tools, and so on; it is about the person. Setting out and creating courses and materials is essential, so people who do not have a background in data and analytics can succeed in that world.

> *My vision and goal would be to both empower and enable individuals and organizations to make smart, data-informed decisions.*

Over time, that vision and project grew bigger. As I went about creating the world of data literacy, I noticed there was more to it than just classes, discussion, and so on; it had become more strategic, working with culture, and more.

My vision and goal would be to both empower and enable individuals and organizations to make smart, data-informed decisions. If I can help drive this type of solution and achievement, then data literacy has been a success.

Alexander: *How should business models evolve to survive and thrive in an increasingly digital world?*

Jordan: This is such a great topic, especially considering the world's situation during 2020 with COVID-19. Organizations have been looking to be more data and digitally driven for a while.

I think organizations were able to recognize there was a need (this was before COVID-19 shut the world down) and they were trying to move forward, but they weren't moving quick enough.

Then the world was completely altered, and digitally transforming was no longer a nice-to-have. COVID-19 forced organizations to truly transform in a quick manner, and they discovered they could do it. Now, did this mean their business models were already in place to be successful? Not even close! In fact, one of the silver linings of the shutdown, at least for businesses, was that COVID-19 showed where business still had gaps. This allowed organizations to work toward filling those gaps.

Business models need to be shifted to adapt quickly. They also need to be focused on cultural shift. Business models focus on a lot of things, but what has been found within the data and analytical world is that culture is the number-one roadblock to data and analytic success. The reality is, business models need to change.

Alexander: How can technology shift the roles and responsibilities of the workforce?

Jordan: Technology needs to be an enabler and not the strategy itself. For far too long, organizations have used technology as the strategy itself, when in reality, the strategy needs to dictate the technology, not the other way around. This is so important because technology should be part of each and every role that exists; it's the same with data and analytics.

For far too long, data, analytics, and technology have not been embedded in the business. That can no longer be the case. We need these pieces embedded into the roles and responsibilities of workers. Having disparate systems and silos does not help the organization to succeed. We should see a shift and empowerment for individuals to use the technology, data, and tools to do their jobs better. Technology and data are enablers and can empower people to succeed! That is how technology should be looked at in roles.

Along with having it within the roles, organizations need to put forth the effort to empower the roles to succeed with the technologies they invest in. This doesn't just mean technical learning, but how these roles can use soft skills to see them succeed.

Alexander: Which technology or digital capabilities are essential for a digital strategy?

Jordan: Sticking with my bread and butter, data literacy is an absolute key skill that organizations must deploy to have a strong digital strategy. Data is a life blood of organizations at this point, and individuals need to be given the ability to succeed with these skills. Another key skill that is much like data literacy is digital dexterity, which is the combination of people with digital skills. This includes the soft skills, the technical skills, and mingling them together.

Both of these things are essential for digital strategy. We are constantly hearing about the technologies that are needed, and don't get me wrong, they are needed. But far too often we forget about all these other pieces that are needed to drive these forward, and it isn't the technical side. Organizations need to focus on the nontechnical, and that is data literacy and digital dexterity.

Alexander: Why is data literacy so important?

Jordan: It is no secret that the world we live in is now a data-driven world. We have seen massive increases in the production of data over the last decade or two. Along with just the increase in data, we are also seeing the increase in tools, connectivity with the Internet of Things, and more. All of this has made data a very, very valuable asset for organizations. Organizations, in turn, have tried to capitalize on their data. To capitalize effectively on data, organizations have invested millions and millions of dollars in tools, technology, and the sourcing of data. Along with that, they have looked to train individuals on the tools and technology being invested in. All the while, there was a key element missing: the human element. Data literacy steps in here.

Data literacy, by definition, is the ability to read, work with, analyze, and communicate with data. The original definition I used came from Emerson University and MIT, but had "argue with" instead of communicate. As organizations have invested their millions in the tools and technology, there has been a common theme throughout the world on the actual usage of these tools and technology: adoption of these things is quite low. By adoption I mean using these tools effectively, not just using them to build a pretty chart. When adoption is low, a common theme runs throughout the blame: the tool is at fault. The tool is probably perfectly fine; the reality is the gap is in the human element.

For an organization to succeed effectively with these different areas of data and analytics, data literacy should have been at the forefront of the mind. This isn't to say that the human needed to be trained first, but there should have been a partnership between the tool training and the human training. We know that most people are not going to school for a background in statistics and mathematics, so organizations need to look to empower individuals with data literacy.

Data literacy then should lead to decision-making and improvement and empowerment of individuals and organizations to make smarter decisions. This is the essence of the value of data for an organization, outside of selling the data. Data literacy improves a workforce's ability to consume data effectively and make smarter decisions.

Alexander: Why do data visualizations have such a strong impact on our decisions?

Jordan: Data visualizations are such a powerful tool within the data and analytical arsenal. One thing does need to be made very clear: data visualizations are not the be-all and end-all of data and analytics. They are just a piece of the analytical puzzle.

Analytics or analysis has four levels: descriptive, diagnostic, predictive, and prescriptive. In some cases, inferential is thrown in too, but I put that within the levels themselves, not on a separate level. Data visualizations really get the journey going, but they don't give us the entire journey. We have to have more skills to make things happen. Data visualizations start us off, but usually are not giving us the "why" behind things. We need the data literacy skills that make that happen.

That said, the question is about data visualization impact. Our visual ability surpasses many others. The ability to visualize and see things is power. Articles, books, and study after study talk about the power of our eyes and visual ability, so we don't need to rehash that here. What we can say is that our ability to visualize and pick things up through our eyes is powerful. That is why visualizations have such an impact!

Alexander: Why is data storytelling the essential data science skill that everyone needs?

Jordan: When we think of data storytelling, we are not thinking about the fluffy stories of Disney or other [more] powerful storytelling, but we are talking about the effective ability of individuals to communicate with data throughout an organization. This skill particularly hits home with data science.

Historically, individuals who work in data science have not had communicating with data at the top of the desired skills list. These individuals have been able to sit and hunker down in their tasks and build their models, analyses, and so on. Well, those days have changed.

Data storytelling is the bridge between the business side and the technology side. There is such a gap there: people on the business side don't know how to talk about and discuss the technology side, and the same is true in reverse. Data storytelling is where someone has the ability to fill that gap with the bridge of communication. We absolutely need this throughout an organization looking to capitalize on data and analytics. Imagine if the greatest analysis ever performed for an organization occurred but the person had no skill to communicate the results and things to be done. That would not be good at all, but unfortunately, we see similar things quite often. We need to have the ability to communicate.

Alexander: How can everyone learn to communicate better with data?

Jordan: Practice, practice, practice. Just look to have conversations. For those who have a advanced knowledge, don't use complicated jargon and terms. Use simpler language. For those without that background and skill, just try, learn, and study. Overall, it is like any language: study terms, words, and so on, and then get out there and practice.

Alexander: Companies usually have plenty of legacy dashboards, the messages of which cannot be seen at first glance. What would a workshop to improve visual data communication look like?

Jordan: Evaluate the legacy dashboards and visualizations an organization is using. In a prior job, I inherited a presentation that was about 75 or so PowerPoint slides long, had one chart per slide, and went to most executives in a company of around 60,000 employees. I eventually distilled all those slides into six charts, total, that had a predictive power to them.

First, determine if the legacy needs to remain in place. If it does, then drive data communication by bringing context to the legacy dashboard. In different cases, people don't know how to find insight because the dashboard lacks true context. Second, we need to teach people about the four levels of analytics and how to drive, understand, and find insight from a dashboard, legacy or not. Third, those presenting the legacy dashboard need to drive effective communication through the visualization.

Alexander: What basic guidelines and patterns should always be considered for a visual expressive dashboard?

Jordan: I love to think of this in terms of the recipients' experience. There are amazing books and dialogue out there on visualization and how to build the right chart, coloring, and so forth. In this case, I will go a different route and give guidelines for the practitioner, so the audience will receive it correctly.

- Understand the audience. Who are you building this for? If it is for executives, make it simple and to the point. If it is for an analyst, provide filtering capabilities. If for a business user, build it simple to understand.
- Understand the end goal. What are you trying to solve with this dashboard? If you are just looking to make a pretty dashboard, stop now! You can have a pretty dashboard that has no value. Bring it around to the end goal and then build that amazing visualization.
- Understand the question. What are you trying to answer? By knowing what you are trying to answer, you improve your chances of making an effective visualization.

Alexander: Whom should you trust with helping you monitor the changes you're making and testing your dashboard prototype to see if it meets expectations?

Jordan: First and foremost, they must be data literate and confident in their data literacy skills. If a person does not have a background that is conducive to improving your dashboard and visualization, then they are probably not the one to help. Second, find those who have these skills but work in a different area. I trust those who don't work in the area more because they may not have the biases that are built up from working in the same area. Third, find the person who has the ability to find insight in data. If the changes you have made make it harder to find insight, there can be large issues in the long run.

Alexander: Why should companies set up an Analytics Center of Excellence as part of their digital strategy? What are some strategies for setting this up?

Jordan: An Analytics Center of Excellence is such a powerful way to drive the data and analytical strategy of a company. I am hit with the question quite often: who should own this? The answer is harder when this center of excellence does not exist. If it does exist, then it is easy to turn to this group to help drive the answers, work, and strategies needed to succeed in a digital strategy. With this sort of strategy, you don't want to be sitting on wishful thinking. Have the right strategy to make this happen.

To drive a center of excellence correctly, there are some key tenets to follow. First and foremost, have leadership buy in from the top. Have you ever tried to implement something like this, but the executive team doesn't buy in? It isn't going to be that successful. Second, make sure you have the right leader in place to build a center of excellence. You need someone with the right skills and talents, both technical and nontechnical, to drive this. Third, make sure you have a strong data and analytical strategy. Without this, the center of excellence will struggle to determine what to do. Fourth, work with the different business units in the organization to set up the right partnerships and understanding. A center of excellence is there to empower the entire organization. Ensure that it isn't just helping one area over another, but has a truly holistic approach to its work. By having the holistic approach, you avoid silos and other issues.

Alexander: What are your personal top three dos and don'ts for an engaging visualization?

Jordan: Good question.

My dos:

- Choose visualizations carefully.
- Choose the right colors to make things stand out.
- Add appropriate filters for analytical work.

My don'ts:

- Don't add charts for charts' sake. Simplicity is truly king or queen.
- Don't add unnecessary colors to try and make it "cooler."
- Don't overthink it. Don't worry about making it the best thing in the world. If you can get value out of it, you have a valuable visualization.

Alexander: Thank you, Jordan. What quick-win advice would you give that is easy for many companies to apply within their digital strategies?

Jordan: Create a library of wins and effective outcomes. A lot of times people question these types of initiatives because they can't see what success looks like. Create a library of digital strategies that have gone successfully, and draw on it. Maybe it is in your supply chain or marketing. But create this library so you can show and empower your naysayers to turn from the negative side to the positive.

Alexander: What are your favorite apps, tools, or software that you can't live without?

Jordan: Being the data literacy guy, I am so focused on non–tool-specific things that I will drive my answer here not from a tool-specific piece but from a work-related piece. I cannot live without public speaking and interacting with people. Even in the virtual world we live in because of the COVID-19 pandemic in 2020 and 2021, I love to be in front of people and convey ideas. Not just convey ideas, but get questions, hear perspectives, and so on.

From an app perspective, I love to meditate and work out, so I will say both the Calm and Peloton apps.

Alexander: Do you have a smart productivity hack or work-related shortcut?

Jordan: I don't know if I would call it a hack, but something that hits home with me is starting my day off with a workout. If I hit a good workout to start my day, the day just goes better. If I don't get my blood flowing and really march forward with a strong workout, the day is not going to be as successful. Don't jump up and start your day looking at your phone, checking social media, and so on. Start by focusing on you, and you can get your day to be an even bigger success. One hack with this: before going to sleep, turn your phone into airplane mode. Then, when you get up you won't be flooded with messages, emails, social media notifications, and so on, that potentially bring fires and negativity. Start your day focused on you!

Alexander: What is the best advice you have ever received?

Jordan: I don't know if I would call it advice, but something that really sticks with me is a quote that is attributed to Albert Einstein, but it almost certainly wasn't he who said it: "Everyone is a genius. But if you judge a fish by its ability to climb a tree, it will live its whole life believing that it is stupid." Regardless of who said it, the message resonates so much with me. We are all amazing individuals and have unbelievable talents, but if we continue to try and fit everyone in the same peg hole, we are in big trouble. Find what you are good at and march forward! Work on your craft and be the genius you are.

Key Takeaways

- Data literacy is not about tools; it is about people. Creating courses and materials is essential so people who do not have a background in data and analytics can succeed.
- Data storytelling is the bridge between the business side and the technology side. This ability to communicate with data is

required throughout an organization looking to capitalize on data and analytics.

- Another key skill is digital dexterity, which is the combination of people with digital skills. This includes the soft skills, the technical skills, and mingling them together.

Chapter 9
Lee Feinberg: Turn Data Visualization and Data Literacy into Strategic Functions

Lee Feinberg, CEO, DecisionViz

Source: Lee Feinberg

Lee Feinberg founded DecisionViz in 2012 to help clients become leaders in the people, process, and culture around data visualization and data literacy.

He has worked for 20 years in the fields of analytics, data visualization, and business intelligence. Lee created the Design To Act® framework as a way to help organizations and individuals apply his knowledge and expertise.

Lee frequently speaks at industry conferences and guest lectures at leading schools, including Columbia University and NYU. He has also served on the board of advisors at Stevens Institute of Technology. Lee graduated from Cornell University with a BS and an MS in electrical engineering.

DecisionViz is a Tableau Silver Services Partner and a Tableau Foundation Contributor. Lee served as a Tableau Ambassador from 2016 to 2020 and on Tableau's Customer Advocacy Board. He also founded and ran the New Jersey and New York Tableau User Groups from 2010 to 2018.

Lee is an avid heavy-metal concertgoer, *Deadpool* is his favorite movie, and he enjoys weightlifting and biking. He's been married for 23 years to Lori; his son, Matt, is a junior in college; and his daughter, Aliyah, is a college freshman.

Alexander: *You are CEO at DecisionViz. What is your mission?*

Lee: We are helping people unleash their potential through becoming data literate.

Alexander: *How should business models evolve to survive and thrive in an increasingly digital world?*

Lee: Data has to be at the center of any digital strategy. And since data visualization is the means to communicate the meaning of the data, that is also strategic. The big idea here is that any strategic function needs a process (imagine if finance did not use balance sheets and income statements). So organizations must have a process in place around data visualization. The typical way of working today is that everyone gets a piece of visualization software, and maybe they receive a bit of formal training on how to operate the software. Then, each person is allowed to use that software however they like — and productivity clearly suffers. This is why organizations continue to wonder why they are not achieving the projected ROI. To operate in a digital world, you must adapt your processes or, in some cases, change them completely.

Alexander: *How can technology shift the roles and responsibilities of the workforce?*

Lee: I'm excited about how technology is providing very powerful capabilities to people who lack technical skills. This allows ideas to take form rapidly by speeding up and simplifying innovation. You can see this in Amazon Web Services enabling startups as well as large companies like Netflix, down to how something like Tableau Software opens access to large databases without any programming. But this shift also places an unanticipated accountability on teams. While the technology provides some automation, typically it's incomplete. The teams have to take on some of the related work. For example, having access to new data requires understanding the data structures, identifying bad data, and writing logic formulas. These are specialized skills that can take years to develop, yet there is often an unspoken expectation that somehow teams will just know how to take on these responsibilities. Of course, that is a bad assumption.

Alexander: *Which technology or digital capabilities are essential for a digital strategy?*

Lee: You need technology that gets data into the hands of everyone in the company, and more importantly, you have to disseminate decision-making. I call this decision democratization; it's the next step beyond data democratization. Data is just there to drive decision-making and action-taking. Most companies use Excel to compile, manage, track, and analyze data. Companies must find ways to automate as much of this work as possible, which will allow them to focus on making decisions and taking action. Outside of the financial investment, the bigger investment required is in cultural change. Leadership needs to put the training in place to help people adopt new ways of working together — not just expect

Leadership needs to put the training in place to help people adopt new ways of working together — not just expect it to happen.

it to happen. And they must demonstrate this behavior; otherwise, frankly, individuals will not be willing to make the necessary changes, and the status quo will prevail. Executives, rather than controlling decision-making, must delegate more of this "power" to individuals and teams, especially since the individuals and teams are usually closer to the truth about the potential upside and downside to specific actions.

While delegating is the necessary first step, it's not sufficient. Executives must enable cultural changes, such as allowing for risk-taking and making mistakes, which are two tremendous human obstacles. Leadership must also train people on the process of making decisions; it's not as simple as telling someone they have the power to make a decision.

Alexander: *Why do data visualizations have such a strong impact on our decisions?*

Lee: We humans are naturally wired to process patterns. Whether it's recognizing an apple, a person, or a bar chart. The amazing thing is that our brain does this automatically for us; it is processing information before we even have a chance to consciously think about that information (don't think about this too much because it will hurt your brain). Imagine that you already have experiences, assumptions, or opinions on a topic and you see a data visualization to which your brain immediately reacts. It starts to make connections from the initial interpretation of that visualization to the thoughts already in your mind. That happens so fast; it starts down the road of thinking about possible conclusions and decisions. For this reason, it's critical to present data in a way that is not biased to show a particular conclusion, but rather to make any insight as clear as possible.

Alexander: *Why is data storytelling the essential data science skill that everyone needs?*

Lee: As data becomes another language everyone needs to speak and read, not just people in data science, data storytelling must be a universal skill. I think about storytelling as one skill in the area of data literacy. If you take the idea of literacy, it is composed of elements including grammar, composition, vocabulary, and storytelling. So we need parallel elements in data literacy. And I want to emphasize the idea that literacy has to address writing and reading. I advocate that the first step is teaching how to author better data stories and then teach people how to read them. In reality you need to do both, but more effort should initially be placed on writing. For example, if you invest more in elevating people's reading skills — but they are reading poorly written stories — that adds very little value to the goals of making decisions and taking action.

The other point I am making is that you can't jump right into teaching people how to write stories without giving them the other foundation elements to build on. Also, the hard truth is that not everyone will reach the same level of skill in authoring or reading stories — just like it is today when it comes to working with, for example, the English language. It's important to recognize that and build a data literacy strategy that accounts for varying levels of ability.

Alexander: How can everyone learn to communicate better with data?

Lee: First, you have to break down the notion of communication into the two parts of writing and reading. Some people will need to develop skills in one of these areas; some in both. Identifying each team member's role in the beginning will help focus where to help them upskill. It will also reduce any pressure they might feel to clarify assumptions about where they are involved in the cycles of decisions and actions.

Outside of the data literacy skills that each person must develop, two significant cultural shifts are equally critical — actually, more critical. Today, work in the field of communicating data is mostly thought of as an activity of making charts and reports — not communicating. The organization has built all of its processes, and its culture, to support work in this way.

To be centered around communication, an organization must change its processes and culture to be consultative, which means asking questions to seek understanding, rather than asking for requirements and not uncovering the intended use and outcomes. While teaching the art of asking questions is straightforward, but requires practice to be truly skillful, the emphasis is more on people being receptive to the questions, especially executives who may feel their authority is not being respected, when in fact it is the opposite. The questions are intended to pull from their experience and knowledge. It will take time and clear successes to make this shift.

Alexander: What skills will managers need to develop to enable data democracy within their companies?

Lee: Trust. Since data democracy will naturally lead to decision democracy, managers will have to trust their teams with the new responsibility of making decisions. They will also have to teach their teams a process for decision-making and help each person to build confidence in making decisions. They cannot assume everything will fall into place without some real effort. Managers will also have to build team members' ability to evaluate decisions and guide their teams on how to test assumptions and hypotheses. Most importantly, leaders will have to be able to recognize which employees may not be comfortable taking on this accountability — and that it doesn't diminish their value to the team. It's not a skill every person can develop or wants to develop.

Alexander: Companies usually have plenty of legacy dashboards, the messages of which cannot be seen at first glance. What would a workshop to improve visual data communication look like?

Lee: I look at data visualization and data literacy as strategic functions, not the activity of making charts and dashboards. So, instead of a workshop, we work with companies to put a strategic process in place — the same way that functions like IT, finance, marketing, HR, and so on have strategic processes. Having said that, the main components of learning the process would be

- understanding the language of visualization, which means the proper use of color, size, gradients, shapes, and so on, and how the brain works with these visual components;
- taking consistent steps to build a clear understanding of the desired decisions and actions;
- making sure the data exists to support the decisions and goals;
- understanding how to create mockups and get feedback in an agile fashion; and
- producing the stories (dashboards).

These steps are just to produce a story; our Design To Act method also covers how to activate, measure, and improve the dashboards so that you can achieve maximum adoption.

Alexander: What basic guidelines and patterns should always be considered for a visually expressive dashboard?

Lee: I have a saying, "Intent before Content," which means you cannot determine the proper way to display information until you understand what it is supposed to do; in this case, what decisions and actions it will support. You need to have flexibility in how a visual data story will be written. However, I do promote the data literacy idea of grammar. When you think about grammar in relation to, for example, English, there are rules about how the language works. If everyone understands and follows those rules, it's much easier to communicate. Each organization must define their own grammar guidelines in a way that best supports their business. For example, do you want to show sales as a bar chart or a list of numbers? What should forecasts and targets look like? Which colors can be used to represent teams? Once this grammar foundation is in place, it will be easier for authors to write data stories and easier for readers, because they are presented with a consistent view of information that they can quickly recognize.

Alexander: Who should you trust with helping you monitor the changes you're making and testing your dashboard prototype to see if it meets expectations?

Lee: I don't think it's a matter of trust, but rather a matter of process. Although you should not trust yourself — the builder cannot be the tester and the customer. At minimum, you need a process for making sure the data is correct, because bad data quickly kills the trust you worked so hard to build. It's best to document real-world scenarios rather than rely on spot-checking a few data points. Equally important, an organization should ensure a consistent user experience. This covers areas such as dashboard load speed, visualization best practices, and grammar guidelines. Think about the standards your company puts in place for its products and apply them to the work of data and visualization. Using this kind of reference point also helps you build a case for why new processes and roles may be needed.

Alexander: Why should companies set up an Analytics Center of Excellence as part of their digital strategy? What are some strategies for setting this up?

Lee: Companies should consider a center of excellence for all core disciplines — finance, marketing, HR, IT, and so on. The more sharing of ideas the better. I don't know the history of why there's a particular focus only on the analytics/data/visualization center of excellence (CoE), but I can imagine it was seen as a way to jump-start and provide a source of support for practitioners. However, most firms are approaching this idea half-heartedly, meaning they typically assign it to someone who already has a full-time job, while running a CoE *is* a full-time job. So from the start, there's a lack of energy and direction. Additionally, the person may not be suited to run a CoE; it takes a special set of skills, like any job — in this case, motivating people to act, establishing an environment for collaboration, setting a strategy and being able to execute, having credibility as a leader in the field and in the company. While a CoE has great potential, I have seen them devolve into an occasional lunch-and-learn event, or the place you go for help with the technology.

Alexander: What are your personal top three dos and don'ts for an engaging visualization?

Lee: Rather than engaging, I'd like to reinforce the ideas of decision-making and action-taking. You can create an engaging visualization that accomplishes neither of these. A visualization must answer the questions, "What decisions or actions would I take?" and "What do I need to see to even consider doing that?" Most people start with listing the data, metrics, and type of charts they want — they have it 180 degrees wrong. These elements come out of answering those two questions. So that's the first don't.

Number two is no pie charts and no donut charts. Seriously, these bother me so much because bar charts and gradient grids are simpler and better alternatives to communicate the data. Number three, well, it's hard to choose. I'd say using your corporate logo and color palettes as the core colors for your visualization. While it's possible these may be viable, most likely they are not. Remember, those colors were chosen for reasons other than a visualization, so you cannot default to assuming they work well. For example, I had a client whose corporate colors were red and black, so all visuals were red and black; even the positive numbers were red. That's just confusing. Work with your corporate communications group to develop a color palette for visualizations.

For the dos, number one is to keep it as simple as possible; don't be enamored with the latest hot viz chart, because most of your readers will not know how to use it and that leads to low adoption. Simple is good if it gets the job of decision-making and action-taking done. Number two is to mimic ideas from great websites. Because the visualization is typically accessed via a web browser, your audience is in the mindset that it's another website; they don't care or have to know what technology it is. They just think it should work like Amazon, Netflix, and ESPN.

Number three, spend the extra effort to remove everything that's not necessary — tick marks, gridlines, bold fonts, color. Don't accept the software defaults. This is the same as when you proofread a document and remove unnecessary words and tighten up the language. You must do the same for visual writing. A cleaner look is easier to interpret and will be more engaging.

Alexander: Thank you, Lee. What quick-win advice would you give that is easy for many companies to apply within their digital strategies?

Lee: When big changes are involved, it's often hard for people to see the possibilities for themselves. Going from where they are to a future state requires a lot of unknowns. So a good start is to create an example of what the future can look like, instead of talking in theories and vague terms. The term *quick* can get you in trouble unless everyone agrees what quick looks like. The results of changing strategy can take months to unfold. A few key points that I stick by are:

- Pick a project that will have moderate visibility.
- Do not choose something that is considered mission critical.
- Minimize dependencies like needing new data sources.

Outside of demonstrating how a new process will work, you must be able to measure the improvement from the current state. If you are working on credit card profit, make sure you can show how the new approach is improving profit. If you are showing quality of patient care, you must know the current condition and specifically where and how the new strategy is working. In the end, all of this work depends on also being able to tell a good data story.

Alexander: What are your favorite apps, tools, or software that you can't live without?

Lee: I have two "secret weapons" that are critical parts of my business.

Fiverr.com is a service I use for "automating" work with people and sourcing skills. I hire a go-to artist and copywriter on a weekly basis. I also hire people to do data research, SEO analysis, and audio transcription. It can take some trial and error to find someone you like working with, but the risk is lower than it is when hiring someone full time.

Zoom is cloud software that helps me share data across other cloud services and automate workflows. I can add WebinarNinja attendees to my ActiveCampaign email list and send myself a Gmail when my company is mentioned on Twitter. Since I am a one-person company, these services let me operate as a larger company, respond faster, and be more efficient.

Alexander: *Do you have a smart productivity hack or work-related shortcut?*

Lee: This may sound strange, but one of my productivity hacks is to take breaks. I follow the Pomodoro Technique of working for 25 minutes and then taking a 5-minute break. It forces me to look away from the screen, stretch, and grab more water (or coffee). Most people believe that you have to keep working at something non-stop, and any interruption is bad. Pomodoro goes on the idea that you become less productive the longer you work on something, and small breaks don't damage your flow of thinking. I'll admit to not sticking to it 100 percent and working through some of the breaks, but even 75 percent compliance is a big plus. I can also share one literal shortcut called TextExpander.[i] It's an inexpensive Mac app that lets you record keyboard shortcuts, and it's a massive time-saver — and prevents lots of typos. For example, "tlv" types out "The Language of Visualization" and "30mcal" gives me a link for "book 30 on Lee's calendar." I have shortcuts for a postscript (P.S.) to close an email and a disclaimer that goes in all my videos.

Alexander: *What is the best advice you have ever received?*

Lee: This is simple; my parents always reinforced the golden rule — "do unto others as you would have them do unto you."

Key Takeaways

- Executives must delegate more decision-making and action-taking power to individuals and teams, especially since the individuals and teams are usually closer to the truth about the potential upsides and downsides of specific actions.

- Leadership must enable cultural changes such as allowing for risk-taking and making mistakes, which are two tremendous human obstacles.
- Data visualization and data literacy can be seen as strategic functions, the same way that functions like IT, finance, marketing, HR, and so on have strategic processes.

Endnote

i   TextExpander website: https://textexpander.com/.

Chapter 10

Sarah Burnett: Fostering a Data-Driven Culture at a Large Global Financial Organization

Sarah Burnett, head of data democratization, at a large financial organization

Source: Sarah Burnett

Sarah Burnett is the head of data democratization at a large financial organisation by day, Tableau User Group Ambassador and Singapore Tableau User Group Co-Leader by night. Sarah's passion is making storytelling clean, clear, and simple by instilling best practices and reducing cognitive load all while using beautiful design. Her creative, direct design thinking allows executives to drive their business with powerful visual insights through data while removing the noise that can easily cloud the story. She has an aversion to 3D pie charts, and one of her goals is to move the world of finance away from unnecessary complexity and into clean, clear, and simple data visualizations. Her education includes a Bachelor of Management Studies degree from Waikato University, Hamilton, New Zealand, and she currently resides in Singapore with her young son, Lukas.

Alexander: You are head of data democratization. What is your mission?

Sarah: We are driving a cultural change to be more data driven, one dashboard at a time!

Alexander: Where do you start, with a bold statement like that?

Sarah: To have people come to a central location to consume their near-real-time data, and to make that information clean and clear, while not only answering the first question they may have but allowing them the flexibility to answer the unknowns as well. To make your information their daily shot of caffeine in the morning.

Historically, data has gone to a few. On our road to data democratization we are making data more accessible; by reducing the barriers to see aggregated data across the organization, we encourage others to look at patterns outside of their immediate realm and start conversations with what is working in other areas. We also build our dashboards with the end user in mind and dig deeper to pull out and understand how they would use the data to drive their business forward, looking at the logical next questions they would need answered.

Alexander: How should business models evolve to survive and thrive in an increasingly digital world?

Sarah: Historically in large organizations technology moved slowly, and the tools were big enterprise stacks. This is starting to change; smaller players are coming in and partnering to provide more cutting-edge solutions. We do not look for one generic solution when it comes to problem solving, but we look out in the community and see what is working there. Seeing so many successfully data-driven nontraditional companies make headway where we did not think it possible has made the financial industry look outside of itself to solve its digital landscape. Where we used to silo data and restrict access even internally, we are now looking at new ways, leveraging the technology to open our data and share where possible. Banks have so much data, and we are now starting to really unleash its value and use it to better serve our customers.

Alexander: How can technology shift the roles and responsibilities of the workforce?

Sarah: I love a good process; using the right tools for the intent they were built for can eliminate so much of the mundane manual legwork. When you can automate your flows and get analysts out of data crunching and into delivering insight, you're empowering your workforce, and you'll start to see results. There is so much value in data and so much effort goes into preparing it, but there's often little time given to exploring it. Having the time for people to be curious about data is where you get to see the real value. I love to build internal communities that are curious and passionate about visualizing and exploring data.

Alexander: Which technology or digital capabilities are essential for a digital strategy?

Sarah: Gone are the days of decentralized data; if you want to be truly digital, you need to democratize your data. Yes, there are some limitations, but if you start with an inclusive mindset, not an exclusive one, and give everyone you can the data, you can really start to see the value.

> *Gone are the days of decentralized data; if you want to be truly digital, you need to democratize your data.*

Alexander: What are the main lessons you learned when you established data democratization for the financial sector?

Sarah: Keep it simple. If you cannot explain your dashboard's purpose in a simple sentence, how are others going to interrupt it? Streamline your access. People do not have time to dig to find your most valuable insights; keep them centralized and accessible. Get the right tools for the job and realize you may need multiple tools to get to the end state. Take your customers on the journey with you, have the deep conversations, understand their business. Create a diverse team to challenge status quo and empower them to be risk takers. Brand your style, that extra gloss on your final output can go a long way.

Alexander: How do you see digital strategies evolving with the maturity of big data processing and AI? How do you prepare for an AI-centric ecosystem as a business leader?

Sarah: AI was a buzzword while people were processing what it really meant. Now there are so many amazing use cases, and we are only starting to scratch the surface. I saw a great example being used for interviewing candidates. This meant hundreds or even thousands of people could be screened for a role before potentially biased shortlisting was done. We all know of cases where a perfect candidate did not even get to the interview stage because their resume was missed in the process. Deploying AI could prevent this.

Alexander: Which innovative AI use cases would be made possible by a tighter data integration?

Sarah: As customers, we are constantly being targeted by marketing campaigns. Using data to understand more about what our customers are likely to be interested in brings value to both sides. In any organization, there is a social and moral responsibility to help our customers, predicting behavior through AI and leveraging that data to develop and offer better products through the use of tighter data integration.

Alexander: How do you face data privacy and data governance concerns when you pitch new ideas?

Sarah: Democratizing data in a highly regulated industry does have its challenges. We operate across multiple markets in APAC and EMEA, each with its own set of restrictions. Ten years ago, financial companies and the cloud were not at the same table, and today that's changing. It is key to build the right partnerships with vendors to understand what tools can give you your required level of data privacy and data governance. Bringing multiple use cases to the conversation has helped me pitch new ideas.

Alexander: Why do data visualizations have such a strong impact on our decisions?

Sarah: A great data visualization can invoke an emotion, good or bad, and lead us to take action. A clean and clear visual can tell a story much faster than a large table of data. We can highlight key metrics by making them big, bold, and at the top; we can quickly show trends with a simple line chart, compare years with multiple lines on the chart, and show how one category is larger than another with a simple bar chart. We can add color to highlight what is key and fade out what is less important. We can add commentary to support the visual. The strongest data visualizations stand on their own, with a clear objective.

Alexander: Why is data storytelling the essential data science skill that everyone needs?

Sarah: When I present a visualization, I like to think those viewing it know nothing about the data I am presenting. This forces me to build the story around it. A whole page of graphs can be as difficult to interpret as can a whole page of tables. If I think to myself, "What are the key takeaways I want the viewer to get from a piece of work?" along with any calls to action on the part of the viewer, and call them out on the page, I can really help the viewer understand without having to go elsewhere.

Alexander: How can everyone learn to communicate better with data?

Sarah: Practice with data you are not familiar with, look at the learnings you had to make on the way, jot them down, and add them to the story. Ask people around you for constructive feedback. Find visuals you love and ask yourself what you love about them. Try and incorporate those principles into your visuals. Find your own style. Realize you will evolve, and do not be too harsh on yourself.

Alexander: What skills will managers need to develop to enable data democracy within their companies?

Sarah: On the road to data democratization you are changing foundational culture and getting people on board with change. Bringing people on that journey is probably the most important part of your role. I have learned over the years that going into an unfamiliar environment and trying to change it all overnight, with a strong sense of entitlement, will not work, but identifying people who have business knowledge and partnering with them and taking them on the journey will increase your chances of success. It is equality important to build a diverse team of passionate people and empower them to build the vision.

Alexander: Companies usually have plenty of legacy dashboards, the messages of which cannot be seen at first glance. What would a workshop to improve visual data communication look like?

Sarah: Working with the business, our workshops go back to basics and ask the question of what is the call to action we need our dashboard to drive. Working closely with the decision-makers, really understanding what nugget of data they are digging for, and making sure that is how we build the story are key. In these initial conversations we keep away from tools and start with pen and paper.

Alexander: What basic guidelines and patterns should always be considered for a visual expressive dashboard?

Sarah: Have a simple, clear objective for the dashboard. Keep fonts, color palettes, chart types, headers, icons, and navigation consistent; develop a style guide. Reduce the clutter; if something does not have a purpose, remove it. Call out key insights. Start with a high-level summary to tell the story; make it interactive, so they can ask more questions of the data and discover their story. Do not be disappointed if people need the lower-level exploratory data — it is hard to cover everyone's needs — just don't make it front and center. Do not use overly complex chart types, just to prove you can build them. Ninety percent of the time bar charts and line charts will tell the story the fastest. Make sure the visual can stand on its own without additional explanation.

Alexander: Who should you trust with helping you monitor the changes you are making and testing your dashboard prototype to see if it meets expectations?

Sarah: Have a process. Developers can get too close to see their own build. Use peer reviews and subject-matter experts, and get business sign-off. You only get one shot at launching a new dashboard, and if the data is not correct or the story isn't clear when it goes live, you may end up losing your key audience.

Alexander: Why should companies set up an Analytics Center of Excellence as part of their digital strategy? What are some strategies for setting this up?

Sarah: Changing the data-driven culture of an organization is a huge transformation that should not be underestimated. Centralizing it can help set best practices and distribute? the load. Make sure you have a diverse and passionate mix of people, including those from traditional organizations and those from the digital world. Empower them to challenge the environment. In addition, find your advocates in the community and leverage them to help you drive adoption.

Alexander: What are your personal top three dos and don'ts for an engaging visualization?

Sarah: Do:

- Know your audience.
- Only present the facts.
- Build a great story from the facts.

Don't:

- Throw up 20 different charts because you want to look knowledgeable.
- Overwhelm your audience with every single thing you found.
- Use size 6 font ... ever!

Alexander: Thank you, Sarah. What quick-win advice would you give that is easy for many companies to apply within their digital strategies?

Sarah: Think big, start small! It's a journey, and the end goal will evolve as your organization does. Bring the right people, with the right passion for change, and empower them to take risks.

Alexander: What are your favorite apps, tools, or software that you can't live without?

Sarah: Tableau and Procreate. I love the way you can quickly explore your data for multiple data sources using Tableau and then pull it all together into a dashboard and make it interactive. Procreate is a great app where I can make mockup visuals as I would on paper, but with the added flexibility of cut, copy, and paste.

Alexander: Do you have a smart productivity hack or work-related shortcut?

Sarah: If you tell someone once how to do something and then someone else asks how to do the same thing, it is time to put it into a living document on a shared community.

Alexander: What is the best advice you have ever received?

Sarah: Find your passion and learn how to incorporate it into your work.

Key Takeaways

- Great visual design can impact all areas and help communicate your message more clearly.
- Get the right mix of people: those from traditional organizations and those from the digital world. This is a balance between what has been done historically and what could be done next.
- Traditionally, banks have tended to shy away from cloud-based, open source technology, but as the platforms advance, so does the governance.

Part IV

Big Data Processing and Cloud Computing

Part IV

Big Data Processing
and Cloud Computing

Chapter 11
Mark Kromer: Leveraging Big Data Analytics and Cloud Platforms for the Next-Generation Data Strategy

Mark Kromer, principal program manager, Azure, Microsoft

Source: Mark Kromer

Mark is bringing game-changing products to market that transform the way we analyze data. He is always searching for new and exciting ways to understand and harness the power of big data analytics and cloud platforms for the next generation of hyper-scale business. For the past 20 years, Mark has focused on data warehouse and business intelligence products and solutions, with the past 10 years focused on big data analytics and cloud-scale ETL. Mark has an MBA and is formerly product manager at Oracle, Pentaho, and AT&T.

Alexander: You are the principal program manager at Microsoft. What is your mission?

Mark: I've spent over 10 years at Microsoft and over 20 years in data and analytics total, so I've been around long enough to witness most of the sea changes and paradigm shifts in this industry. In the Microsoft Azure Data Factory product group I focus on the convergence of two of the most seismic shifts in our industry during these past two decades: cloud and big data. My mission is to drive the most end-user value out of our products through obsessive customer-driven focus. Since I am responsible for cloud ETL (extract, transform, load) at scale, the way that I help businesses achieve their ultimate ROI with Azure data services is through ridiculously easy and intuitive user experiences that make seemingly impossible data integration and transformation projects possible.

Alexander: How should business models evolve to survive and thrive in an increasingly digital world?

Mark: I like to talk to business decision-makers and technologists about finding business value from data points that were previously obfuscated or completely hidden because their companies may have been trapped in legacy solution approaches and mindsets. In the cloud data world, it is important to break out of the preconceived approaches of data carving and endless iterations on requirements for the most common business reports. Those are bread-and-butter requirements just for your business to survive. But as you evolve your thinking in the digital world, as a technologist, you can drive better decision-making in your business by providing access to data points that your business decision-makers never knew were possible. Rather than wait for the business to come to you with new requirements, treat your raw data assets like gold and mine those data assets in the data lake. Data wrangling, data prep, data transformation, and aggregated, curated data presented to your business users provide new insights to do more than just stay afloat; they give your business a strategic advantage.

Alexander: How can technology shift the roles and responsibilities of the workforce?

Mark: My area of focus is cloud-based big data and analytics. The value that mining and processing big data at scale in the cloud can bring to business is the value of data democratization. If we can harness the power of data-driven decision-making and data insights throughout an organization, we can provide all areas of business with the business insights needed to improve business performance and to make everyone in the organization feel empowered with data. The organizational transformation of data democratization means trusting your workforce to make data-driven decisions by extending data and intelligence across organizational silos. Cloud-first data modernization architectures, where all forms of available raw data are swept through a data lake and into business models, made available across business organizations, are the key to breaking down those silos and leading to a data-driven business strategy.

> *As you evolve your thinking in the digital world, as a technologist, you can drive better decision-making in your business by providing access to data points that your business decision-makers never knew were possible.*

Alexander: Which technology or digital capabilities are essential for a digital strategy?

Mark: To really have success in these cloud-scale analytics and data processing scenarios that I've described, there are three key components that you need to implement as part of a digital data strategy.

- Data processing pipelines
- Scaled-out processing engine
- Serving layer

In Microsoft Azure, the manifestation of those components is Azure Data Factory, Azure Databricks or Synapse Spark, Synapse SQL Pools, and Power BI.

You need to have a way to manage ingestion of vast amounts of structured and unstructured data into bottomless storage for your data lake and a way to process, transform, and conform that data at scale, which is where Spark really shines.

Finally, that data needs to be molded into models that serve business users so that they can drive better business decisions. Oftentimes, you'll need to clean the raw data that is ingested into the data lake to make it usable, not only by business users for reporting but also by data scientists. Cleaning data for data quality and addressing duplicate data are two of the most important areas to get right to provide meaningful data for business decision-makers. Each target audience, from business decision-makers to data scientists, will have different data requirements for data engineers to refine the raw data in different ways. Data scientists may build predictive models that can surface to business users in product strategy as what-if scenarios to make product portfolio decisions. Marketing leaders can take these new, more real-time insights and devise target marketing campaigns based on these new data points.

Alexander: Why is a data strategy an essential element within every company's overall digital strategy?

Mark: Put simply, a digital strategy requires a data strategy. You are going to need to put together a plan that includes mechanisms for consuming large amounts of unstructured raw data, cleaning it, processing it for modeling and business intelligence, and serving that refined data to decision-makers. That means leveraging utility-based cloud services to quickly stand up big-data cloud-scale processing. The ability to scale those services on demand without needing to procure and provision on-premises hardware and software is where the rubber meets the road in a modern data strategy. That's how you enable your business to prepare for a digital strategy. Essentially, you'll focus on making massive amounts of data into a strategic business advantage by leveraging the flexibility and scalability of the cloud.

In most cases, you are going to augment your existing legacy data strategies with these new cloud-based data-lake approaches. This is an important concept to plan for. You should look for ways to include your existing data warehouse analytics in the available marts and models available to your data scientists and business users. Even in the case of greenfield solutions that are born in the cloud, summarized data in star schema models (traditional analytical models common in data warehouse scenarios) is still very valuable, so do not ignore that requirement.

Alexander: *How much of the collected data is typically being used today? To what degree can the business leverage the data in a timely fashion?*

Mark: Think of the classic analogies. The iceberg analogy or the 80/20 rule very much applies here. In those analogies and rules, the hidden part of the iceberg, or the 80 percent, is the untapped intelligence that has not yet been realized by processing data in a way that was never possible before. A modern cloud-based data architecture can process data from unconventional and unstructured sources like sensors, social media, logs, and so on. Data pipelines that can transform that data into actionable summarizations via Spark and store it in analytical data pools, combined with your legacy existing data assets, is how you get ROI out of these large-scale endeavors. In the early days of data warehouses, we used to say that even the most optimized analytical models took advantage of only around 10 percent of the data available to the business. Cloud-scale analytics in a digital world means taking data from many more sources, with varied quality and velocity, and increasing the percentage of refined data presented to your business.

Alexander: If companies collect all this data, what new questions are they able to answer? What decisions and actions could be made that would drive value?

Mark: When you modernize your data strategy to cloud scale and data lakes, there are a number of new and very interesting use cases that become available. Let me describe two important scenarios that come to mind that do a good job of illustrating these benefits:

> **Near-real-time marketing and product feedback:** These take advantage of cloud analytics to collect social media data and marketing surveys for immediate voice-of-customer feedback. Without digital strategies, prior mechanisms for collecting this type of product and marketing feedback typically demanded costly third-party surveys, which were conducted with long delays between the time of a product launch and the time that the collected data was available to be turned into decisions. Commonly, the results were gleaned through traditional analytics, which prevented accurate attribution. Collecting mass amounts of immediate data from social media, email, and so on improves your product launches and marketing campaigns. To do this, you'll leverage data lakes in the cloud with bottomless storage, data processing pipelines that can transform and conform data to models at scale using Spark, machine learning modeling tools, and business intelligence tools for the business decision-makers in marketing and product teams.
>
> **Elastic scale for seasonal business and anomalies:** Cloud-based big data analytics solutions present you with the opportunity to scale up capacity, storage, and processing quickly and without the need to overprovision. In the past, data engineers would need to request hardware and capacity for worst-case scenarios, or they planned for marketing blitzes or seasonal business spikes, like around holiday shopping seasons. Digital data strategies let you budget your capacity based on normal operations and then scale up during seasonal business spikes, unforeseen global events, and planned advertising blitzes. A digital data engineer will build

data ingestion and processing pipelines that utilize scale-out capacity, which will maintain the same daily business logic but leverage the ability to elastically scale Spark, Data Factory, Synapse Analytics, and so on.

Alexander: *How do you see digital strategies evolving with the maturity of big data analytics and AI? How do business leaders need to prepare for an AI-centric ecosystem?*

Mark: Cloud-scale data processing means having access to more data than any team of humans can ever accurately make sense of. There absolutely needs to be a strong application of AI and ML to data lakes to make them manageable and valuable. I've seen too many projects fail to deliver on promises of providing business value because the data provided is too messy, incomplete, and missing context. AI and ML provide automated ways to sort that out. But the data engineer is the key role in this process to bring vast amounts of data to the data scientists and their ML models. So, cleaning, prepping, and transforming the raw data for processing into ML models is crucial for success here.

Alexander: *Which innovative analytics and AI use cases would be made possible by a tighter data integration?*

Mark: In the world that I live in every day in ETL and data engineering, one of the more interesting use cases enabled by tightly coupling with AI for big data analytics processing would be the use of AI for classification and quality of the data in the lake. Data cleansing is crucial to the success of your data strategies, and data lakes notoriously contain messy raw data that requires manual intervention. In many cases, the cleaning and classification processes fall into the ETL process through business rules. But that is time-consuming and error-prone. Data cleansing and classifying sensitive data can be automated through AI and are important areas to include in your data strategy.

Alexander: *What are your thoughts on the cost of cloud-based services compared to on-premises installations?*

Mark: When deciding between on-premises and cloud, companies often perform a total cost of ownership (TCO) analysis to weigh the direct and indirect benefits with the price. However, adopting a cloud-based, an on-premises, or even a hybrid cloud model can provide additional benefits that may not correlate with a specific dollar amount.

I'd recommend evaluating your ongoing cost of ownership, including licensing fees, maintenance and support costs, implementation costs, networking costs, and so on. Sometimes moving to the cloud may seem like an additional, recurring expense to consider, until you consider the cost of maintaining a system in house or having to upgrade to a new system.

With cloud technology, upgrades to the software are generally included in your maintenance fees, giving you immediate access to updated versions of software without the time and expense of system upgrades. Cloud technologies offer continuous access to IT support, scalable storage capacity, and real-time access for an increasingly mobile workforce.

Specifically, in regard to modern data strategies, you will need the scale and flexibility that big data processing in the cloud provides. Procuring and overprovisioning massive clusters of compute and storage resources cannot compete with the consumption-based pricing model in the cloud and the time-to-production enabled with dynamic and elastic scale.

Alexander: Besides total cost of ownership, which are the top arguments for companies to use cloud-based services? When do they stick to an on-premises solution?

Mark: The ability to bring massively distributed compute, bottomless storage, and ephemeral services should make cloud-first architectures the obvious choice when building a modern data analytics solution. In the past, procuring the physical and human resources to build, manage, and maintain a compute environment on the scale needed for these projects was a nonstarter for most businesses. With cloud bringing the power of big data analytics with elastic scale, the only reason at this point to maintain an on-premises presence is to live out the depreciation and software license life cycles. This is why beginning the journey to the cloud with a hybrid solution is an ideal starting point when you've already established a data warehouse and analytics infrastructure on prem.

But hybrid solutions will become untenable over time due to duplicate costs and code.

Alexander: What are typical scenarios for a hybrid cloud architecture? What would such an architecture look like?

Mark: With the exception of the occasional greenfield net-new data project in the cloud, most digital modernization projects are hybrid in nature, though many have the goal of becoming fully cloud based over time. If you're not standing up a new solution architecture born fully in the cloud, then you'll likely start with a lift-and-shift approach to existing data and data systems, followed by migration of your code to cloud services. A long-lived hybrid strategy would entail maintaining legacy software, hardware, and support licenses for databases and data stores that can communicate with cloud-based services. In most cases, this will mean that you'll set up a communication link from your data centers to the cloud provider, similar to Microsoft's Express Route with Azure. Your network administration team will then establish firewall rules and network peering rules so that you can access data in cloud and on prem. It is important to keep in mind that these network routes can become saturated at times or "laggy." So for a digital data engineer moving to the cloud, I highly recommend that you establish a staging pattern whereby your primary use of that on-premises data is to pull the data in chunks and stage it in your cloud data lake. This way, your cloud-based pipeline and analytics processing engines can treat that data as any other in the lake without worrying about constant connectivity speeds and availability to your on-premises network resources.

Alexander: How do you face your customers' data privacy and data governance concerns?

Mark: Everything we've talked about so far is predicated on the idea of building a data lake in the cloud as a way to quickly land and then process raw data for different end user requirements. That data will frequently have personally identifiable information (PII), payment card details, sensitive business intellectual property, and so on. It is vital to prevent your business from leaking sensitive information and to properly classify your data assets as classified or personal. In some extreme cases, regional data regulation may require you to completely delete files or information that has been collected. Make sure to understand related General Data Protection Regulation (GDPR) or similar constraints that you are required to work under. Common tools to help with this area of data-lake management and privacy include metadata catalog and classification tools like Microsoft Azure Purview. Removing sensitive data or masking can be performed inside Azure Data Factory data processing pipelines.

Alexander: Thank you, Mark. What quick-win advice would you give that is easy for many companies to apply within their digital strategies?

Mark: This is where you can take advantage of a key value proposition of cloud data engineering. The serverless nature of the infrastructure needed to build a complex big data analytics solution makes it quick and easy to just stand up an entire analytical solution like Azure Synapse Analytics from a web portal. You'll instantly get an ETL tool, bottomless storage, Spark and SQL distributed compute engines, data governance, and ML tools without needing to build any infrastructure.

If you already have an existing well-established data analytics in your business, a good way to get started down the modernization path is to start small with a single business area that is currently modeled in your data warehouse and business intelligence models. Reproduce the ETL and data models in cloud platform services and begin to get a sense of the difference in approach and architecture from on premises. Once you've gotten your feet wet, now take a look at something new. Hook up an event-based feed to your company's Twitter feed and build a net-new ETL pipeline that analyzes the JSON produced by the Twitter API and map that to your existing business models.

Alexander: What are your favorite apps, tools, or software that you can't live without?

Mark: I would have to say that no matter what role I've had in the data ecosystem over my two-plus decades in this area, simple editing tools for viewing and modifying all of the many different types of file formats that you are going to encounter will serve you well. Something along the lines of Visual Studio Code, Notepad++, or Sublime are vital parts of a data engineer's toolbox. As a modern digital transformation data engineer, you're going to be challenged by working with and understanding many file formats. Prepare yourself with tools that can help you make sense of the schemas and contents of parquet files, JSON, Avro, ORC, and even legacy CSV and XML file formats that you'll frequently find landing in your lake.

Alexander: *What is the best advice you have ever received?*

Mark: Never stop questioning, learning, or trying. That was from one of my very first managers right out of college. If you aim to make a difference in the world, I'm sure those three attributes will also serve you well as a modern digital data engineer. As you move into cloud data architectures, expect a lot of new challenges and some slightly different ways to solve problems that may seem very familiar to you. You'll be able to leverage your background in data modeling, ETL, data quality, and machine learning. By applying those same approaches to cloud analytics, you'll quickly adapt to unstructured raw data in your lake. And by updating your chops in the cloud, you'll learn to appreciate how easy it can be to adapt to large, complex data architectures.

Key Takeaways

- A next-generation data strategy is going to include moving massive amounts of raw data into data lakes and processing that data into business-friendly data points. Be prepared to include data classification and data cleansing services in your final solution to address data privacy and data quality.
- With a cloud-based digital data strategy, you'll now be able to scale complex data services on demand without needing to procure and provision costly hardware and software.

Chapter 12
Dr. Henna A. Karna: Racing to Last Place — The Criticality of an End-to-End Data Strategy

Dr. Henna A. Karna, managing director of Re/Insurance and Risk Management Solutions, Google; and the former CDO of AXA XL

Source: Dr. Henna A. Karna

Henna is a highly respected global leader with more than 25 years of experience leading innovation across digital/data in high-tech, CPG, risk management, and insurance industries (across vendors, brokers, and independent agents). She has led businesses and advised Fortune 500 companies on digital innovation and disruption and has designed and developed patent-pending technology and applications in the field of genetic algorithms, behavioral analytics, deep neural nets, and digital-data technologies.

Henna currently serves as managing director of Re/Insurance and Risk Management Solutions at Google, leading Google Cloud's global insurance strategy and solutions, including a cloud-based software-as-a-service (SaaS) data and analytics platform for insurers, reinsurers, brokers, and so on. Previously, Henna served as chief data officer and managing director at AXA XL, the Property and Casualty, Specialty Risk, Risk Management, and Consulting entity of global insurance giant AXA SA.

Over the course of her career, Henna has served as the global actuarial CIO and managing director for AIG. Earlier in her career, Henna held positions at Affinnova and John Hancock Insurance and held cryptology-related roles for the U.S. government. She has also served as an adjunct professor of statistics in the entrepreneurial program at Babson College.

Henna holds an MBA from Massachusetts Institute of Technology (MIT), a bachelor of mathematical sciences degree from Worcester Polytechnic Institute (WPI), and a master's degree and doctorate from the University of Massachusetts.

Alexander: *As the managing director of Re/Insurance and Risk Management Solutions at Google, you have a strong focus on cloud-based data and analytics solutions. How did you get started in the data and analytics domain?*

Henna: My first love is mathematics. It has been a character-defining passion in my academic life that persists through my professional career. It was a language that I found both creative and intellectually stimulating and helped me advance through many of the other areas of work that went from the basics of data to genetic algorithms to storytelling and relational analysis to social physics and network effects, and so on.

The field of data and analytics really helps me apply what has become a foundational part of my nature. I don't see this as a quantitative field alone. The power of data and analytics is the balance (and illusion) between knowledge and wisdom — the bringing together of information/insights with creative analysis.

I remember making one of my essays about the difference between knowledge and wisdom. This balance is a combination of what is explainable with data and what is assessed by experience. I bring this lens to my work. Most of my research, most of my work, is connecting the dots between what information provides to us and how we leverage our intuition and wisdom to test and evolve our thinking by it.

Alexander: *How does your research experience help you today?*

Henna: Both mentally and tactically. Research is often a non-linear effort, and there is nothing as serious a teacher of resiliency as the gravity of the "test-and-learn" research world. The beauty of mathematics is that there are many ways to solve a problem. We must bring that mindset to the table. It is a mentality in perfect harmony with authentic leadership. For example, my team is a highly diverse group of brilliant individuals from numerous fields, and I see in them the ability to devise solutions in dramatically different ways — we are constantly thinking, learning, envisioning, relearning, and so on. This mindset of diverse thought is the greatest attribute of a life-long learner — a seeker of knowledge and teacher of wisdom.

One more viewpoint fits here as well. In traditional firms, the world of data has been a subset of IT or systems. It resulted in the suffocation of data maturity due to lack of data expertise, data culture, and data literacy. There was minimal investment toward the data itself, and most of the technology investments went to commonly understood IT activities. Today, we need to upend this and bring data to the front and center. Yet, the momentum of the traditional IT approach creates an unreasonable expectation of any CDO or CDAO.

Consider Newton's first law, which states that "every object will remain in uniform motion unless compelled to change its state by the action of an external force." Translating Newton's law to teams and team momentum, we need to assume people don't change, even when asked to. In fact, they are driven to succeed within the situation they are currently measured in and likely consider themselves rather successful within that status quo. To change is not their goal. Hence, for a CDO or CDAO to change the status quo of decades of minimal data literacy and expertise is nearly impossible.

However, the company that delineates data from IT thoughtfully and deliberately will achieve the greatest outcome across both fields and will create a highly balanced, optimized, and necessary partnership.

In comes the "research mindset." If we go back to the basics, data by its nature is very different from IT. Data and analytics projects are more akin to scientific analysis and clinical trials than to IT initiatives, which are more easily related to linear workstreams, such as software lifecycles or service level agreements. Data projects typically start with user problems or opportunities, which may be speculation. They move on to data-driven assessments about particular outcome, generate hypotheses, identify relevant data sets, and build the appropriate data solution. Data projects require an iterative development model (to increase data maturity and reduce unmanageable shortcuts) with incremental benefits for users who need deliverables yesterday. This is much like research work. The data development process I have applied in our team is highly iterative, provides a split across sequential and cyclical workstreams, and allows for the predictability needed for extensive monitoring and flexibility in the process for business prioritization. (The premise of our data development process comes from my MIT training on dynamic work design, which states, "Creative work is invisible and more variable, so workflow is harder to monitor. The trick is to make invisible work visible.")

Alexander: *Before joining Google, you were the chief data and analytics officer of AXA XL, an insurance company operating worldwide. Could you tell me more about your chief data officer role at AXA XL?*

Henna: In the chief data and analytics officer role, there are three major components: (1) manage and evolve the central data and analytics talent for the enterprise; (2) design, execute, and transform the data and digital transformation of the firm; (3) ensure a first line of defense for all data across the enterprise.

In CDO-speak, this is considered both defensive and offensive data work and is much discussed in literature today. However, what is different is the success criterion that we have set with regard to the work we are doing.

The success criterion is not the usual single source of data. Our success criterion is very particular to the strategic business imperatives of the firm. We measure throughput of our colleagues' value-driven work, reusability of our data assets, the holistic depth of our data insights and connectivity of the data across the insurance value chain, and so on. Our driving force is top-line profitable growth and bottom-line analytical processing efficiencies.

However, our ultimate goal is something very personal to me. It is to trailblaze our industry into the digital current. The importance of this is increasingly obvious — not because of fear of being displaced by an InsurTech or the digital-native firms, but because our world needs to become safer and smarter. Our bread and butter are risk management and mitigation, and that is an economic balancer. Firms like ours, with the size and global presence we have, have an intrinsic responsibility to make sure we can provide resiliency to our economies, governments, and businesses. We must be on a solid footing to be able to help immediately during a global crisis, a natural catastrophe, or an uncanny, serendipitous event. To do this, we must know our customers, understand their risks and needs, and be able to very thoughtfully respond in a way that lets them take immediate action. And, to do that, we must be digitally capable and analytically advanced. This is the responsibility that my division and I have for our firm and industry.

Alexander: How should our business evolve to survive and thrive in an increasingly digital world?

Henna: We have to change our approach to our customers and hence the fundamental business model of our firm. I do not see this as a higher calling. It is simply a digital world where frequency of interaction is table stakes, but the depth of the relationship is paramount.

A business needs to pivot on each of nine principles. These pivots are highly nuanced and equally precise (Figure 12.1).

Moreover, transparency and authenticity are the new norms of firms that will thrive in a digital world. Hence, we have to make it obvious that our customers come first. Questions that research indicates we should ask ourselves are the following:

- Are we obsessed with understanding the customers' decision journeys cyclically, and have we embedded them in our core business?
- Are we using unprecedented levels of data precision to identify flaws in existing value chains and create value on new frontiers?
- Do we have our senses open to react to another wave around the corner, or have we gone as far as to create the waves ourselves by iterating and developing for tomorrow?
- Have we institutionalized cross-functional collaboration, flattened hierarchies, and built environments to encourage the generation of new ideas?

Figure 12.1 Principles of yesterday versus orientation of tomorrow
Source: Dr. Henna A. Karna, Managing Director, Re/Insurance and Risk Management Solutions, Google and the former CDO of AXA XL.

Alexander: You mentioned the value chain. Is the value chain also connected to an end-to-end data strategy? How is a solid end-to-end data strategy designed?

Henna: The value chain concept is interesting in the context of a traditional firm versus a digital one. In our world today, the value chain consists of a submission for a policy, through understanding its risk implications, limits, and reserve requirements, to ensuring portfolio management across the variety of risks both in a micro and macro view, to understanding and responding to a claim that is made. For our firm, which specializes in commercial, B2B, and highly complex risk, this process can be rather intense. However, the net result of our value chain today is fundamentally transactional and limited to two to three customer touchpoints, and at the most is helping our customers detect and restore from risks. In a digital world, the boundaries of our value chain start to extend far beyond just the two customer touchpoints into a more bidirectional, 24/7 model that allows us to help our customers to proactively predict and prevent risks. In this new value chain, we build a trusted partnership with our customer, and that partnership is all predicated on the data (or insights) we can provide that is most critical for them.

An end-to-end data strategy brings the value chain to life. For example, data from historical claims across numerous industries in the commercial space would allow our pricing models to determine nuances to our new submissions in real time. The power of the data is the connectivity of information across correlations and causations that are not easily noticed across the value chain due to traditional, siloed workstreams.

A solid, end-to-end data strategy considers the evolution of the firm and moves the current traditional value chain toward the value chain in a digital world. This is paramount for any data strategy being designed today, in any industry. The delta between the current and target value chains needs to reflect the goals we have with our customer partnership and the behavior our firm is looking to achieve. Once we know this target state, we can acknowledge the

A solid, end-to-end data strategy considers the evolution of the firm and moves the current traditional value chain toward the value chain in a digital world. This is paramount for any data strategy being designed today, in any industry.

types of evolutions required to achieve that goal. And, in the several digital and data transformation programs that I have run, it has always come down to the data strategy to realize the benefits. A solid data strategy will further democratize data and the leveragability of it across the value chain all the way to the ownership of it.

It is also important to realize that an end-to-end data strategy will enforce a culture change. First and foremost, the firm will have to disrupt itself before it considers truly disrupting its value chain for its customer base. Culture and data strategy are highly in sync; we cannot divorce the two. There is an intrinsic interdependency between culture and technology. Data provides direction and culture drives adoption. Culture is tied to human experience. It is inseparable from anything we do. It's tied to who we are, our existential needs. It is core to our fundamentals, and without it we can perish. Data and technology are derivatives of that. We could argue that everything is a derivative of that.

If we want to operate in a world that is entirely quantifiable through the use of data, which is perhaps a digital-transformation end state, data and culture become cyclical. The genesis is culture, which will drive innovation, and innovation will leverage technology to get the art of the possible. And then culture becomes the adoption mechanism. And, if we get this right, it is an exponential function.

Alexander: *Which skills need to be developed from scratch, and which skills can be scaled up?*

Henna: A wise person once said, "Everything in business can be copied except for talent." It is quite true. Our people, how we upskill them, and how they embrace the firm's mission are all core to our strategy. Data talent is a very specialized skillset and in high demand in all industries, across all countries. I have a rather basic talent equation that we use to measure each one of these variables and track their impacts quantitatively: $T = A + B + C + D$; where $T =$ total skills required to sustainably live in the target state; $A =$ skills within a central data and analytics function; $B =$ skills across the power users of data across the firm; $C =$ skills across the network of partners; $D =$ skills we need to get to T. The key is that D has three parts that need to be thoughtfully considered in a talent strategy: $D1 =$ trainable skills; $D2 =$ untrainable skills; $D3 =$ skills you need that are either highly niche or highly commoditized that we do not need within our colleague DNA.

To answer the skills question, so basically D1, we include a combination of foundational data literacy skills combined with business acumen and embedded machine learning and/or basic analysis. There is no one skill that overshadows any other, except that the principle of training is that it is not about the data but the usage of the data for business implications. We must train all skills, be it data quality or artificial intelligence, with the business complexity and visibility to top-line impact (see Figure 12.2). We do not see data as back-office or behind the scenes, and that has made a tremendous difference in our talent retention and optimization.

Alexander: *What does that look like? How does your internal training on data governance work?*

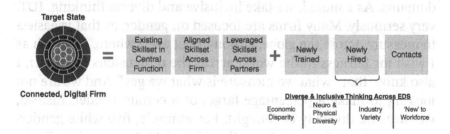

Figure 12.2 Diverse and inclusive thinking is a crucial component for a connected, digital firm.

Henna: There are two differentiators in our talent strategy that I have established within our division. The first is an inverted pyramid with a rotation approach that deploys colleagues to work-streams mapped to their skills and interests — I call these *X-treme teams*. The second is something I call *ambition planning* where we encourage our colleagues to sit in the driver's seat of their career lattice and thoughtfully plan, assess, and discuss their career growth for both depth and breadth of skills alongside their tenure in the firm.

The X-treme teams are based on the military research of the "extreme performance teams," whose understanding of human nature really impressed upon me the dynamics we needed to suc-ceed in a high-intensity, high-speed transformation program.

In the ambition planning work it became important for me to lead by example and transparency. Unfortunately, not all of us are lucky to have managers who realize that leaders create other leaders. Hence, not all managers put in the effort to help pro-vide direction for their direct reports — leaving many unaware of the possibilities to learn and achieve more. I do believe that we humans need a goal that is ambitious enough to inspire us, even if it is surrounded by unpaved roads. Transparency is crucial in trust, and this effort has the means to bring trust to a higher level in our division.

Lastly, one critical aspect of our training has been the constantly humbling experience of being surrounded by experts across many domains. As I shared, we take inclusive and diverse thinking, IDT, very seriously. Many firms are focused on gender, as that is easiest to measure across the globe, although not everywhere. As much as I wish for fairness in the world across the dimensions of gender, I also know that "what we measure is what we get." And we are not looking to make a percentage target of a certain gender. Instead, we measure diversity of thought. For example, five white gender-homogenous colleagues from the United States, Sweden, South Africa, Russia, and Singapore may create a rather diverse group. Hence, I really believe IDT is not about the physical attributes of any one person, and I do not agree to measure this. Instead, I have created four areas of IDT that we measure.

- Colleagues from backgrounds of economic disparity
- Returning military or government and new to corporate
- Neuro and physical diversity
- Industry variety

This has made our world of collaboration and perspectives extremely rich and robust. Frankly, our team ranks as one of the best in our firm, and I am sure would be one of the rarest in the world of data.

Alexander: *What software experience should graduates bring as a plus if they are looking for a job in the data domain?*

Henna: A few experiences would be meaningful, such as behavior analytics, digital product development, data visualization, data content design, and so on. Of course, artificial intelligence, machine learning, natural language processing, and skills such as deep neural nets are all becoming table stakes to have dabbled in. I think the typical programs are already teaming some coding, some basic data, and so on. We do also look for expertise in R, Shiny, Python, and Java.

We need more data visualization and data content design skills. These are areas of training that demand more translation of quantitative information into layperson words. This ability to translate is extremely necessary as we progress in the data field.

Beyond those skills, though, I look for solution finders. Strong performers are people who can ask different questions and think beyond symptoms to look for root-cause analyses. They are people who are intellectually driven to not only understand their technical language but understand the business implications as well as opportunities. The bottom line is that data is a business function.

Alexander: *How important is a data strategy in the insurance space?*

Henna: A data strategy will make or break an insurance company.

Many articles identify data as the new oil. Oil is considered to be one of the most important commodities of the world. IT is a driver of the world economy and a dominant energy source. It is so central to many things. I suppose it is a cute analogy (although I am not a fan of it). Oil is oil, and data is data. Data has enabled us to quantify things we could not before — but data is not new to our insurance industry. I know it is not as cute a saying, but the reality for our industry is that data is blood. Oil is just fuel. Having a meaningful and well-done data strategy is the only way to sustainably create skills to become data-driven and analytically savvy, while also becoming technically advanced and compliant.

Alexander: How do you see data strategies evolving with the maturity of big data processing and AI? How do you prepare for an AI-centric ecosystem as a business leader?

Henna: AI is evolving aggressively now, although it is a 20-year-old space. In terms of commercial impact, it is early days to tell what the most impactful and sustainable business benefits will be in industries like insurance. Predictable data sets are starting with robotics automation, but the learning pieces are in much earlier stages. There is an incredible amount of AI today where we are mapping language and structure. Deep learning, certainly at scale, has just started. The way AI becomes of value is based on scale. Of course, it comes down to the data.

As part of our data strategy, we work closely on assessing the right data for the AI to be trained on. We establish a multitude of AI algorithms to balance bias and cross-analysis. Our data ecosystem has an embedded AI approach and ensures we are creating proper velocity by our AI capabilities. However, we are very aware that AI is not a magic trick or a solution for all problems. Hence, I have coined a statement in our department to make sure we note balance, which is simply "Mind + Machine." We don't want only the machine, probably ever.

Being a bit dramatic, the AI engine could be the thing called God, if only everyone would just focus on training it, and do so objectively. That would be something. But that is an ungodly, highly complex task. To say it less controversially, the long pole is not in the ability to develop more and more intelligent AI only. The capacity to develop more intelligent AI is not a known limitation, nor is the storing of the data needed for training. It is more the training itself and enablement issues that we must solve for.

The best way to optimize AI is to leverage it at the elemental level — whether it is for data governance, business semantic calculations, business triage, automated submissions, and so on. The worst that we can do is to create multiple AI instances where our workflow becomes broken and disjointed but has AI behind it. That would result in insufficient data for our AI to be eloquent in any area of the workflow, and we would not be gaining enough velocity across the workflow. On the other hand, if we leverage AI at the architectural level to solve a flow of data knowledge for analytical processing, we will find untapped insights and perspectives.

Alexander: *How will AI change the way people analyze their data? Will Mind + machine accelerate data democracy? Will it further reduce the time-to-insight by guiding the analysts?*

Henna: Data democracy is at the heart of empowering our colleagues with data, and is as much a technology play as it is a business play. If we can create data assets that can be co-shared, co-evolved, our information will be more meaningful and relevant across our value chain. With AI, this is much more possible. The example I would use here is the ability to build user behavior and real-time segmentation, recommendations, and quantitative perspectives within the data platform. Not only do we need data to be democratized, but we need AI to help accelerate patterns and perspectives quickly. This embedded capability will be a game changer in the actionability of our data.

Alexander: *Which were your most impactful data strategy campaigns?*

Henna: The most successful strategy I have worked on most recently has been to shift the weight of influence we have with third-party relationships. Today, many of these situations are driven by the third parties as opposed to a quantitatively based dialogue (that is, based on data) for a more balanced partnership model.

The way we have done this is with our data, information, and analysis. Our industry is heavily caught up in a price war, and we need to convert that into a values war. The value we generate comes from the insights we can gain from cross-analysis of our data across the firm. For example, we can look at cyber across multiple parts of the firm. We can now analyze business continuity across cargo, marine, aerospace, and across various exposures, like pandemic risk. The level of insights and analysis we can now gain from our data strategy enables us to bring a level of perspective and validation of viewpoint to the table with our third-party colleagues. This has increasingly changed our conversations with them, enabling us to be more thoughtful and measurable about our negotiations. Additionally, it has added more relevance to our partnership with our end customers and clients.

Alexander: How do you face data privacy and data governance concerns when you pitch new ideas?

Henna: Data privacy and compliance is a great weapon to wield, as any firm must first be transparent in its data requirements. This builds confidence with our partners and clients and allows us to structurally treat our data with the rigor and respect that we have not prioritized in the past. In the end, our job is to build value with our data to better our business value to our customers. The line we must always ensure is that our data is only used to improve our customer value.

Our data architecture has been built for compliance, traceability, lineage, history, access, and controls. These were not afterthoughts. The more proactive and transparent we can be on requirements, such as private and sensitive data, the more flexibility we will gain as a next step.

Alexander: Which further challenges or obstacles do you foresee insurance companies and other companies with huge amounts of customer data facing?

Henna: There are emerging groups to support CDO/CDAOs across the globe that I have been part of. We gather from different companies, different industries, and different phases of our careers. Yet, the problem seems to be the same. Every company that is not native digital has competing approaches. How to maximize the data has become an intellectual debate in most companies, and I think that creates handcuffs in terms of where a company can go. We have not pushed the CDO/CDAO to be clearly accountable for the data monetization and commercialization. This results in many individuals aiming to do this in different ways, with different degrees of investments — all resulting in yet another version of a siloed data landscape.

Large volumes of data should allow for more AI-driven analysis and more cross-functional insights. It also results in having more people pulling the data in different directions. The way we have conquered this is by forcing the story to be bigger than any one department or executive leader. Like a unified corporate business strategy, a unified data strategy helps everyone row the boat in the same, or a similar enough direction.

The other point to note here is that the weight of historical data and near-real-time data is starting to become questionable. As we think about the upcoming challenges, what type of data is used and to what degree and why, will become a mathematical balancing act, and data and business experts will have to work together to find their secret recipe here.

Alexander: What advice can you give other companies that are at a very early stage, and what is your advice for established companies that want to establish a data strategy?

Henna: We have to be customer-centric. Before Tesla came to the market, when we bought a car, we thought about the family size, miles per gallon, maybe the acceleration, and maybe the impact on the environment. Today, Tesla has changed the basis of competition. It doesn't matter anymore whether we can go from 0 to 60 in 2.5 or 2.9 seconds. New attributes such as environmental protection and sustainability got into focus for the customers.

A really solid data strategy will move the firm to change the basis of competition. To do so, though, we have to reimagine the needs of the customer and work backwards.

Alexander: What are your favorite apps, tools, or software that you can't live without?

Henna: I love the book summary app Blinkist, as I like to read books very quickly. Certainly, a lot of CEOs do that as well. So that's one of the apps that I think is quite great.

Alexander: Do you have a smart productivity hack or work-related shortcut?

Henna: Of course, we're looking for something like a quick and easy thing, but to me this is a philosophical thing. Many people say: do what you love so that work isn't work.

I say it the other way. Ideally you do what you love, but you have to also love whatever you're doing. My biggest productivity hack is that I love what I'm doing. I didn't plan to be in insurance. I didn't plan to be running this particular team. In some ways, it's all serendipity. But I really do philosophically believe that if you love what you do you, the constraints become opportunities.

I think that's been our biggest productivity hack. My team today has the highest productivity in our enterprise. I really attribute it to making sure that they love what they do. As leaders, we make sure of these three things:

- They know their goals.
- They know how they are doing against their goals.
- They know someone cares if they succeed.

Alexander: That productivity hack is very applicable and a good connection to the last question. What is the best advice that you have ever received?

Henna: I really enjoy quotes and gather them for inspiration. I have several I keep on my phone to always refer to when difficulties present themselves. However, the advice I would want to always keep close to my heart is the importance of time. As long as we are alive, we have time. That is the only thing we have. We don't have assurance of much else in life. But by the fact that we are alive, time is a momentum we can appreciate. With that in mind, how we spend time becomes our greatest and most critical decision every day. Hence, I have lived life as if every day is my last day. I work with that in mind. I hug my children with that in mind, and I try my best to pay it forward with that in mind.

Key Takeaways

- Data strategy will enforce a culture change. Culture and data strategy are highly in sync, we cannot divorce the two.
- Data democracy is at the heart of empowering our colleagues with data and is as much a technology play as it is a business play.
- AI is evolving aggressively now. There is an incredible amount of AI today where we are mapping language and structure. Deep learning, certainly at scale, has just started. The way AI becomes of value is based on scale. And, of course, it comes down to the data.

Chapter 13
Mohamed Abdel Hadi: The Future of Data-Driven Business

Mohamed Abdel Hadi, vice president for SAP Data Warehouse
Product Management & Strategy, SAP

Source: Mohamed Abdel Hadi

As vice president for SAP Data Warehouse Product Management & Strategy, Mohamed Abdel Hadi (Mo) is responsible for the entire cloud and on-premise portfolio.

A pioneer in the data and analytics industry, Mo has been with SAP for more than 12 years in different management positions, with a focus on analytics and data throughout his entire career.

Mo provides a strong technical market- and customer-oriented vision for new products and technology-driven development projects. As a leader of a global organization, his focus is to deliver best-in-class analytics and data warehouse products to customers and strengthen SAP's position in the converging markets for data and analytics.

Mo speaks or moderates frequently at top industry events:

- Transforming Data With Intelligence (TDWI)
- German-Speaking SAP User Group (DSAG)
- Americas' SAP Users' Group (ASUG)
- Business Application Research Center (BARC)

Mo also receives invitations from companies such as Accenture, McKinsey, and KPMG to consult and speak about digital transformation and how data and analytics can help to turn data into actionable insights, support decisions, and enable data democratization.

Alexander: You are vice president for SAP Data Warehouse Product Management & Strategy at SAP. What is your mission?

Mohamed: Early in my career I worked as a CFO assistant in Dubai. In this position, I spent a significant share of my time collecting, consolidating, and analyzing data to create insights and drive the company's success — oftentimes experiencing the limits of self-service ability and the need to involve IT even for small requests. Even in large companies, analytics is in many cases still a highly manual process, with limited business-user empowerment. Therefore, I was excited to move on to help companies to make better use of the data they have available. I had previously worked in analytics and was excited to take on the role as VP last year. My focus is to deliver best-in-class analytics and data warehouse products to customers and partners. My mission is to enable data democratization in companies with our products and accelerate companies' transitions to making decisions based on data rather than on opinions.

Alexander: How should business models evolve to survive and thrive in an increasingly digital world?

Mohamed: The increasing digitalization dramatically changes both how companies operate internally and how they provide value to their customers. In terms of internal operations, modern technology allows companies to increase both the speed and quality of decisions made — and together with my team I work on providing the necessary foundation to make this happen day to day. In terms of products and services offered, digitalization opens up new opportunities for reaching customers and serving their needs. As a result of the digital transformation, we see that customers' expectations have changed significantly — both in the B2C and in the B2B contexts.

For instance, customers no longer look for products but rather solutions that fulfill their needs and that they can consume easily as their needs change (ad hoc, on demand, subscription-based), which modern technology-enabled business models can offer. The revenue-generation side of the business models also change — oftentimes starting with a freemium model that significantly lowers the adoption barrier and provides the foundation to start for free and extend as required. Lastly, modern business models increasingly open up and include the broader ecosystem to unlock additional sources of value and revenue. Many companies consider themselves not only as product or service providers but also as playing a key role within a digital ecosystem — as either ecosystem or marketplace providers or participants. All these changes depend on having the necessary digital and technology foundations to make this happen and take advantage of modern cloud-based architectures that can be easily and flexibly provisioned, used, and scaled. Being able to generate value out of the data generated in this process becomes more and more a key competitive differentiator.

Alexander: How can technology shift the roles and responsibilities of the workforce?

Mohamed: As a result of these technology shifts, roles and responsibilities evolve significantly. For example, in my focus area we see a tremendous elevation of the responsibilities and requirements of knowledge workers and subject-matter experts working in business departments. They now work with digital solutions and data independently from IT. Traditionally, there had been a pretty clear segregation between the IT and business departments. In the data and analytics context, business departments specified requirements for analyses and reports and handed them over to IT to implement. These times have changed. We see that business users increasingly work directly with operational and strategic data and analytics on their own within their strategic and operational decision-making processes. Budgets for digital initiatives more and more move from the IT to the business teams, and new roles emerge. Analysts confirm this perspective. In a recent session with International Data Corporation (IDC), I learned that they identify 25 percent of knowledge workers as belonging to the so-called Gen D—data natives who live and breathe data in their day-to-day jobs.

Alexander: Which technology or digital capabilities are essential for a digital strategy?

Mohamed: It largely depends on the digital strategy, but in general I see three important enablers that drive a digital strategy to success. First, the company needs to identify which roles and skills are needed, hiring and training employees to be able to define a viable strategy and execute on it. A chief digital officer with the respective organization can shape this strategy and should closely align with enterprise architecture management to ensure the overall fit of initiatives within the companies' business capabilities and IT architecture. The implementation—especially of data-related strategic initiatives—oftentimes requires new skills and a supporting company culture on both the IT and business sides to make this happen. Companies should think about establishing new roles like chief data officer (if not already present) as well as data scouts and data strategists to empower their organization to be data driven.

Business-side users need to be trained to work with data in their day-to-day jobs. Luckily, modern tools make this easy, allowing for a more business-user–centric understanding of data-management features.

Second, to enable their digital strategy, companies need to build the required technological foundation. Implementing change is oftentimes inhibited by complex system architectures that have been built and extended over decades and are hard to change. In contrast, current modular microservice and cloud-based architectures allow for flexibility, scalability, and quick time-to-value and are an essential part of companies' digital strategies across industries.

Last, the success of every digital and data strategy largely depends on whether employees support it and see the value in their day-to-day activities. I see that oftentimes providing the technology is not enough, but companies actually have to transform their culture to become truly digital and data driven and reap the value of related initiatives. Therefore, thinking about how the core principles and culture would need to change as a result of digital and data strategies (for example, advancing from a "need-to-know" to an "allowed-to-know" principle) and which initiatives can be launched to make this happen is a critical success factor.

Alexander: Why is data warehousing an essential element within every company's overall digital strategy?

Mohamed: For the past two decades, data warehouses have been—and continue to be—the central places and single sources of truth for managing and working with critical company information. This is important for many reasons—making the right decisions is only possible on a high-quality foundation, and having a reliable source of truth is important for fulfilling companies' legal and regulatory requirements. At SAP, we are committed to helping companies turn the increasing data volume into lasting business value and make smarter, more sustainable decisions. With SAP Data Warehouse Cloud, we looked not only at how we store and manage data but also how we connect data with business context and unlock data insights for business users—empowering them with collaborative, self-service capabilities while ensuring quality and governance. Deriving business value from increasing data volumes should be easy and accessible. With SAP Data Warehouse Cloud, we changed the paradigm of what data warehousing can do. Companies now have the ultimate flexibility to connect and collect data from a variety of sources and extract insights in real time. We empower business users to connect their data, share it securely, and run analytics on their own—collaborating in business terms and using the tools of their choice. Prebuilt content packages provided by SAP and partners further accelerate the time to value—and keep complexity to a minimum. SAP Data Warehouse Cloud helps remove data silos and integrate data in a central place—bringing the data back to the business.

Alexander: How much of the collected data is typically being used today?

Mohamed: In any company 50 percent of the data is not used today. The rest of the data is mostly accessible, but the quality of the data is in a lot of cases still not 100 percent assured.

Alexander: If companies have sufficient high-quality data, what new questions are they able to answer? What decisions and actions could be made that would drive value?

Mohamed: Companies would get a live, 360-degree view of their customers and be able to improve the entire customer experience; customers would enjoy an individualized product; and marketing and service could be personalized based on insights for a segment of one.

Employees would be freed of mundane, repetitive work and could concentrate on activities and decisions where their unique human abilities bring greatest value.

Similarly, entire supply chains could be streamlined, leading to lower costs and an improved environmental footprint for a more sustainable future.

Employees would be freed of mundane, repetitive work and could concentrate on activities and decisions where their unique human abilities bring greatest value. These are only the first glimpses of concrete use cases that can be achieved based on data that already exists today, which would be integrated with relevant additional data sources and then leveraged in a data-driven company.

Alexander: How do you see digital strategies evolving with the maturity of big data analytics and AI? How do business leaders need to prepare for an AI-centric ecosystem?

Mohamed: Developing and operating a predictive analytics platform will remain a challenge for quite some time. Companies will need to consciously invest and focus on a portfolio of relevant use cases comprising quick wins as well as more long-term scenarios. Such a portfolio approach allows them to gather experience as an organization that is learning and demonstrate tangible value to critics while avoiding putting all eggs into one basket.

Data literacy on all levels of the organization will play a critical role: companies need to upskill internal talent and hire externally in order to be able to drive these projects. At the same time, users of these systems will need basic statistical knowledge in order to understand the limitations and capabilities of those solutions and be able to decide also when to not lean on them.

Alexander: Which innovative analytics and AI use cases would be made possible by a tighter data integration?

Mohamed: Advanced, AI-supported analytics can point users to relevant insights and alert them to pertinent changes in business metrics. Systems can identify links to adjacent data sets and propose pulling them in on demand, for example, comparing business results with industry benchmarks.

Humans find it particularly difficult to wrap their heads around complex interactions involving multiple variables, such as market share changes affected by product introduction, price changes, competitor actions, and promotional activities all at the same time. AI-based systems can uncover such multidimensional relationships and drivers with ease, simulate various scenarios, and propose the best possible way forward. Similar scenarios exist for all lines of business and all industries, and they very often live at the intersection of integrated data, advanced analysis through AI, and human judgment to make the final call.

Alexander: Besides total cost of ownership, which are the top arguments for companies to use cloud-based services? When do they stick to an on-premises solution?

Mohamed: Customers are going to the cloud to accelerate projects, connect to the external world, and adopt new technologies. Also, the flexibility in building new business models in the cloud are much simpler than in an on-premises world. On the technology side we built our SAP Business Technology Platform (SAP BTP), which empowers companies to become intelligent enterprises with one strong end-to-end offering. Our collaboration with Microsoft, for example, gives us the flexibility to run our applications on a solid platform. Customers are sticking with an on-premises solution mostly if they have security concerns or are not allowed to go the cloud because of specific regulations.

Alexander: What are typical scenarios for a hybrid cloud architecture? What would such an architecture look like?

Mohamed: Imagine the customer has different SAP on-premises business applications, such as S/4 HANA and SAP BW, and is looking for a way to accelerate their data and analytics across the company. We are able to connect via our hybrid technology from the data warehouse cloud, for example, to the back-end system even without replicating the data. This immediately gives the customers a nice start to building their first use cases on top of their back-end systems in a hybrid approach and also being able to include their cloud-based data with a common semantic layer across different clouds (see Figure 13.1).

Figure 13.1   SAP Data Warehouse Cloud

Alexander: How do you face the data privacy and data govern-ance concerns of your customers?

Mohamed: Customers are currently very open to investing in cloud technologies but are still deciding which kind of data they want to move into the cloud. Of course, there are still sensitive industries with very strong regulations. But especially during the COVID era there are a lot of global initiatives that will help to accel-erate the acceptance of cloud technologies. With a hybrid approach, customers are willing to invest in cloud technologies because they can decide if they want to move sensitive data or if they want only to connect virtually. In addition, modern methods for data anonymi-zation and data masking provide measures to further protect sensi-tive data in the cloud. This is, for example, used for the Zero Suicide Platform, which is developed by HarrisLogic, to help slow rising suicide rates.[i]

Alexander: Thank you, Mo. What quick-win advice would you give that is easy for many companies to apply within their digital strategies?

Mohamed: There are always negative opinions, and innovative digital strategies have a low priority in some companies. Companies should just start to think like startups and establish this agile digital culture from top to bottom. Senior management should act as role models toward new strategies and, for example, create new roles, like a chief digital officer who could help to evangelize across the company on that topic.

Be agile, just do it!

Alexander: What are your favorite apps, tools, or software that you can't live without?

Mohamed: Spotify, Amazon Prime, Clubhouse, WhatsApp ☺

Alexander: Do you have a smart productivity hack or work-related shortcut?

Mohamed: Always be visible and be open to learning new things and accepting challenges. Don't hesitate to get real feedback.

Alexander: What is the best advice you have ever received?

Mohamed: Don't stop learning. Always try to give more than expected. And always find a good balance between work and private life.

Key Takeaways

- Traditionally, there was a pretty clear segregation between the IT and business departments. These times have changed. Business users increasingly work with operational and strategic data and analytics on their own within their strategic and operational decision-making processes.
- Implementing change is oftentimes inhibited by complex system architectures that have been built and extended for decades and are hard to change. In contrast, modern modular, microservice, and cloud-based architectures allow for flexibility, scalability, and quick time to value, and are an essential part of companies' digital strategies across industries.
- Companies should just start to think like startups and establish this agile digital culture from the top down.

Endnote

i   Meyerhoff, Robin, "HarrisLogic Uses Technology to Help Slow Rising Suicide Rates," November 14, 2018 (news.sap.com/2018/11/harris-logic-sap-technology-slow-rising-suicide-rates/).

Chapter 14

Tatyana Yakushev: Data Visualizations and Cloud-Powered AI as Strategic Assets for Next-Gen Analytics

Tatyana Yakushev, principal engineer, Amazon Web Services
Source: Tatyana Yakushev

Tatyana Yakushev is a principal engineer at Amazon Web Services working on Amazon QuickSight. She has been working in the data analytics and data visualization space since 2006. Prior to joining Amazon, she worked as a software engineer or manager at Microsoft, Tableau, and Predixion Software.

Alexander: You are a principal engineer at Amazon Web Services. What is your mission?

Tatyana: Principal engineers at Amazon Web Services are strategic members of product teams, helping to build and manage flexible, architecturally sound systems aligned with business needs. Since data analytics is near and dear to my heart, my mission is to make Amazon QuickSight the preferred service for our customers.

Alexander: How should business models evolve to survive and thrive in an increasingly digital world?

Tatyana: To discuss how business models should evolve to thrive in an increasingly digital world, first we need to talk about the shift to the cloud and the changes it brings. Why are organizations moving their IT infrastructure to the cloud, and why are they doing it so quickly?

- The first reason is cost. With the cloud, you don't have to lay out the capital up front for the servers and the data centers, and you instead get to pay for it as you consume it as a variable expense. If you've ever had to provision infrastructure, you know you could decide to provision on the low side. Then, if it turns out you don't have enough, you create a customer outage; most people don't choose this option. You could instead provision for the peak, but you rarely sit at the peak for long. In the cloud you just provision what you need — if it turns out you need less, you give it back to us and stop paying for it. That variable expense is lower than what virtually every company can do on its own.

- While cost is often a conversation starter, the number-one reason that enterprises and governments are moving to the cloud is the agility and speed with which they can change their customer experience. If you look at most companies' on-premises infrastructure, to get a server typically takes 10 to 12 weeks (sometimes longer), and then you have to build all this surrounding infrastructure software, like compute and storage and database and analytics and machine learning. In the cloud, you can provision thousands of servers in minutes and access a variety of services to get from an idea to implementation several orders of magnitude faster.

What helps organizations thrive in an increasingly digital world? What separates successful organizations from the rest? The biggest differences often come down to a few key factors.

- First, the senior leadership team needs to be aligned and truly committed to the changes. They need to be setting clear direction and expectations for the rest of the organization to get everyone on the same page and working toward the same thing. It's easy for others to do nothing or block things if the leadership team isn't making the transition a priority and building a culture for change.
- Then, the most successful organizations start with an aggressive top-down goal that forces the organization to transition faster than it would organically.
- Third, it's really important that organizations are trained on the technologies and comfortable with the concepts as part of the whole process.
- Last, sometimes organizations can get paralyzed if they can't figure out how to transform every last workload. There is no need to boil the ocean. It is useful to conduct a portfolio analysis, assess each application, and build a plan for what to transform in the short term, medium term, and last. This helps organizations get the benefits for many of their applications much more quickly, and it really helps inform how they move the rest.

Alexander: How can technology shift the roles and responsibilities of the workforce?

Tatyana: Recent technological advances are transforming the way we work, play, and interact with others. These technological advances can create enormous economic and other benefits but can also lead to significant changes for workers.

These technological advances allowed organizations to pivot in the face of the COVID-19 pandemic by providing services remotely and having part of the workforce working from home.

Technological advances allow us to automate routine work and help people focus on more creative tasks. According to a recent McKinsey report,[i] "Nearly all occupations will be affected by automation, but only about 5 percent of occupations could be fully automated by currently demonstrated technologies. Many more occupations have portions of their constituent activities that are automatable: we find that about 30 percent of the activities in 60 percent of all occupations could be automated. This means that most workers — from welders to mortgage brokers to CEOs — will work alongside rapidly evolving machines. The nature of these occupations will likely change as a result."

Automation will increase demand for people with advanced technological skills. Social, emotional, and higher cognitive skills and complex information processing will also see growing demand.

Alexander: Which technology or digital capabilities are essential for a digital strategy?

Tatyana: Artificial intelligence (AI). Even though we have learned to use or even depend on assistant technologies such as Alexa or Siri, in the grand scheme of things, most organizations are still in the very early stages of adopting artificial intelligence. AI will continue to transform every single business.

Alexander: Why do data visualizations have such a strong impact on our decisions?

Tatyana: Good data visualizations show the most important information needed to achieve one or more objectives. This key information is consolidated on a single computer screen so it can be monitored and understood at a glance. Having the information presented in a graphical form allows us to leverage the power of the visual perception, focus on key elements first, notice trends or outliers, and explore further to get the full picture.

Alexander: Why is data storytelling the essential data science skill that everyone needs?

Tatyana: Data analytics can be divided into two broad areas: exploratory analysis and explanatory analysis.

- Exploratory analysis is what you do to understand the data and figure out what might be noteworthy or interesting to highlight to others.
- Explanatory analysis is what you do when you have something specific that you want to communicate to somebody specific. This is where storytelling skills become critical.

Since almost every data scientist needs to communicate their findings to other members of the organization on a regular basis, storytelling becomes an essential skill for every data scientist to master. While many data scientists can build an OK story, it takes years of practice to become a pro in drawing your audience's attention to the things you want them to see, providing the right level of details to answer most common questions without overwhelming the audience, and building a memorable story that others will remember after leaving the meeting and when making a decision.

Alexander: How can everyone learn to communicate better with data?

Tatyana: Step 1 is building data-driven culture within the organization so that decisions are made by looking at the data instead of gut feeling. Step 2 is practicing and learning from others.

Two of my favorite books on the topic of data visualizations are

- *Information Dashboard Design: Displaying Data for At-a-Glance Monitoring* by Stephen Few
- *Storytelling with Data: A Data Visualization Guide for Business Professionals* by Cole Nussbaumer Knaflic

Alexander: What basic guidelines and patterns should always be considered for a visual expressive dashboard?

Tatyana: Many data scientists and data analysts focus on the technical aspects of the problem when building a dashboard, such as getting access to the data, figuring out how to automate data transformation pipelines, and figuring out how different metrics are computed. I want more people to think like a UX designer before they start to do any work.

Interview your audience to understand their needs. A great way to do it is to ask them to teach you to do their job as if you were a new member on the team. Listen to understand what information is important for them to take an action or make a decision. Understand where and when they look at the information, what other systems they use, and how they collaborate with other people within or outside of the organization.

Alexander: Companies usually have plenty of legacy dashboards, the message of which cannot be seen at first glance. What would a workshop look like to improve visual data communication?

Tatyana: When helping others build and improve existing dashboards, I like to focus on eight areas:

- Content organization within a dashboard
- Picking the right chart
- Proper use of colors
- Techniques for highlighting what's important
- How and when to use captions, labels, and description to help people understand the content
- Providing necessary context to help compare results to target, another time period, or results in another region
- Techniques to reduce chart junk, remove unnecessary or repetitive information, and increase data-to-ink ratio
- Adding interactivity to dashboards

Before and after examples help people understand and remember the content.

Alexander: Whom should you trust with helping you monitor the changes you're making and testing your dashboard prototype to see if it meets expectations?

Tatyana: Sometimes people forget that dashboards are software applications that benefit from well-established software validation and deployment processes. It might be OK to quickly build a dashboard and share it with the team if everybody is very familiar with the data, the scope of work is very clear, and the dashboard is used by only a handful of users. In other cases, you can adopt processes used by big technology companies. These include the following:

- Automated tests to make sure that data pipelines are functioning correctly and the data is accurate and fresh
- Use of version control systems to track and approve changes and to roll back to the previous version if anything goes wrong
- Early validation by a subset of users to catch problems before they affect everybody
- Usability research to identity if the dashboard meets expectations and how it can be improved. Make sure that this research is done by observing a diverse set of users, including people with different roles, different experiences and backgrounds, different geographic locations, color vision deficiency, or other visual impairments.

Alexander: Why should companies set up an Analytics Center of Excellence as part of their digital strategy? What are some strategies for setting this up?

Tatyana: Becoming a data-driven organization takes time and the efforts of many people. Selecting the right analytics tool and building the necessary dashboards is only a small part of the journey. An Analytics Center of Excellence (ACoE) can help streamline analytics efforts across the organization and steer all of your efforts in the right direction. The ACoE can be responsible for these tasks:

- Setting up your organization's analytics vision. How do you prioritize investments in different areas? How do you measure the business impact?
- Building a technology blueprint. What data, tools, and capabilities will help your organization remain ahead of the competition in the future?
- Establishing standards and best practices to be used across the organization. Besides helping your organization complete analytical projects better and faster, it can help you stay compliant with applicable laws and regulations.
- Managing programs and controlling funding. Should your organization pay to acquire third-party data? How much should you be spending on licenses, salaries, and other expenses?

- Skills development. The analytics area is continuing to grow very quickly. This means that people working on analytical projects need to continuously learn about new tools and techniques and will greatly benefit from knowledge sharing.

When establishing an ACoE, it helps to

- define clear areas of focus,
- secure funding or headcount and establish partnership with other parts of the organization that benefit from the ACoE's work the most,
- build a balanced team with regard to areas of expertise and skills, and
- define demonstrable success criteria and celebrate successes.

Alexander: The Fourth Industrial Revolution is inseparably tied to the vast amounts of data needed to train artificial intelligence. How has this revolution impacted your work at Amazon Web Services?

Tatyana: With the rise in compute power and proliferation of data, machine learning has moved from the periphery to become a core part of businesses and organizations across industries. Gartner forecasts that AI-derived business values are projected to reach $3.9 trillion in 2022.[ii]

AWS has tens of thousands of machine learning (ML) customers who are using ML to drive efficiencies, create new revenue streams, and innovate on behalf of their customers. These companies span many industries, including healthcare and life sciences, finance, technology, retail, media, and entertainment, as well as the public sector.

Alexander: Which AI use cases would you see as essential to contributing to any organization's digital strategy?

Tatyana: Good machine learning use cases solve real problems for our customers' businesses and can help to gain support and adoption at the organizational level. To assist customers in choosing the right use case, we have prioritized seven horizontal machine learning use cases, which are applicable across a number of industries.

Personalize Customer Recommendations Amazon Personalize can help applications and websites tailor content to a user's behavior, history, and preferences, boosting engagement and satisfaction. For example:

- A video streaming website can help users discover additional shows that they may be interested in by providing recommendations on the home screen based on past viewing habits and demographics.
- A retailer can recommend items similar to a selected item on a detail page.

Discover Accurate Information Faster with Cognitive Search AWS makes it easy to combine previously siloed data sources into a central location and use natural language questions instead of simple keywords to get the answers faster and more accurately from unstructured content. Internally, this allows organizations to improve employee productivity, accelerate research, and make faster and better decisions. Externally, organizations can delight their customers with a superior experience and easy access to the information they need.

Forecast Faster and More Accurately Amazon Forecast is a fully managed service that uses machine learning to combine time-series data with additional variables to build forecasts. It requires no machine learning experience to get started. You only need to provide historical data, plus any additional data that you believe may impact your forecasts.

Analyze Rich Media Assets and Discover New Insights The AWS Media2Cloud solution makes it easy to import the media content, such as video, audio, and text, into the cloud and then rapidly analyze what the content contains (objects, spoken audio, activities, and so on). Based on these insights customers can build their business use cases, such as content search (internal and external), language detection, audio and text translation, ad classification and targeting, subtitling and localization, content moderation, and so on.

Add Intelligence to the Contact Center   AWS offers solutions that add intelligence to your contact center tailored specifically to your business needs, whether you are building a contact center from scratch or integrating services into existing partner contact centers.

Identify Fraudulent Online Activities   Amazon Fraud Detector is a fully managed service that makes it easy to identify potentially fraudulent online activities such as online payment fraud and the creation of fake accounts.

Automate Data Extraction and Analysis   Organizations have long struggled to process documents efficiently to make them easy to search and access. With Amazon Textract and Amazon Comprehend, AWS helps customers build and maintain a smart index of their document stores. Amazon Textract and Amazon Comprehend use automation and natural language processing to extract and classify documents, and to produce insights that are meaningful to the business.

Alexander: Because so much data is needed to train AI algorithms, how can organizations and companies stay ahead of legal, regulatory, and ethical issues associated with collecting and applying data?

Tatyana: AWS continues to talk to customers, researchers, academics, policymakers, and others to understand how to best balance the benefits of AI technologies with the potential risks. One of the goals of these discussions is to create guidelines for ethical use of AI technologies. The other goal is to encourage policymakers to consider these guidelines as potential legislation and rules in the United States and other countries.

Alexander: Is there a way for citizens to own their data instead of organizations and companies owning fractions of it?

Tatyana: Many countries have laws and regulations to protect citizens' fundamental right to privacy and the protection of personal data, such as General Data Protection Regulation (GDPR) in the European Union. Many requirements under these laws and regulations focus on ensuring effective control and protection of personal data. AWS offers services and resources to help you comply with regulatory and compliance requirements that may apply to your activities. These include the following:

- Encryption of personal data
- Ability to ensure the ongoing confidentiality, integrity, availability, and resilience of processing systems and services
- Ability to restore the availability of and access to personal data in a timely manner in the event of a physical or technical incident
- Processes for regularly testing, assessing, and evaluating the effectiveness of technical and organizational measures for ensuring the security of processing

Alexander: What types of professional roles will we see evolve alongside the development and increasing use of AI across the industries?

Tatyana: The job market of the future will be characterized by human-AI cooperation rather than competition. With increased use of AI, people will be able to do their work better and faster. AI will allow people to spend less time on mundane tasks, such as finding the right information, and more time on creative tasks and human-to-human interaction. For example, a doctor might spend less time entering medical information and more time talking with a patient to make a data-driven decision regarding the best course of treatment. Employees who previously lifted and stacked objects can become robot operators, monitoring the automated arms and resolving issues such as an interruption in the flow of objects.

We will continue to see increasing demand for data analysts and cybersecurity specialists.

Alexander: How do you develop your team's AI skills?

Tatyana: We've been using machine learning across Amazon for more than 20 years and have thousands of engineers focused on machine learning across the company. To help advance our team's AI knowledge, we run a machine learning university (MLU) program. Most of the same courses used to train Amazon employees are available online at no charge[iii] (you only pay for the services you use in labs and exams during your training).

Alexander: What skills will managers need to develop to be able to work with AI?

Tatyana: Technology companies and departments looking to adopt AI will need to learn how to plan and run their software development programs. AI solutions often require a higher number of experiments and iterations relative to non-AI solutions. This happens because results of training AI models are difficult to predict ahead of time. Managers will need to learn how to set the right goals for their teams, track progress, and help teams focus on the right priorities. Being able to bridge the communication gap between data scientists, engineers, and businesspeople is very beneficial.

Alexander: Thank you, Tatyana. What quick-win advice would you give that is easy for many companies to apply within their digital strategies?

Focus on customer needs and work backward to develop new experiences. Most successful companies got ahead not by competing head-to-head but by rethinking the entire experience.

Tatyana: Focus on customer needs and work backward to develop new experiences. Most successful companies got ahead not by competing head-to-head but by rethinking the entire experience.

Alexander: What are your favorite apps, tools, or software that you can't live without?

Tatyana: I like LinkedIn. It helps me stay connected with people working in my field, discover news, articles, books, and courses.

Alexander: Do you have a smart productivity hack or work-related shortcut?

Tatyana: I take time to review my plan for the week, write down what I plan to accomplish, and see how I've done against my goals the previous week. This helps me spend my time more efficiently and not forget something important.

Alexander: What is the best advice you have ever received?

Tatyana: "Take actions to move toward your goal, regardless of whether you know how each one is going to work out or not." It is not uncommon for people to think that somebody else is more qualified, more capable to achieve something. Women are especially affected by this. Nowadays, I ask myself, "What is the worst thing that can happen?" make peace with it, and move forward.

Key Takeaways

- Most successful companies got ahead not by competing head-to-head but by rethinking the entire experience. Focus on customer needs and work backward to develop new experiences.
- AWS Well-Architected Framework is a great resource for customers to apply best practices in the design, delivery, and maintenance of AWS environments.
- AI will allow people to spend less time on mundane tasks, such as finding the right information, and more time on creative tasks and human-to-human interaction.

Endnotes

i McKinsey Global Institute, "AI, automation, and the future of work: Ten things to solve for," June 1, 2018 (www.mckinsey.com/featured-insights/future-of-work/ai-automation-and-the-future-of-work-ten-things-to-solve-for).

ii Gartner, "Gartner Says Global Artificial Intelligence Business Value to Reach $1.2 Trillion in 2018," April 25, 2018 (www.gartner.com/en/newsroom/press-releases/2018-04-25-gartner-says-global-artificial-intelligence-business-value-to-reach-1-point-2-trillion-in-2018).

iii ML training website: aws.training/machinelearning.

Chapter 15
Kerem Tomak: Designing a Digital Strategy for the Financial Sector

Kerem Tomak, global chief analytics officer,
ING Group
Source: Kerem Tomak

Dr. Kerem Tomak studied mathematics, economics, and information systems in Turkey and the United States. He embarked on his professional career as an assistant professor at the University of Texas, Austin. Dr. Tomak brings more than 15 years of experience as a data scientist and an executive. Prior to his current appointment as the global chief analytics officer at ING Group, he was the founder and head of the big data, advanced analytics, and AI division at Commerzbank AG as well as a supervisory board member of Main Incubator, a subsidiary of Commerzbank. He has expertise in the areas of hybrid multicloud architectures for scaling data-driven products, AI and machine learning applications in retail and financial services, digital transformation, omnichannel and cross-device attribution, price and revenue optimization, promotion effectiveness, yield optimization in digital marketing, and real-time analytics. He has managed midsize and large analytics and digital marketing teams in Fortune 500 companies, including Google and Yahoo, and delivered large-scale analytics solutions for marketing and merchandising departments for retailers like Walmart and Macy's in the United States. His outside-of-the-box thinking and problem-solving skills have led to four patent awards and numerous academic publications. He is also a lecturer at the Frankfurt School of Finance and Management in the applied data science master's program as well as a sought-after speaker on big data and BI platforms for analytics.

In this interview with Kerem, we are going to explore the importance of an end-to-end data strategy and how this is connected with AI, analytics, and data democracy.

Alexander: You are global chief analytics officer at ING Group, a multinational banking and financial services corporation. How did you get started in the data and analytics domain?

Kerem: I come from a pretty quantitative background, and I have always been intrigued by the use of computers to solve real business problems. So much so that I started consulting for companies of various sizes at age 18. After a mathematics degree with an economics minor, I got interested in econometrics and hence started to learn more about data analysis, modeling, testing, and so on. It was when I was consulting for a startup in Austin, where I was a professor at the University of Texas, that I got really interested in building solutions to real-world problems.

Problems I started to tackle involved price optimization, assortment planning, revenue management, and so on, all using data and analytics. I was exposed to building real-time, large-scale, data-driven products at Yahoo, which helped me learn more about what it takes to get from ideation to implementation of algorithms in production. A/B testing with real traffic before handing over a product prototype to engineering units is an extremely valuable experience in my field. I used Hadoop before it was open source, and we were doing things now considered big data and data science before these terms were mainstream. From building algorithms, I then moved on to building teams.

I started with smaller teams and learned concepts of management, skills matrix, promotions, hiring and firing decisions, and so on. As the size and scope of the teams grew, complexity—both in product delivery and team culture—also grew. While I was building teams, I had to navigate matrix organizations. I quickly learned what worked and what didn't in gaining success in these environments. I still try to get my hands dirty when I get a chance in order to stay current in tools and techniques in data science.

Alexander: Before joining ING Group, you were the executive VP of big data, advanced analytics, and AI at Commerzbank, a major bank in Germany with subsidiaries around the world. Could you tell me more about your role at Commerzbank? How does your professional background (Google, Yahoo, and so on) help you?

Kerem: I was the founder of the big data and advanced analytics (BDBA) function at Commerzbank as part of its divisional board of executives. I was also the founder of a startup under Main Incubator focused on data and analytics monetization. My career had been in Silicon Valley, so the natural next step was to take a global role such as the one I had with Commerzbank. The international makeup of tech companies like Google and Yahoo allowed me to bring a more inclusive team leadership focused on transparency and pragmatic adoption of ideas into Commerzbank and take both a thought leader role and a functional leadership in the bank. As such, I was both an expert in data and analytics as well as a digital transformation leader for the bank.

Alexander: *How should business models evolve to survive and thrive in an increasingly digital world?*

Kerem: There is no foolproof approach here. I can point to some key characteristics of winning strategies. One of these is to build a "fail-fast, learn, and optimize" culture. This is where all digitally savvy companies should strive to excel, since they all know that if they do not achieve this, they will be disrupted. An important driver of innovation is being able to test any and all ideas possible about a product and a business model. It is of course easier when there are plenty of resources to allocate to this task.

However, even in the absence of resources, the mindset should be there. How else can we know what will work in the marketplace and what is no longer working? Generally, this approach, when implemented in the right way, allows an organization to curate product, process, and structure ideas from all levels of the organization. These ideas are then tested either in a lab setting or in real market tests using well-established A/B testing approaches or any other statistical design of experimental methods. Design of experiments is an area in statistics that focuses on applying statistical methods in the appropriate choice and setup of an experiment.

Once the validity of an idea is scientifically or directionally proven, one can go forward with a go-to-market strategy. Fine-tuning after each step of learning allows the optimization of products brought to the marketplace. If, on the other hand, the idea does not work, it is still important to understand why it does not work and either try again or kill the idea. If this is the general culture of the company, innovation will make business models thrive. At the core of it, though, it always starts with the customer. There are many examples in history where very futuristic and novel products failed due to lack of customer adoption, such as General Magic, Google Glass, Fuel Band, Segway, Google Nexus One, and so on. This also happens with digital business models.

Another characteristic of a winning strategy is to "increase proximity to the customer and scale through digital, direct, or through other platforms." Note that both this and the previous characteristics critically depend upon the scalable use of data and analytics to drive insights and intelligence in support of these strategies. Digital channels allow customers to have a plethora of alternatives when they look for products and services. This constant access to information is putting pressure on all companies to be better at understanding their customers, provide better and proactive services, and be better at after-sale support and reach. Companies either build their own platforms (for example, Facebook, Google, and so on) or join existing platforms to increase their presence in digital channels while also scaling their operations to meet their customers' demands. The strength of the platforms is pushing further the need to digitize to be able to connect to these platforms.

Alexander: How can technology shift the roles and responsibilities of the workforce?

Kerem: Technology is shuffling and flattening the traditional roles and responsibilities of the workforce. On the one hand, it is allowing the workforce to connect globally and expanding the time and space of interactions; on the other hand, it is increasing the need for face-to-face meetings for more strategic decisions. Technology can increase and deepen the collaboration across an organization as well as speed up delivery timelines when used correctly. I support the approach of remote work, and I believe that one has to have flexibility when it comes to working from wherever on the globe. Companies today have to find and compete for talent globally. This cannot be done by opening offices all around the globe. Technology can support connecting members of a global talent pool to each other.

I should also mention the importance of data fluency of the workforce. We talked about key characteristics of successful digital businesses earlier and I mentioned that at the core, data and analytics play a key role. In fact, almost all decisions in a business need to be based on or supported by facts. This is a tremendous change in the way job definitions are written these days. Many of the digitally savvy companies include data/analytics as a desired competency of a job candidate at any level. A growing number of companies declare data fluency as a requirement for their employees. Obviously, training employees on the importance of data and insights is only half the battle. Data needs to be "liberated" and provided to all employees by default. As a benchmark, companies like Airbnb and Lyft claim they make 50 percent of their overall data treasure open to all employees. Enriching the ideation, testing, and decisioning flow of their employees, companies hope to lead and remain competitive in the marketplace.

Alexander: *Which technology or digital capabilities are essential for a digital strategy?*

Kerem: As of today — as it is impossible to forecast technology — there are some key technologies that are pillars for a digital strategy: public cloud, data science, API, CI/CD.[i] If we agree that any given brand needs to support customers wherever they are and whenever they need a product or service, then the cloud allows the scalability needed to achieve this, APIs offer microservices a framework for modular buildup of customizable products, CI/CD allows fast deployment of solutions, and data science brings the intelligence needed to understand customer needs and product improvements. Altogether you have the basics of the digital capabilities needed to support any digital strategy.

Alexander: *What are the main lessons you learned when you established an organization as part of a digital strategy for the financial sector?*

Kerem: There is a stigma around regulated industries where people think technology cannot be easily used or traditional organizations cannot change and adapt. I do not believe this is true. I came to realize that even the regulators want to learn technologies such as deep learning, cloud, and so on, in order to more effectively regulate the use of such technologies in financial services. In the absence of true expertise in the ranks of the regulatory bodies, regulations cannot achieve their targets. The fear of regulation hence stifles progress in digitalization of the financial sector for companies with histories longer than a decade or two.

For the fin-techs, use of technology enables them to bypass or disrupt existing companies, but customers still drive the adoption of financial services. Here, lessons from retail apply. Companies need to be customer-centric, and digital strategy starts with the customer. Understanding what the customer needs from a brand must shape the digital strategy of that brand. For example, in Silicon Valley, almost everyone uses technology to search and buy products, using their devices and paying digitally; cash has almost completely disappeared. In Germany, cash is still king — although COVID-19 may change that — so assuming that a digital strategy based on a Silicon Valley approach will work in Germany may be a fatal mistake.

Alexander: How do you see digital strategies evolving with the maturity of big data processing and AI? How do you prepare for an AI-centric ecosystem as a business leader?

Kerem: Data and algorithms are key for the success of any AI-centric digital strategy. As I said earlier, digital strategy starts with the customer. Increasingly, AI enables more intelligent interfaces and touchpoints anywhere, anytime. I have to also stress that we are using AI in the most narrow sense of it today. The most important breakthrough in AI was the use of deep learning at scale, which is nothing but machine learning—a concept going back to the 1950s and established as a technology solution by the 1980s, so we are not talking about anything new here! At the core of deep learning, we still have massive dependencies on clean data and scalable compute infrastructure. Use of public cloud technology becomes doubly important for the adoption of AI.

> *Use of public cloud technology becomes doubly important for the adoption of AI.*

Alexander: Algorithms have been used in the banking business for many years. What can other sectors learn from the experience in the financial sector?

Kerem: For regulated industries, algorithms are more scrutinized, and data is more controlled. Even so, algorithms that work within this domain can be used in other fields, and vice versa. Essentially, algorithms accomplish a similar purpose no matter what industry we look at: create a set of rules which can be translated into a set of instructions for a computer to execute. For example, an algorithm that predicts purchase intent of an online browser can be modified to also predict the purchase intent of a store visitor. Similarly, a model that predicts credit risk of an individual can be used to predict insurance risk of the same individual.

Alexander: Could you give some insights on Commerzbank's hybrid multicloud architecture?

Kerem: Sure. On premises, we have a data lake production environment consisting of major sources of data and Cloudera tools to scale. Each business unit has its own lane for the tools and data it needs, and each business follows a self-service approach to analytics and BI development and deployment. In addition, the BDAA unit has a dedicated data lake for our own testing and development for a variety of topics ranging from fraud detection algorithms to customer churn prediction models. This enables us to experiment with new technologies, tools, and ideas. We are then able to bring what works to production on the main lake. These lakes are also connected to the cloud providers, Microsoft and Google. We use a hardware-based security module to encrypt the data we transfer to the cloud. This allows us to manage our own private key and ensure no one else has access to the cloud environment we are using.

Alexander: How do you decide which vendor's cloud service to use for a certain scenario? When do you stick to an on-premises solution?

Kerem: It depends on the capabilities and solutions each cloud vendor provides. Google has great tools for AI, and Microsoft provides integration with Microsoft 365, which we use across the enterprise. We choose a solution provider based on the use case and end goal. For business-critical workloads, data we cannot port to a public cloud environment due to regulatory or data protection rules; we still need on-premises solutions, but at a much smaller scale.

Alexander: How do you face data privacy and data governance concerns when you pitch new ideas?

Kerem: First, we wrote a data playbook and made it available to everyone in the bank. This playbook has everything one needs to know about regulatory and legal aspects of data, its use, cloud architecture, and security concepts. The playbook is in a sense "operationalization of the *Data Protection Manual*." Next, we created a Privacy Council, which has this book as its bible when assessing the fit of a use case before allowing it to be deployed in the cloud. It can also discuss other use cases which have to do with the use of data anywhere in the bank.

Alexander: Thank you, Kerem. What quick-win advice would you give that is easy for many companies to apply within their digital strategies?

Kerem: Not sure if it is a quick win but any digital strategy must take data and analytics seriously. It needs to consider how to use this capability early on in the evolution of the strategy. If this step is missing, I do not see a successful digital strategy coming to fruition.

Alexander: Before moving to Germany for Commerzbank, you had been working in the United States for many years. What are the key differences that you have discovered comparing Europe and the United States?

Kerem: Europeans are very sensitive to privacy and data security. The European Union has set a high global standard with its General Data Protection Regulation (GDPR[ii]). Data protection made in Europe is a real asset and has the potential to become a global blueprint.

Also, Europe is very diverse — from language to culture to different market environments and regulatory issues. Even though immense progress has been made in the direction of harmonization in the European Union, a level playing field remains one of the key issues in Europe, especially for banks. Technology adoption is also lagging in some parts of Europe. Bigger infrastructure investments, wider adoption of the public cloud, and 5G deployment are needed to stay competitive and relevant in global markets, which are increasingly dominated by the United States and China. This is both an opportunity and a risk. I see tremendous opportunities everywhere, from IoT to AI-driven B2B and B2C apps, for example. If adoption of the public cloud lags any further, the European Union risks falling behind on AI development and innovation. Finally, I truly enjoy the family-oriented work-life balance in Europe, which in turn increases work productivity and output.

Alexander: What are your favorite apps, tools, or software that you can't live without?

Kerem: My iPad Pro, iMac Pro, Adobe Lightroom, Google Workspace, Microsoft 365, Python, Tableau, WhatsApp, and so on.

Alexander: Do you have a smart productivity hack or work-related shortcut?

Kerem: Every day I spend at least an hour reading articles my network shares with me on LinkedIn. It helps me keep abreast of what is going on around the world in my field. I also pay attention to publications coming out in my field, both academic and business. I try to read at least one quantitative book a month and more if possible in the business press.

Alexander: What is the best advice you have ever received?

Kerem: My father once told me, "The wisest man is the one who knows that he does not and cannot know everything. Son, just focus on being the best at what you do and never stop learning." To this day, this is the best advice I ever got.

Key Takeaways

- The "fail-fast, learn, and optimize" culture is where all tech companies thrive, since they all know that if they do not achieve this, they will be disrupted.
- Bigger infrastructure investments, wider adoption of the public cloud, and 5G deployment are needed to stay competitive and relevant in global markets.
- At the core of deep learning, we still have massive dependencies on clean data and scalable compute infrastructure.

Endnotes

i   CI/CD refers to the combined practices of continuous integration and either continuous delivery or continuous deployment. The CI/CD practice forms the backbone of modern-day DevOps operations.

ii The *General Data Protection Regulation (EU) 2016/679 (GDPR)*, also known as *DS-GVO* (from the German term *Datenschutz-Grundverordnung*), is a regulation in EU law on data protection and privacy in the European Union and the European Economic Area. The GDPR's primary aim is to give individuals control over their personal data and to simplify the regulatory environment for international business by unifying regulation within the European Union. GDPR official text: `eur-lex.europa.eu/eli/reg/2016/679/oj`.

Chapter 16
Christy Marble:
Connecting the Dots Across
the Customer Lifecycle

Christy Marble, chief marketing officer, Pantheon
Source: Christy Marble

Christy is a seasoned global SaaS growth marketing expert and currently chief marketing officer of Pantheon, a leader in the WebOps[i] space. She has overseen successful digital, martech,[ii] and go-to-market transformations; product, ecommerce, and ecosystem launches; acquisitions and integrations; successful rebranding; market expansion; and multibillion-dollar brand and portfolio growth over the course of more than 30 years in marketing. When she was CMO of SAP Concur, Christy's B2B marketing teams led rapid channel, vertical, and international market expansion, growing the pipeline from $200 million to beyond $1 billion. As CMO of Visier, as a business-to-business marketing executive at Vertafore, E-centives, and Claritas, and as a consumer marketing executive at Sallie Mae, she has led successful SaaS product commercialization and go-to-market strategies, corporate and consumer brand launches, customer segmentation, and digital marketing programs. Christy is a global advisory board member of the Sales & Marketing Strategy Institute (SAMS) and an advisor to Fenix Commerce. She holds an MBA from the Anderson School of Management at UCLA, a CMO Program certificate from the Kellogg School at Northwestern University, and a BA in sociology from Pepperdine University.

Alexander: You are chief marketing officer at Pantheon. What is your mission?

Christy: We have an amazing team at Pantheon, including a team of executives who founded Pantheon with the vision of a better way to build websites by applying proven best practices in software development to the web. Our mission is to make the open web a first-class medium that delivers results. Our turnkey SaaS WebOps platform empowers marketers and business stakeholders to take control of the end-to-end website experience. By enabling cross-functional teams to collaborate and to test and deploy website changes in an iterative fashion to improve web experiences and achieve measurable business results as they go, we have eliminated the need for high-risk, all-or-nothing "relaunch" events.

Alexander: How should business models evolve to survive and thrive in an increasingly digital world?

Christy: The pace of digital innovation continues to accelerate, and just as the bubonic plague made way for the Renaissance, we are in for a digital acceleration beyond our wildest dreams in this decade and thereafter following COVID. Already we have seen the acceleration of both biotech and cloud technology during COVID. In biotech we are seeing crowdsourcing and machine learning aiding in the development of experimental drugs and vaccines. We are also seeing pharmaceutical companies launch websites in just a day or two from concept to go-live to recruit participants for vaccine trials. Leveraging WebOps and marketing automation, they secure 30,000–40,000 participants within weeks. Likewise, universities have been able to collect longitudinal studies over the course of the pandemic to track thousands of individuals on a daily basis. I have participated in the Stanford University research since last spring by completing a daily survey. Johns Hopkins University, through one of its data technology partners, has also been a first-mover in releasing worldwide data on the spread of the pandemic. All of these are examples of companies using technology for good and using the internet to provide access to important information for everyone.

When we think of the business models that are thriving, we can see that it is the organizations that are collaborating cross-functionally and across company boundaries to see a need and to find a way to meet that need quickly. These organizations are able to do this because they are not beholden to the long, drawn-out, enterprise-wide technological roadmaps, capacity restraints, blackout dates, and resourcing queues of prior decades. Instead, they have embraced the agility of the cloud. They break projects into bite-sized chunks — applications and microservices that they can develop, test, and get to market quickly, and just-in-time technology to respond to the immediate needs in the marketplace. In the SaaS space, go-live isn't a once-a-month or once-a-week scenario, but it is a steady process that enables constant releases, testing, iterating, and improving. These are the business models that are experiencing the greatest levels of success. It is not an era of caution, but an era of exploration and adventure. The new frontier is digital.

Alexander: How can technology shift the roles and responsibilities of the workforce?

Christy: There have been some interesting and encouraging dynamics that have arisen out of the movement toward a fully remote workforce beginning in 2020. The first that I find exceptionally promising is a leveling of the playing field that has taken place with video conferencing. Specifically, the advantages of height and loud voices frequently enjoyed by males in leadership and management have been minimized all the way from elementary school well into the business world. In video conferencing, everyone is the same height, and while it is possible for one loud voice to dominate in-person conversations, meetings, and classes,[iii] the digital technology may actually be having the opposite effect. Virtual meetings may more readily hold hubris and domination in check, and when all workers are remote, each individual has the ability to participate; chat functionality helps to ensure that. There is a level of equality and inclusion that is rising.

My team has recently adopted a new strategy to increase dialogue during our monthly virtual "all-hands meeting." We have begun to supplement Zoom with an app that enables team members to submit anonymous questions and ideas during the meeting. This gives each team member the means to contribute in real time in the way that they are most comfortable, without having to have the loudest voice. Some have video on and "unmute" to participate in discussions, some use the Zoom chat, and others contribute anonymously via the app.

In the early days of computer technology, we saw the rise in power, influence, and purchasing power of the IT department inside of companies. This was especially prominent through the 1990s and 2000s. Huge budgets, multiyear enterprise initiatives to design custom technology, huge data warehouse initiatives, and centralization of processes and systems were common. Then toward 2010 and beyond, as cloud technology advanced and people across organizations began to be able to use data to drive business strategies — and results — we saw a pivot toward business functions gaining the autonomy to select and implement their own technology.

This included the rise of marketing technology and the marketing stack, as well as the CMO. Prior to this it was relatively rare for the most senior marketing person within a company to report to the CEO or to have a seat at the executive table or the boardroom. But empowered with customer data and the ability to collect that data on the web and analyze it all the way through the revenue cycle to drive measurable business results, the role of marketing became elevated within companies. So did the pressure on CMOs to drive growth.

When I was in the consumer marketing space, I was once asked by the chief financial officer exactly what additional marketing budget would be required to drive an additional $10 million in revenue in that fiscal year. Not much later, I was doing a call center visit, and I joined the president and the CEO on their jet to go through the models and determine the feasibility of making that investment. It was the fastest flight from Florida to the DC area that I had ever taken, and likely the most stressful one. But we committed to the plan, and we achieved it, because we had invested in the data and analytics to be able to track our go-to-market process from the first touch to fulfilment.

With CRM, sales automation, and marketing automation systems, this closed-loop digital strategy is just as vital in the world of B2B marketing as consumer marketing today. These are not competitive advantages, they are table stakes for growth marketers today. Your finance partner is your best friend, and you manage your marketing budget through a SaaS tool like Allocadia or Plannuh; then tracking return on marketing investment (ROMI) can become a core input into your forecasting and decision process. Free trials and freemiums are common digital acquisition strategies in the B2B space. And, good-better-best capability bundling, where multiple SKUs are bundled together into three pricing tiers, of which buyers most commonly purchase the middle tier, has become a common digital pricing strategy employed by software product marketers within go-to-market motions. The P&L model for these packages is usually grounded on simplifying the selling process to remove friction and increase sales productivity. These pricing strategies are designed to increase revenue per sale while contributing to increased sales productivity, and reduced marketing costs that create desirable customer acquisition cost (CAC) ratios, which in turn help drive favorable valuations and the potential for deeper investments in growth.

Alexander: Which technology or digital capabilities are essential for a digital strategy?

Christy: A critical thing for marketers to consider is that more than any other function within the company, it is the marketer's role to know their audience and to bring that knowledge to every interaction, along every stage of the customer life cycle.

The companies that really do this well are the companies whose marketing teams think about it from the mindset of the audience. That is harder to do than it might seem, so many companies miss the mark. The key to this is creating strategies for meeting your customers where they are, for giving them a voice, for getting to know them, and for bringing them value. Digital communities, review sites, Net Promoter Score surveys, and social media are all great places to start. The companies that do it well tell stories about highly successful customers who are doing innovative things. Customers who have driven huge growth, achieved significant breakthroughs, have become more efficient, saved time, cut costs, increased revenues, won awards, and maybe even saved lives. These marketers know what their customers value and what drives their success, and they work hard to deliver that value over and over again.

It seems so obvious. Customer, Company, and Competition have been hailed as the three Cs of marketing strategy for every marketing student since their introduction in 1982 by renowned Japanese business strategist Kenichi Ohmae.[iv]

Before the era of connected computing, consulting firms that supported the leaders in customer data capture and analysis in the financial services industry were innovating the confluence of data, technology, and strategy to establish a competitive advantage. This was often achieved through strategic change management designed to employ technology to drive down the costs of professional labor—what we now call automation. Even then, before the concepts of online customer journeys, customer life cycles, and digital experience had been coined, it was the companies that focused on their audience, on their customers, that were able to differentiate to win.

Early big-data leaders collected data not for the sake of building big databases and fancy data warehouses but to answer questions about customers and gain customer insights. With the power of the internet the boundaries of personal data have blurred and access has increased. Even the ownership and use of structured data, such as data collected in forms, and unstructured data, such as videos and photographs, have proliferated in marketing programs and artificial intelligence. Digital technology ranging from websites to social media to the internet of things (IoT) has given marketers access to seemingly limitless amounts of data. But at the same time marketers' task of turning all that data into usable insights has become exponentially more complex.

That is the challenge of the marketing technology stack. There are now thousands of specialized marketing technologies — microservices — that we string together within our technology stacks to run our marketing strategies. For fun, just do an internet search for *marketing technology stack*. If you select the Images tab, you might quickly become overwhelmed. You might even come across the Martech5000 landscape.[v] Each of those technologies provides a marketing capability, collects data, and likely includes a separate isolated reporting tool that marketers can use to see the results of a small component of their marketing programs. At Concur I counted 20 baseline technologies that each field marketer had to be proficient in using in order to effectively do their job. Imagine how much time it takes to train a new marketer to a level of proficiency.

It seems overwhelming, but that brings me back to this unrelenting focus of the most successful marketers: how you bring value to your audience, to people who buy or use your product or service, or to people who influence others to buy your product and service. There are some core frameworks that help keep marketers focused on what matters most: audience personae, customer life cycles, customer journey maps, customer touchpoints, and a few key metrics.

Alexander: What are the main lessons you learned when you established a digital strategy? How is a coherent digital strategy designed?

Christy: I have a very simple rule of thumb that has been tried and true through every digital marketing strategy for every company, every client, and every team throughout my career. It has two parts, and it has never let me down: *It is always about the customer, and first do no harm.* In a digital marketing strategy I apply the life-cycle construct to how I define our audience. When I use the word *customer*, it intentionally applies to the entire customer from beginning to end. This is deliberate, because in cloud technology, our data shows that we interact with our audience at every stage of their customer life cycle, whether we choose to recognize and influence it or not. Across our customer life cycles, we interact with people before they become customers, as they are considering whether to become customers, when they are customers, and even when they choose to no longer be customers. The best digital marketing strategies, in the highest-growth companies, reach customers at each of those stages either directly or indirectly—and deliver value. This means the marketing experiences improve the customer experience and shape the way customers feel about the company all along the way. When you really get this right, you can earn advocates at every stage of your customer life cycle.

From a visual representation standpoint I use both a circular/fly-wheel and a linear representation of the customer life cycle, depending upon how I am using it (see Figure 16.1). For interactive white-boarding exercises when mapping

> *I have a simple rule of thumb that has been tried and true through every digital marketing strategy for every company, every client, and every team throughout my career. It has two parts, and it has never let me down: It is always about the customer, and first do no harm.*

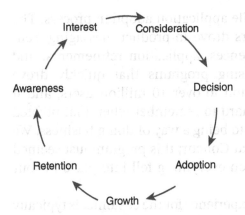

Figure 16.1 Customer life cycle

elements of a digital experience, it's easier to map activities to a horizontal line. However, for time-sequencing a customer demand experience, the circular visual better captures the flywheel effect. The point is not to get hung up on the visualization, but focus on the moments that matter in the customer experience.

This level of customer advocacy can become a superpower when your digital strategy is thoughtfully designed to deliver your customer a *better way* to do something. This requires the discipline to consistently capture and apply customer insights at every stage of the customer life cycle and to then apply the insights to improve customer processes and experiences. This applies to every function in the company, including marketing processes, sales processes, contract processes, invoicing processes, implementation processes, and support processes. For the customer, they are all connected. They are all aspects of how they experience your product, but for your company those are distinctly different (likely siloed) departments, using multiple different systems and technologies. Make sure to design and architect your strategy first. Design it to deliver a better experience for your customer and then select and integrate the technology to achieve that. Technology should fit the strategy, not the other way around.

When I was at SAP Concur, one of our biggest product adoption successes was from a 10-customer advisory group with whom we designed and tested our mobile application adoption process. The insights from those customers drove in-product messaging, self-service guides, digital experiences, application refinements, and communication and advertising programs that quickly drove mobile adoption from 2 million to over 10 million users, and it accelerated from there. It is hard to remember when that pivoted from being a program launch to being a way of doing business. We liked the term *automagically* at Concur; this program just seemed to automagically take off when everything fell into place for our customers.

That seemingly effortless experience for the customer is typically the result of very well researched, hypothesized, tested, refined, and retested strategies and processes. I remember having dinner with a friend who mentioned he had just been at our headquarters that week testing some of our new software. User experience testing was core to our product development strategies. The people who tend to be really good at this are gritty, resilient, humble, and really committed to listening, learning; then trying, failing, and asking for help or more feedback; and then putting something out there again until they succeed. Then the ultimate reward is when customers love the results and tell others. Advocacy.

This customer journey process was not a once-and-done exercise. In the years that I led various marketing divisions at Concur, and as the business grew and evolved, we repeated the exercise multiple times to ensure the strategies that we created were centered around delivering better ways to bring value to our customers. When we ran through this customer-journey mapping process later in the business unit that supported small and midsize companies, that convergence was much earlier in the customer journey because our free trial introduced the ability to use the applications before they actually bought them. Eventually the company grew and became more complex, and we progressed to mapping an end-to-end customer life cycle with many varying customer journeys along the way. They represented experiences of different partner channels, web and digital programs, and business units to ensure we made thoughtful and deliberate decisions based on the customer experiences at each intersection along the way. This informed digital experiences that we delivered, advertising campaigns and response flows, brand and creative, how we enabled our referral partners, our market development representatives (MDRs), our sales teams and our customer success teams, and within the product itself. It also required data and processes to feed information into those touchpoints, to trigger messaging based on a customer or user activity, and to track and measure customer activities across those touchpoints and within the product itself.

Alexander: *How much of the collected data is being used today? To what degree can the business leverage the data in a timely fashion?*

Christy: One of the things that has frustrated me in my experience working in the cloud software industry is how much data is collected and how much goes to waste. As a marketer I watch closely the marketing investment that we make toward lead generation. Especially in high-growth companies it can be easy to get excited about the volume of inbound leads that you attract but never convert. This is especially true in paid search marketing. You acquire leads that never intend to buy your product but are in your database, withering. I don't want to pay for leads that just go to our database to die. If lead generation to conversion rates are 10 to 20 percent even on very targeted campaigns, that means 80 to 90 percent of those leads are not being used.

Even more important is a fast response to the leads that you attract who *do* match your ideal customer profile and are showing buying intent. In B2B marketing those are often referred to as MQLs (marketing qualified leads), and a best practice is to get them to a human within five minutes. That is one of the most important elements of the highest-performing demand generation programs, yet sales and marketing teams rarely achieve that high bar. The longer the response time between an inquiry and a human conversation, the less likely you will turn that lead into a customer. Every moment matters.

A few core metrics are essential to a B2B team's ability to run successful digital growth marketing programs (see Figure 16.2).

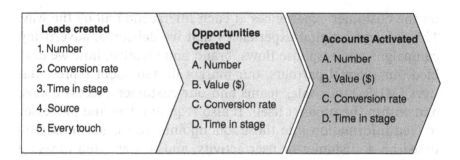

Figure 16.2   Core metrics for digital growth marketing programs

These align to the marketing and sales stages of the customer buying journey and should be tracked for every channel you can measure. When tracked at every stage, from the first point of contact in the journey to the point where a deal is won or lost, they give marketers powerful insights that empower them to make the right investments and decisions about which customers to target and which programs to modify, kill, or invest in. When marketers are armed with self-service access to this data all in one place through Tableau, they can begin to layer the cost data to measure ROI and decide the right choreography of activities and which steps to take to accelerate success and drive growth or diagnose mistakes.

In SaaS businesses, where revenue generation requires user transactions, and in free-trial or programmatic revenue models, it is particularly important for marketers to track these metrics all the way through customer adoption. In one of my small-business marketing programs, our digital marketing campaigns were driving significant growth in opportunities created and contracts signed. Our contracted revenue growth numbers were higher than any other segment, and in aggregate the return on marketing investment for our digital campaigns looked higher than break-even, which was our goal for first-year sales. We started to explore increasing our digital spend in this channel by a significant amount. But thankfully, before we turned up the investment, we extended our reporting to track post-contract adoption. We found that only 50 percent of new customers had begun using the product within 30 days of signing, and by the end of the first year we had 30 percent customer attrition in that segment. Those customer-side metrics negated our marketing investment. This led us to pivot our marketing investment toward customer-side programs to improve the customer onboarding process for that segment to increase adoption and reduce year-one attrition before we invested more money in top-of-funnel digital campaigns.

Even knowing this, I have faced many roadblocks when trying to get these metrics tracked. The processes are not standard anywhere. Systems and processes have to be created. They typically require cross-functional alignment and multisystem process changes that can take weeks or months to achieve — even in the smallest companies.

The most common obstacle is the absence of date stamps for every activity at every stage in Salesforce or Marketo or between other combinations of sales and marketing automation systems. Fix it. Fast.

Alexander: *How do you see digital strategies evolving with the maturity of big data processing and AI? How do you prepare for an AI-centric ecosystem as a business leader?*

Christy: A colleague and I were talking recently about what can be solved by AI and what contains nuances that require human interception. What level of individual privacy and identity do we protect, and what are we willing to give up for convenience? I am enrolled in the CLEAR airport security program. It has significantly reduced the time that I have had to wait in TSA lines. However, for reasons I cannot fully explain, I am willing to provide my fingerprint but not a retina scan. Now I am noticing every time I go through that my fingerprints take multiple passes to read and the assistant keeps asking for my retina scan. Every time I go through, I get the "ID-required" error. It makes me wonder.

I can see opportunities across our web and digital experiences to improve everything from routine website maintenance to who is prompted and when by our online chat functionality or routed to a voice conversation with an SDR or a customer support representative.

As much as I love the convenience of telling Alexa to add items to my grocery list, I still find it creepy when she tells me she doesn't recognize my voice and asks me to tell her my name. When I apply that to the workplace, I continue to be biased toward putting the customer at the center of these types of strategies and using the centrality of the customer to guide the strategy. Where AI can improve process automation and integration of analytics on already existing data sources, I am eager to test, learn, and iterate. But when customer, employee, or personal data privacy is in question, I draw the line.

Alexander: Which innovative AI use cases would be possible by a tighter data integration?

Christy: A company whose CMO I have spoken with is doing some innovative work around applying machine learning to digital A/B testing in order to improve customer website experiences and improve conversion rates.

Additionally, the ability to really measure the terms and effectiveness of search engine optimization (SEO) and paid search management, which are data-rich environments, begs for a truly integrated AI-driven approach to optimization and outcomes.

We have begun to use conDati to pull data from all of our different digital marketing channels into their AI analytic systems to get a fully integrated view of our multichannel marketing and inform what levers we should pull to drive growth.

I would definitely like to see better buyer-intent data out there in the market from all of the various data providers, content syndication, and digital at tech providers. My teams have had success with predictive modeling solutions such as Mintigo and now 6sense. We have had varying levels of success with marketing attribution models, but they can be very complex to validate and action across multichannel marketing programs.

Alexander: Could you give some insights into how the Pantheon WebOps platform contributes to the changing digital strategies?

Christy: Successful corporate digital strategies now involve hundreds, sometimes thousands, of rapidly evolving websites, applications, and other digital experiences that cross-functional

WebOps teams spanning marketing, IT, and development must string together to serve their business and their customers.

WebOps teams that use Pantheon value the agility of deploying website changes as they are ready rather than holding them for weeks or months for a big launch or relaunch. Our clients are able to leave the big behemoth relaunch behind and adopt a continuous development strategy for their websites. Web developers appreciate the automation of routine updates, so they spend less time on maintenance and have the peace of mind that they are on Pantheon's infrastructure so their site can seamlessly and immediately scale to respond to enormous traffic spikes when their digital programs are wildly successful. The multitenant, container-based architecture supports unlimited on-demand development environments to allow for parallel development, testing, and training and enables organizations to run as many instances of a site as needed for development and to manage all of their websites from a single dashboard.

This became essential as the pace of digital transformation accelerated in a matter of weeks in 2020, with workforces relocating from offices into employees' homes as the COVID-19 pandemic spread. Organizations ranging from Ivy League universities to public schools, retailers, banks, technology companies, and pharmaceutical companies were called on to pivot their go-to market strategies from brick-and-mortar to the web and virtual overnight. Digital agencies, political campaigns, banks and community organizations, and anyone supporting retail and sales across multiple industries called on their WebOps teams to adapt and respond with speed and agility.

When I was CMO at Visier, we were a client of Pantheon, and with a small and agile web and digital team of three people we were able to rebrand and re-architect our entire website without even a minute of downtime and with no interruption to our business or marketing strategy. The team would deploy changes weekly, even sometimes daily, including personalized audience journeys and solution, customer success, and partner navigation. We were also able to perform personal experience testing to collect feedback from customers and apply their feedback almost immediately to improve the website experience. When the pandemic hit, we were able to quickly pivot our strategy to add a COVID response section where we hosted feedback forums and virtual forums for the HR industry to share best practices and learning about how to support our employees through this time.

Alexander: How do you face data privacy and data governance concerns when you pitch new ideas?

Christy: Data privacy is an opportunity for companies to really demonstrate their values and commitment to what is best for their customers. By considering data privacy from the standpoint of what matters most to your customer the answers become quite clear and can be a competitive advantage for your company.

At SAP Concur, when CASL, Canada's Anti-Spam Legislation, was announced, we were just a couple of years into our Canadian market launch and were just building momentum. The laws were new, and we struggled to interpret them, but we ultimately recognized that even though we had made a significant investment in our demand efforts, we had built a database of more than 200,000 contacts in the market that were not compliant. The right thing to do for those contacts was to remove them from our database. So we did.

The groundwork that we had done for CASL was valuable to us when the General Data Protection Regulation (GDPR) arose in Europe. By then we had been acquired by SAP and were well into our global expansion strategies. We had digital marketing programs running in at least 20 different countries managed by distributed marketing teams in markets such as mainland China, Japan, the United Kingdom, and Germany. The Concur SaaS-enabled technology and digital marketing subscription management gave us the ability to personalize the customer-data-handling experience based on the governing privacy regulations of their location. Our local marketing teams in each market ensured that we did not attempt a one-size-fits-all global approach to GDPR. We understood and respected that the value placed on personal privacy in Germany is different from that of customers in the United States or in mainland

China, and we executed our strategy accordingly. Additionally, to ensure compliance and prevent errors, we hired TrustArc to audit and document our processes.

Alexander: *Thank you, Christy. What quick-win advice would you give that is easy for many companies to apply within their digital strategies?*

Christy: Always be researching, collecting data, turning that data into insights, and using it to find new ways to deliver value to your customers.

Always layer in the human element. Not just the data points, but how they connect together all along the customer life cycle. Act like every moment matters because it does.

Alexander: *What are your favorite apps, tools, or software that you can't live without?*

Christy: I was a late adopter of Alexa, but now I cannot imagine buying groceries or listening to music without it. I have a love-hate relationship with the GPS in my car. I'm not sure how I would have gotten through 2020 without Zoom, and as a marketer I am frequently in Salesforce looking at pipeline performance — or, better yet, in Tableau. The best end-to-end life-cycle data sets my teams have used have been built in Tableau, unburdened by the reporting limitations of the many microservices and technologies that collect data and create processes for marketing programs. And my teams have experienced measurable success using predictive lead scoring from Mintigo in the past. Currently we are an early adopter of 6sense and conDati, an AI-powered marketing analytics platform.

Alexander: *Do you have a smart productivity hack or work-related shortcut?*

Christy: First, focus on just one or two major things at a time and doggedly pursue them. Second, if I am struggling with a decision or with a complex challenge with no obvious solution, I always sleep on it. Our brains are amazing magical things if we give them the time and space to dream. I cannot count the times that I have suddenly been awakened from a restless or even deep sleep in the middle of the night by the answer to a big question, the eureka moment of discovering the missing piece to a technical puzzle, or the solution to a big business challenge.

Alexander: What is the best advice you have ever received?

Christy: Be true to yourself and trust your instincts. The more you apply data, the more you are able to identify things that do and don't pass the sniff test. When something doesn't look right, trust your instincts and dig deeper, peeling back another layer of the onion.

Key Takeaways

- Deliver value at every touchpoint. Marketing leaders own the role of audience experts for the company. When they fully embrace this responsibility, they will lead and require data and digital strategies that enable their marketing teams to have the insights they need to deliver value at every touchpoint.
- Connect the dots across the customer life cycle to deliver a frictionless experience. Every marketing microservice typically has its own reporting. That is nice, but it won't get you the macro results that your customers, your executives, and your shareholders demand. You need to close the loop on your data, end to end across the entire customer life cycle to forecast, achieve, and deliver results.
- The consumerization of B2B marketing removes the distinction between users and buyers. In this era of digital transformation, as companies adopt cloud technology, the user experience becomes paramount, fueling product-led growth. In the business-to-business SaaS and PaaS space, this introduces a new level of complexity to marketing leaders. Cloud software marketers are leading the consumerization of B2B software by embracing previously distinct go-to-market strategies that put purchasing power for the product in the hands of the end user.

Endnotes

i WebOps (web operations) is a domain of expertise within IT systems management that involves the deployment, operation, tuning, maintenance, and repair of web-based applications and systems. WebOps can be described as DevOps for web applications.

ii Martech is the blending of marketing and technology. Anyone who is involved in digital marketing is working with martech, since digital by its very nature is technologically based.

iii Cline, Jay, "The Rise of Women and Introverts During the Big Shutdown," December 26, 2020 (www.linkedin.com/pulse/rise-women-introverts-during-big-shutdown-jay-cline/).

iv Ohmae, Kenichi, *The Mind of the Strategist: The Art of Japanese Business*, New York: McGraw-Hill Education, 1991.

v Brinker, Scott, "Marketing Technology Landscape Supergraphic (2020): Martech 5000 — really 8,000, but who's counting?," April 22, 2020 (https://chiefmartec.com/2020/04/marketing-technology-landscape-2020-martech-5000/).

Chapter 17

Data Strategy as an Essential Component of the Digital Transformation Journey

According to Forrester, between 60 percent and 73 percent of all data within an organization goes unused for analytics.[i] Nearly 30 percent of the so-called global datasphere will be real-time information by 2025, IDC says.[ii]

This real-life example is based on an engagement at a telecommunications company (telco). The telco wanted to better understand its customers' usage patterns (mobile, landline, internet services, various bundles) and network performance to assess potential new products and other bundle configurations. However, the telco was unable to get a complete picture of its data. It was nearly impossible to access the highly decentralized data for ad hoc analysis and machine learning. So, employees downloaded data manually and processed it on desktop machines, which led to many limitations in quality and quantity and made governance challenging.

Three Elements of a Data Strategy

The telco's goal is to manage data as a corporate asset. A data strategy was required to leverage all their data. This data strategy was meant to embrace various isolated and sometimes redundant big data initiatives and analytics practices that were not well orchestrated in the past.

The telco's data strategy (see Figure 17.1) has these three core elements:

- Big data
- Analytics
- Decision-support tools

Strongly aligning these three core elements as part of the data strategy should drastically increase the business value of the data.

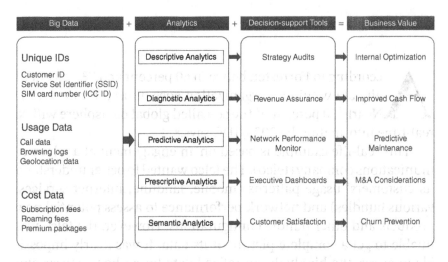

Figure 17.1   Three elements of a data strategy adapted for the telco's typical requirements

Big Data

There are four key issues that the telco must overcome if it wants to tame big data: volume (quantity of data), variety (different forms of data), velocity (how fast the data is generated and processed), and veracity (variation in quality of data).

The ongoing digital transformation of our lives has created an enormous amount of data about almost every aspect of those lives. Every website we visit, every link we click, every search engine term we enter, and every purchase we make is recorded and associated either with our online identity, if we have accounts with the sites we visit, or in systems that save our sessions through cookies or digital fingerprinting.

Once gathered, data across the enterprise is typically stored in silos belonging to business functions (vertical silos), to business units (horizontal silos), or even to different projects within the same division (segmented silos). Making this data a valuable and useful asset will require breaking down the silos. This may not be so easy to accomplish, due to ownership issues, regulatory concerns, and governance practices.

Analytics

Collecting data alone does not generate value. The completeness of the advanced analytics stack and the complexity of the applied models determine how smart the insights will be and therefore how deep the level of business impact will get. The main goal of advanced analytics is to help organizations make smarter decisions for better business outcomes.

Only a few years ago, advanced analytics was based almost entirely on a complex tool chain and plenty of scripting in gnuplot,[iii] Python, and R. Today, self-service analytics platforms enable us to analyze our data at the speed of thought, to connect to our data sources in seconds, to add dimensions and measures by dragging and dropping, and to get insights faster than ever before.

It is crucial to leverage the entire mass of data, as it enables us to make observations and ask questions along the entire analytics stack using five types of data analysis methods:

- **Descriptive analytics "describes" things:** Descriptive analytics describes what happened, characterized by traditional business intelligence (BI). It is a glimpse into the past. Examples include visualizations and dashboards to show profit per store, per product segment, or per region.
- **Diagnostic analytics "diagnoses" the issues:** Diagnostic analytics, which is also known as *business analytics*, looks into why something is happening and is characterized by reports to further slice and dice and drill down into data. It answers the questions raised by descriptive analytics, such as why sales went down in a particular region.
- **Predictive analytics "predicts" future possibilities:** Predictive analytics determines what might happen in the future and needs larger domain expertise and tool sets, including machine learning. Examples include regression analysis, credit risk assessments, and forecasting which product segments are likely to perform better in the next quarter.
- **Prescriptive analytics "prescribes" the right course of action:** Prescriptive analytics identifies the actions required in order to influence a particular outcome ("What should I do?"). Examples include portfolio optimization and recommendation engines that answer which customer segment should be targeted next quarter to improve profitability.
- **Semantic analytics asks "What does it mean?":** Semantic analytics examines data or content to identify the meaning, suggests what you are looking for, and provides a richer response. Examples include emotion and sentiment analysis and latent semantic indexing to understand social media streams and to track brand popularity.

Prescriptive and semantic analytics might be tough to implement, especially if the telco needs to find a way to classify semistructured data, such as social media streams.

While looking to apply sophisticated models, the telco should not forget to collect the low-hanging fruit and see that they put in all the quantitative information, such as revenue data, to scale out their diagnostic capabilities.

Decision-Support Tools

Now the telco needs intuitive tools that integrate data into sustainable processes and apply analytic models to generate information that can be used for business decisions. Depending on the stakeholder, the outcome might be presented as a self-service web front end, such as a network performance monitor that allows predictive maintenance, or an executive dashboard that provides the CFO with the latest numbers for upcoming M&A activity.

An important consideration for decision-support tools is user acceptance. Decision-support tools should be easy to use and should not make processes more complicated. Instead, designers should consider adding buttons that trigger actions directly from the user interface.

Result

We provided the telco's data scientists and analysts with the ability to access and use data residing in its Azure data warehouse quickly and easily on an ad hoc basis. Azure Synapse Analytics enables a quick, one-step process to deliver all live data needed for a fast and responsive visual analysis system. The data scientists and analysts have full access to all rows, all dimensions, and all metrics — allowing them to see, understand, and analyze millions of rows and mashups of data with very little help from IT.

All of the telco's analysis can easily be shared with product managers, business development, and marketing, enabling much better collaboration on new product introductions.

With this new data strategy, the telco is able to use its data and extract insights on customer buying patterns by region. As a result, the telco introduced local products to meet regional market demand with an estimated impact of $76 million in new revenue.

Chief Digital Officer as Key Driver of the Data Strategy

The chief digital officer (CDO) was significantly involved in the setup of the data strategy — with some influence from the chief risk officer (CRO) and the chief marketing officer (CMO). The CDO role had been introduced just recently at the telco.

CDO is a new position gaining popularity in many industries. Unlike the head of IT, the CDO's background is almost never purely technical, but rather includes two or more business units or areas. The CDO is almost always tech-savvy, with excellent understanding of the latest technology and trends. The CDO usually has an autonomous role and advises the CEO on the migration strategy that will lead to the digital organization. CDOs are not in charge of the whole IT strategy, but they control the "transformational journey" to the digital age and need to have tight relations with business units.

Key Takeaways

- Many companies have big data initiatives and analytics practices that are not well orchestrated. A data strategy should embrace these isolated initiatives and hence leverage data to generate additional business value.
- Strongly aligning the three core elements, big data, analytics, and decision-support tools, as part of the data strategy should drastically increase the business value.
- A chief digital officer is an excellent driver for a data strategy, as the CDO's background is typically tech-savvy with great understanding of various business units and their needs.

Endnotes

i Gualtieri, Mike, "Hadoop Is Data's Darling For a Reason," Forrester, January 21, 2016 (go.forrester.com/blogs/hadoop-is-datas-darling-for-a-reason/).

ii Reinsel, David, et al., "Data Age 2025: The Digitalization of the World," November 2018 (www.seagate.com/our-story/data-age-2025/).

iii gnuplot is a command-line program that can visualize mathematical functions and data interactively, but has grown to support many noninteractive uses such as batch processing and scripting. gnuplot was first released in 1986 and is freely distributed. Website: gnuplot.info/.

Part V

Artificial Intelligence

Chapter 18
Bora Beran: Vast Amounts of Data Are Key for AI and Automation

Bora Beran, director of product management, MongoDB
Source: Photography by Ayla Beran.

Bora holds a PhD from Drexel University and is a reviewer of several scholarly journals in the area of technical computing. Prior to joining MongoDB, he worked at Descartes Labs, Tableau Software, Windows HPC Server, and Microsoft Research, developing tools and infrastructure for visualization, knowledge representation, large-scale computational modeling, and machine learning.

Alexander: You are the director of product management at MongoDB. What is your mission?

Bora: At MongoDB, our goal is to build a database that "just works." Historically, data management has been a painful process. Too much up-front design, difficult to scale, difficult to respond to changing requirements, too many knobs to manually tune, works in one scenario but not so well in others hence requiring you to maintain multiple copies of your data on different systems . . . we basically make these problems go away so you can focus on analyzing data and building your applications regardless of scale and where it needs to be: on-premises, in the cloud, or Internet of Things (IoT) devices on the edge.[i] We offer the best-in-class developer experience, built-in seamless syncing between distributed edge devices, automatic scaling, automatic healing and maintenance, transactional guarantees, fault tolerance, speed, and so forth. Because in order to meet the needs of modern applications, database technology needs to become ubiquitous and invisible.

Alexander: How should business models evolve to survive and thrive in an increasingly digital world?

Bora: Digital transformation changed both the way we build (design, develop, and so forth) and the way we sell products (find and reach customers, distribute the product, transact a sale, and so forth). Today you can start a business with little funding and disrupt industry behemoths as cloud infrastructure lets you start small and scale with ease, while social media gives you a channel to reach potential customers without a massive marketing budget. If your product is a physical good, you can go directly to consumers instead of having to pay stores for shelf space.

For some businesses this means efficiency improvements; for example, add an AI chatbot to scale customer support or use a machine-learning model to predict out-of-stocks for improving logistics operations, improving the bottom line. However, in industries with slim margins that compete on pricing, these efficiency gains could make the difference between success and bankruptcy.

For others, the change happens at a more fundamental level and can be very disruptive; think mailing DVDs versus video streaming, video rental store employee picks versus machine-learning models providing personalized movie recommendations, or the businesses where data is the core asset from which the value is derived, as in digital service brokerages and social media companies. These blue oceans are where the best new business opportunities lie as the incumbents (if they exist at all) that built large businesses on old technologies get too complacent, focus too much on sunk cost, and resist change.

Sometimes what appears easy on the outside might take a lot of work because of the way business is structured and data is siloed. Omnichannel personalization is a great example of this, yet it changed the market in such a way that customer expectations shifted, so now everyone has to keep up to survive.

In short, it is an arms race between businesses where data is the most important weapon, requiring more data sources, larger data volumes, and technology to unlock the data's potential. Every business will need to adapt to this new norm, but the how will vary.

Alexander: *How can technology shift the roles and responsibilities of the workforce?*

Bora: The past will be a good predictor of the future here. Take the First Industrial Revolution, for example. It fundamentally changed how people worked and where they lived. It led to the emergence of big cities, new jobs to operate machinery in factories, and the invention of middle management to coordinate large-scale operations.

The Third Industrial Revolution gave us the knowledge workers, which led to a new, more empowering approach to people management, and a few decades later made remote work an acceptable practice with the help of the Internet. Today with advances in AI and robotics, we are starting to see this transformation in manual work as well, even for tasks that require extreme precision, such as remote surgeries, not to mention use of unmanned aerial vehicles (UAV) in military settings for many years now.

While we see some of the trends introduced by the First Industrial Revolution being reversed, overall patterns haven't changed that much. A lot of these advances we've seen so far follow the same formula: step 1, machines are operated by humans; step 2, machines take on some low-level, repetitive task, and humans get involved when things get complex; step 3, the task gets fully automated.

Think about the temperature and pressure regulators for steam engines; we've moved from analog or mechanical to digital. Tasks are getting more complex, but automation has been around for decades. Today it is all about IoT and AI, but the principle is fundamentally not that different.

On the positive side, broadband access and robotics will reverse the employment trends that led to urbanization and level the playing field for many workers by removing geographic and physical — traits or abilities — limitations. On the negative side, distributed work will create a significant imbalance between supply and demand by making a much larger pool of workers available to employers while automation eliminates jobs.

During the First Industrial Revolution, while the economy grew, the general population didn't benefit from it for the first 100 years; in fact, for the bulk of the population, that is, workers, the living standards declined in the beginning. Unfortunately, I think we'll see the same pattern as robotics and AI uptake increases in the industry. It will get worse before it gets better as the workers being replaced by robots need to be retrained, and some may not be able to integrate into the post-AI workforce.

Alexander: *Which technology or digital capabilities are essential for a digital strategy?*

Bora: The world is becoming much more data-driven. So, the technologies that enable collecting and managing large amounts of data and AI to make sense of all that content have become the key capabilities for success. In one of my previous companies, we applied machine learning to satellite imagery to predict crop yields at continental scale with very high accuracy, help our clients to gather competitive intelligence, and identify potential supply chain disruptions from thousands of miles away.

> *The technologies that enable collecting and managing large amounts of data and AI to make sense of all that content have become the key capabilities for success.*

This was made possible by technologies like convolutional neural networks coupled with the massive reduction in the cost to build and launch Earth observation satellites, which significantly increased the pace at which we can collect data. To give you an idea about the scale, while five years ago we could get a full picture of the earth roughly every two weeks, now we can get daily updates with much higher image resolution. Considering all the public and commercial satellites today, that corresponds to roughly tens of petabytes of new data per year. Sensors, of course, go well beyond those installed on satellites, and with IoT going mainstream, similar increases in data volumes and computing requirements will apply to many industries: manufacturing, utilities, logistics, and fleet management, to name a few.

We also have to mention the importance of cloud computing, as it eliminates the need for large up-front investments on computing infrastructure, which is important because it both enables experimentation and makes dealing with high-demand variability in day-to-day operations possible without sacrificing performance. Data scientists can now rent large computing clusters for data cleaning, analysis, and model training without breaking the bank. With hybrid cloud and on-premises solutions, this gives companies a lot of flexibility in finding the right balance from budgeting and regulatory requirements standpoints.

Alexander: *The Fourth Industrial Revolution is indivisibly tied to the enormous amounts of data needed to train artificial intelligence. How has this revolution affected your work at MongoDB?*

Bora: Our customers are collecting higher volumes and different types of data and expecting more flexibility. Our mobile database (Realm) is being used for edge-computing use cases, and high-volume data ingestion for IoT analytics is becoming much more common. We are seeing more tiered storage in practice where recent operational and frequently accessed data stays in low-latency storage, as older data goes into the more affordable, long-term archival storage.

While scenarios that involve inference using pretrained models rely on recent data, for model training purposes we often see customers accessing data across multiple tiers simultaneously; hence, we made it possible to seamlessly integrate results in a single query without having to worry about where their data is stored. Another common trend is unstructured and semistructured data becoming common information sources. Our flexible document model and data lake puts us in a unique position compared to many databases that perform suboptimally (if at all) when data lacks a rigid structure.

Alexander: *Which AI use cases would you see as essential to contribute to any organization's digital strategy?*

Bora: There are several use cases that are applicable to organizations of any type, such as employee and customer retention,[ii] lead qualification, spam and fraud detection, personalization, and demand forecasting. Recent improvements in image recognition and natural language processing also allow digitization of paper processes with unprecedented accuracy, making information retrieval and document workflow tracking much more efficient, timely, and less prone to errors.

Alexander: *Which further AI use cases would be possible by a tighter data integration?*

Bora: Industrial production and supply chains provide some great examples that speak to the value of integrating multiple data streams.

Going all the way back to the beginning, to the extraction of natural resources, the first step is prospecting. At this step, locating ore or oil deposits efficiently and with high accuracy requires magnetometers, hydro- or geophones, and many sensors that can measure different spectra of light. In earth observation, sensors often operate in the so-called tip-and-cue fashion, where a sensor takes coarse measurements over large areas to identify a prospect, which triggers a higher resolution sensor to scan the same area to confirm it. In the case of mining, further verification is done using land-based sensors. This process is driven by machine learning, where the ground truth is fed back to the system as training data. For farming, while instruments vary, the story overall isn't that much different either. Many sensors need to be calibrated to work together to identify health and growth stages of plants.

When it comes to manufacturing, data on consumer behavior, available stock, and shelf life help forecast the demand to ensure the right amount of product is manufactured by finding the right balance between potential waste and keeping shelves stocked. During manufacturing, data collected from sensors and operating environments supports predictive maintenance, minimizing production disruptions and product defects and improving employee safety.

As the goods are shipped, monitoring them in transit using radio-frequency identification (RFID) chips and cameras (with the help of computer vision) allows operators to identify bottlenecks in the logistics infrastructure, bringing more predictability to restocking schedules and making it possible to trace back any potential mishaps to the source.

Once the product hits the shelf, to run a successful omnichannel strategy the retailer needs to collect and integrate user data across channels (mobile, web, in store) so the offers can be personalized for each customer to maximize sales. It does not end there: in the not-too-distant future, with smart packaging, not only will we see products being automatically reordered for us before they run out, but that data will also be used further upstream to better balance supply and demand.

Alexander: Is there a way whereby citizens own their data instead of organizations and companies owning fractions of it?

Bora: This will likely be the case in domains like healthcare soon. Regulations like HIPAA already limit what companies can do with your data, but with wearable devices and affordable genetic testing services, individuals are starting to become sources of significant data about themselves, which they should own, without a doubt. Most wearables have settings to keep data private already.

Most patient record sharing is currently a manual process with very limited flexibility. We need a digital-rights-management system where patients can grant specific institutions access to data for fixed periods of time and even limit what the data can be used for. So that in the not-too-distant future, as AI healthcare services become more reliable and mainstream, patients could easily share their data to get personalized prescriptions, exercise and dietary regimens, health insurance discounts, and so forth. Blockchain ledgers might be a part of the solution for this. Some car insurers already have a somewhat similar opt-in data-collection program where drivers can log and share their driving habits for discounts on their insurance payments.

In general, the adoption of more regulations like the General Data Protection Regulation (GDPR) in Europe, the Personal Information Protection and Electronic Documents Act (PIPEDA) in Canada, and the California Consumer Privacy Act (CCPA) will shape this moving forward.

Alexander: What types of professional roles will we see evolve alongside the development and increasing use of AI across the industries?

Bora: There will be many roles that will be augmented by AI. Take security operations center (SOC) analysts, for example: they will spend less time watching for well-established patterns and more time on deeper analysis to identify relationships and root causes. Lawyers, doctors, and scientists will get help from AI's information-extraction capabilities to quickly scan through large numbers of documents like legislation and journal papers to stay up-to-date on the latest developments in their fields. More experiments will be conducted via simulation, making "computational" not just a prefix for specializations like physics, chemistry, or biology but rather part of the core curriculum.

In manufacturing, we will see operators working in robotic suits and exoskeletons or controlling machinery remotely, and technicians will be needed to service and maintain the robots. In national defense we will see roles specific to AI technologies like cybersecurity research against adversarial attacks on neural networks,[iii] and social sciences will extend to cover machine and computational ethics.

Alexander: What are your thoughts about the path to artificial general intelligence (AGI)? Can AI ever achieve general intelligence? How far are we from AGI?

Bora: Deep learning so far has given us the ability to automate a lot of mundane work through components specifically designed for particular tasks, but lack of an overarching structure limits what machines can do with high-level cognitive tasks. Even though there are cases where this works to some extent, such as transfer learning, models overall tend to generalize poorly, and in many business domains there isn't enough data to create models of acceptable quality. This makes it difficult for deep learning to be a panacea by itself.

But there might be another path.

I studied knowledge graphs and reasoning and inference as part of my PhD dissertation, which are the building blocks of symbolic AI. I believe the convergence of the two approaches, neurosymbolic AI, will be the next step toward AGI and already has many meaningful applications. I was the head of product at a machine learning startup that applied deep learning to satellite and drone imagery a few years ago. We had a 16-petabyte overhead imagery archive, and we even augmented training sets with synthetic data, but for certain structures, architecture had such variation that it was difficult to train an accurate model.

To the human eye, however, classifying the same images was a trivial task. So we decided to let the users express their knowledge in our tool. For example, if the AI couldn't identify schools out-of-the-box correctly, we could define school as a building with yellow buses, a baseball diamond, or a football field nearby. We were able to achieve significant accuracy gains by combining deep neural networks and a symbolic AI approach this way. There are several companies using such approaches in genetics, medicine, and chemistry (for example, computer-aided retrosynthesis) as well to run in-silico experiments.

Traditionally symbolic AI has been used in expert systems with rules manually created by human domain experts. Today this could be easily automated where a deep learning model like RNN/LSTM (recurrent neural networks/long-short term memory) parses text to build relationships in the form of an ontology, which in turn can improve the quality of deep-neural-network applications like conversational AI.

That being said, there is no guarantee that this combo will take us far enough, so it is still hard to meaningfully forecast how many years away we are from AGI. There could be another AI winter around the corner. If I had to guess, I would say no sooner than 10 years.

Alexander: *There are concerns that AI can become a threat once AI reaches the level of an artificial super intelligence (ASI). What do you think about ASI and a recursive self-improvement loop?*

Bora: It is certainly a possibility, but I don't expect it to happen in my lifetime. Though, I'd predict within a decade we'll achieve virtual omniscience and omnipresence through telepresence, IoT, and various forms of surveillance for good or bad. This is not a matter of tech breakthroughs at this point but rather how fast widespread implementation efforts can move, given monetary, legislative, and societal speed bumps. Since there will be too many things to monitor in real time than what's humanly possible, this will all be handled by AI, which as a side effect will give the machines access to orders of magnitude more data to learn from and more incorrect causal associations to deduce.

Of course, monitoring without corrective action has very little value, so AI-enabled machines will need to be able to predict outcomes and act on them. This will be the point in time when we handover the keys to the kingdom. If AI can turn off your pacemaker, insulin pump, or brain implant, or shut off the engines of the plane you are on, who is to say that it can't also be considered omnipotent. At which point all we can hope is that it is also omnibenevolent; otherwise, we will be in big trouble. Such a threat could materialize much sooner than ASI if we're not careful, because it could just result from algorithmic error and an overeager optimization process going awry.[iv] But in the longer run, I don't think it is far-fetched to think that a super intelligent AI will treat us the same way we treated other species and underdeveloped civilizations in the past.

Alexander: *Thank you, Bora. What quick-win advice would you give that is easy for many companies to apply within their digital strategies?*

Bora: Set meaningful, business-focused goals; take hype with a grain of salt; and don't start with inflated expectations of what you expect technology to accomplish for you. There is no silver bullet. Far too many big-data and data-science projects fail for these reasons.

Don't get too comfortable. Always be on the lookout for emerging technologies that could nullify your competitive advantage. Disrupt yourself while you're still ahead if you want to avoid being disrupted by a competitor.

Alexander: *What are your favorite apps, tools, or software that you can't live without?*

Bora: Kindle. I read a lot. I have also automated as many mundane tasks as possible, using grocery subscriptions, robotic vacuum cleaners and lawnmowers, and smart thermostats and light switches, so I can focus my time on things that matter.

Alexander: *Do you have a smart productivity hack or work-related shortcut?*

Bora: I create blocks of uninterrupted time where I don't respond to emails or instant messages or engage social media. I have playlists for different parts of my day: high beats-per-minute tunes paired up with full-spectrum light early in the morning as I go through emails, instrumental music during focus time, nature sounds as I end my workday. Once you get into the routine, it is surprisingly effective in keeping you focused.

Alexander: *What is the best advice you have ever received?*

Bora: Many people are too protective of their ideas and worry that if they told someone they would steal them. However, really valuable, substantial ideas are almost never things you can just overhear and claim to be your own. Ideas that are easy to steal are simple ones and hence should be easy to part with. Jim Gray used to say, "Success has many fathers; many of them have never met the mother."

Early on, I learned to let go of these kinds of concerns, which contributed to my becoming not only a good team player and a leader but in many cases also a major influencer. In product management especially, given that you're measured by the success of your products, it is much more useful to openly share ideas within your teams and cultivate a culture of trust, teamwork, and innovation. Spend that time validating those ideas to make sure only the ones that meet a real market need get worked on.

Key Takeaways

- Cloud computing eliminates the need for large up-front investments on computing infrastructure, which is important because it both enables experimentation and makes dealing with high-demand variability in day-to-day operations possible without sacrificing performance. Data scientists can now rent large computing clusters for data cleaning, analysis, and model training without breaking the bank.
- Citizen-owned data will likely be a fact of life in domains like healthcare soon. Regulations like HIPAA already limit what companies can do with your data, but with wearable devices and affordable genetic testing services, individuals are starting to become sources of significant data about themselves, which they should own, without a doubt.

- Deep learning has given us the ability to automate a lot of mundane work through components specifically designed for particular tasks, but lack of an overarching structure limits what machines can do when it comes to high-level cognitive tasks.

Endnotes

i   Edge computing moves the computation and data storage away from cloud data centers toward the edge of the network, exploiting IoT devices, mobile phones, or network infrastructure to perform tasks and provide services on behalf of the cloud. Edge computing saves bandwidth and improves response times. Notable edge applications include home automation systems, cloud gaming services, autonomous and connected cars, smart cities, and smart industry (Industry 4.0).

ii Identifying customers who are likely to churn and incentives that are most likely to succeed in retaining them (for example, different product bundles, loyalty benefits, discounts).

iii An adversarial attack would be, for example, feeding a signal to a machine learning model that would result in malfunction. Computer vision is especially prone to these kinds of tricks. Here is an example on this topic: https://www.sciencedirect.com/science/article/pii/S209580991930503X.

iv Typically, these tools look for the optimal way to solve a problem given a set of constraints. If you forget to add a constraint, for example, it can decide to kill all humans to reduce pollution.

Chapter 19
Andreas Kopp:
Responsible AI in Practice

Andreas Kopp, digital advisor for AI Business Solutions, Microsoft
Source: © Studio Gleis11/Jens Schierenbeck

As a Microsoft digital advisor, Andreas Kopp advises enterprise customers on the strategic planning and implementation of digital business solutions. His focus is on applied business AI solutions, including medical imaging and fraud detection. Furthermore, he specializes in practical solutions for the responsible use of AI systems. Among these are AI interpretability, algorithmic fairness, privacy-preserving analytics, and machine learning with the differential privacy concept.

Alexander: You are a digital advisor for AI business solutions at Microsoft. What is your mission?

Andreas: We guide large commercial and public organizations during the whole lifecycle of digital transformation initiatives. A typical project starts with envisioning workshops that involve business and technology stakeholders. Once a target vision and plan are defined, the realization phase often involves many customer and external participants delivering a broad range of specialized activities. A digital advisor's responsibility is to ensure everybody strives toward a common big picture in this phase. Furthermore, we track the realization of objectives and business value when the first minimally viable products (MVPs) are in place.

Several digital advisors also cover a dedicated subject area. In my case, it is artificial intelligence, which is a great passion of mine. My main focus is business AI applications like medical imaging, forecasting, and fraud detection. Moreover, I work on frameworks and tools for a responsible AI approach, including transparency, algorithmic fairness, and privacy-preserving machine learning.

My current customer engagement role is being the lead digital advisor for Siemens. I am also working with Azure AI–related product groups at Microsoft on responsible AI tools. I recently finished a whitepaper and interactive demos on differential privacy and just started similar work in transparency and fairness. The primary goal is to help enterprise customers use these concepts.

Alexander: What exactly is responsible AI? What is the role of government, and how can organizations put it into action?

Andreas: Let's start by looking at where we are in the journey toward intelligent systems. Recent innovations and the media hype should not obscure that the AI revolution is still ahead of us. It is one of the most transformative innovations that can add substantial value to the world. Like all groundbreaking inventions, AI poses significant new challenges. It is in our hands to shape this future responsibly.

The AI revolution is still ahead of us. It is one of the most transformative innovations that can add substantial value to the world. Like all groundbreaking inventions, AI poses significant new challenges. It is in our hands to shape this future responsibly.

If you follow the discussion about AI-related challenges, you observe quite a spectrum of concerns.

First, there is the fear of fundamental imminence from the technology: will there be an artificial super intelligence (ASI) that surpasses our intellectual ability or even becomes a significant threat to humanity?

Second, there are discussions about the effects on society and the world of work. In particular: will more jobs be lost than created by AI?

Third, there are the concerns that arise from AI applications in today's practice: how can we ensure the transparency of algorithm-based decisions and prevent discrimination and abuse? Who is ultimately responsible for the behavior of AI systems?

There is a broad consensus — even among technology enthusiasts — that an effective regulatory framework is needed to minimize negative impacts on people and society without blocking the opportunities of AI. Policymakers, researchers, AI practitioners, and the tech industry currently discuss appropriate ethical principles and their application in practice. For instance, Microsoft has established a binding framework for its product development and customer projects (Figure 19.1).

These principles have led to Microsoft announcing in summer 2020 that it will stop selling facial recognition technology to police authorities in the United States until a human-rights-based

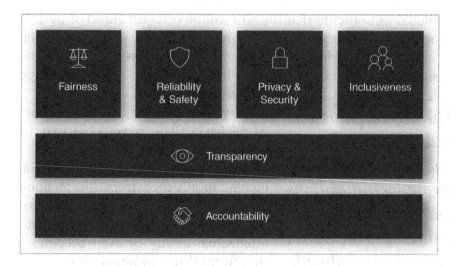

Figure 19.1   Microsoft's responsible AI principles

regulation for its use is in place. Other technology companies have taken similar steps.

In practice, the question arises of how these principles are put into concrete terms for the respective applications (for example, medical diagnostic support, evaluating loan applications, and assessing résumés in recruiting).

A proven starting point is to estimate possible adverse effects for the parties involved and those indirectly affected by AI-based systems. The harms assessment is a structured evaluation of possible adverse effects from the use of AI systems. A comprehensive set of potential harms like physical or emotional injury, denial of consequential services, human rights abuses, and damage to social and democratic structures is considered during the assessment.

By integrating the perspectives of heterogeneous stakeholders, creative techniques are used to answer the following questions:

- Who are the parties involved in and affected by the system that we are creating?
- How might the system be used (including potentially unintended cases)?

- What are the possible adverse effects or damages?
- Which measures are necessary to minimize the adverse effects?

Alexander: How can technology shift the roles and responsibilities of the workforce?

Andreas: In past technological revolutions, innovations have created more jobs performing newly emerging tasks than have been lost due to the workforce reduction effect. That said, there is no guarantee that this will be the case in the future, especially with artificial intelligence. Many routine activities have already been replaced by robotic process automation (RPA).

Occupations typically consist of several activities with varying degrees of complexity. According to the U.S. Bureau of Labor Statistics, the frequently used example of a radiologist's job consists of 30 distinct tasks. Analyzing medical images, in which AI systems already perform well, is only one of them.

Delegating tedious and often exhausting routine tasks to intelligent machines also provides opportunities for reinventing work. A positive effect might be that the time freed up can be used for personal consultations with citizens and customers, for which today there is often not enough time.

In the midterm, activities that require human skills like communication, empathy, creativity, or multidisciplinary thinking won't be eliminated. Nevertheless, we have to continuously learn new skills as AI systems eventually tap into more domains. But we must also consider the limits of the human ability to adapt to significant changes. For example, imagine a longtime truck driver whose job just got replaced by autonomous vehicles.

Alexander: What mechanisms will exist in the employment marketplace to enable that person to find a fulfilling new career?

Andreas: The McKinsey Global Institute estimates for the U.S. economy that roughly 50 percent of the tasks performed in today's workplace can be automated. That does not mean that the same percentage of jobs are affected since a typical occupation involves several activities, as the radiologist's example shows. Nonetheless, as happened in previous technological transformations, several jobs will be eliminated. Other disciplines will change significantly due to the augmentation of human competencies with artificial intelligence. A positive example would be the radiologist who can spend more time with patients and less time staring at computer screens. The third effect is the creation of entirely new occupations we can't even imagine today. For example, some of my coworkers at Microsoft are engaged as *envisioning advisors*. Their job is to help customers envision how they can best use new technologies like augmented reality in their businesses, including the imagination of completely new use cases. Although this job has been around for a few years, most people probably don't understand what the occupation is about when they hear the title.

A primary concern is when it is tough for employees to transition from existing jobs to new occupations. This skill mismatch might lead to a situation where we see noticeable unemployment and many open positions simultaneously.

The truck driver's scenario might be an extreme example since we assumed that the occupation is rationalized entirely. For most professions, this won't be the case for the foreseeable future. These occupations will change as artificial intelligence and other innovations find their way into everyday working life, but they likely won't disappear. Labor market economists have a good assessment of which current activities are likely to be affected by automation. For example, standardized white-collar activities that can be easily digitized and are associated with comparatively high wages are at risk.

So what can we do about it? I advocate a proactive approach to promote competencies or job profiles already during education that will not be affected in the foreseeable future. Society should help apprentices make an informed decision regarding the future viability of their qualifications.

Proactive support for existing careers is also encouraged. We all know that lifelong job profiles are becoming increasingly rare. Here, the awareness and personal responsibility of the individual should be strengthened. In many cases, leeway must first be created if, for example, the individual situation does not offer options for further education on one's own initiative. Therefore, some government stewardship will likely be needed to ensure that the time and financial resources are available for accompanying training and education. Researchers expect a noticeable overall increase in productivity through artificial intelligence. One regulatory responsibility would be to reallocate a part of this value creation to ease the transition of existing workers into the jobs of the future.

Alexander: *You mentioned interpretability and transparency as critical principles for AI ethics. What exactly is the issue?*

Andreas: Today's machine-learning systems don't follow explicitly human programmed rules. Instead, they learn to derive insights from sample data. For instance, if you show the computer enough examples of malignant and benign tumors in medical images, it learns to distinguish relevant patterns and finally to recognize malignant tumors in new images.

Growing neural networks drive this progress for computer vision, processing unstructured text, and other tasks. For example, GPT-3[i] — one of the most powerful networks for processing natural language — reaches an incredible size of 175 billion parameters. Provided that sufficient training data is available, such networks produce very accurate predictions, already exceeding humans' performance in many domains. That said, many algorithms, and neural networks in particular, do not provide any justification for their projections. Since humans do not explicitly program them, we also do not know which general rules they follow.

Transparency is the prerequisite for trust. For instance, if a physician is faced with an AI prognosis that she cannot comprehend and that contradicts her assessment, she will most probably ignore it. If, however, she gets a meaningful justification, she can clarify whether the AI is wrong or has discovered a relevant pattern overlooked by her. Both occur in practice. Hence, under the heading AI explainability, work is currently being done on methods that make AI systems and their predictions more transparent.

Microsoft is approaching the topic from two sides. On the one hand, we are improving intrinsically transparent AI algorithms, called glass-box models.[ii] These are fully explainable, but their performance sometimes falls behind the more complex black-box algorithms. On the other hand, we are developing methods that aim to explain these black-box models.

The example in Figure 19.2 highlights areas in a picture that an image captioning algorithm found relevant to describe the scene.[iii]

Alexander: *Fantastic example! You also highlighted fairness. What does it mean if an algorithm is fair as opposed to biased?*

Andreas: Algorithms follow given (learned) rules and, unlike people, are not influenced by factors such as loss of concentration, fatigue, or moods. Nonetheless, we have seen several examples of biased AI systems: women are frequently disadvantaged when it comes to granting loans or applying for jobs in the tech sector. AI systems also work less reliably in the case of ethnic minorities. For instance, a person with dark skin who is convicted of a crime often gets a lower social rehabilitation rating than a person with light skin.

The reason for this behavior lies in the training data. If, for example, the data is biased because, in the past, women were disadvantaged in credit approval decisions, the AI learns to adopt this behavior. Such discrimination often occurs subtly, even when gender is not explicitly included in the data set. In such cases, women might be discriminated against because their salaries are often lower than those of men, but this, in turn, is an essential variable in lending decisions. Hence, the cause of unequal treatment can be found in the job market and is not directly attributable to the bank.

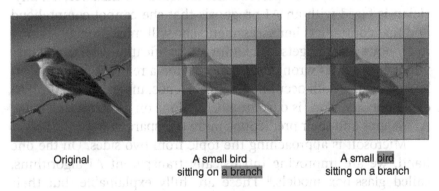

Original   A small bird   A small bird
sitting on a branch   sitting on a branch

Figure 19.2   Uncovering relevant areas to explain an image captioning model

To make these subtle forms of discrimination visible and adjust them, various methods (for example, Microsoft Fairlearn) are available. There are several concepts for measuring and managing fairness. While each concept looks reasonable on its own, they lead to different, potentially contradicting, consequences. Therefore, the appropriate fairness metric for a given application needs to be selected thoughtfully, involving business domain, ethical, legal, and data science perspectives.

Furthermore, there is a trade-off between fairness and predictive accuracy. Practice shows that one can maximize predictive quality at the cost of the fairness objectives and vice versa, as Figure 19.3 illustrates.

We see predictive accuracy and disparities in lending decision outcomes for men and women for an unmitigated model and several alternatives provided by the Fairlearn tool. The red model represents the default machine-learning result: an unconstrained model

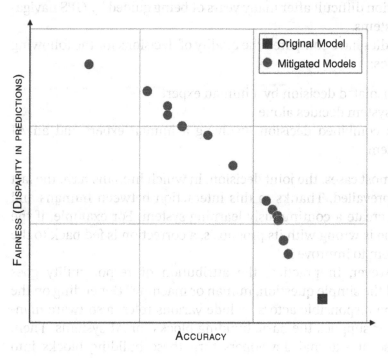

Figure 19.3   Fairness-accuracy trade-off

constantly optimizes predictive accuracy. Fairness is not taken into consideration at all. The blue dots show alternative models that better meet the selected fairness metric.

Alexander: That sounds like there are promising ways to improve transparency and fairness. What about accountability? Who is responsible for the decision of an AI system that impacts the lives of real people?

Andreas: There is broad consensus that we must not outsource the responsibility for decision making to algorithms — especially when there is a significant impact on human lives. Unfortunately, it is tempting to rely on AI to justify decisions with negative consequences. A bank employee may emphasize to the customer his commitment in the event of a favorable credit decision. However, in the case of rejection, many will be tempted to ascribe the decision to "the system." Moreover, humans tend to unlearn cognitive abilities due to automation. Many car drivers today find map-based navigation difficult after many years of being guided by GPS navigation systems.

Studies have compared the quality of decisions for the following scenarios:

- An isolated decision by a human expert
- AI system decides alone
- The combined decision involving a human expert and an AI system

In most cases, the joint decision, in which humans have the last word, prevailed. Thanks to this interaction between humans and AI, we create a continuously learning system. For example, if the machine is wrong with its prognosis, a correction is fed back to the AI system to improve it.

However, in practice, the attribution of responsibility goes beyond the simple question, human or machine? Depending on the case, the responsible actors include various roles: a software manufacturer supplies the basic building blocks for AI systems. Then, in-house or external developers turn these building blocks into an application, often reusing publicly available open source components. Internal departments or external suppliers provide training data that builds the essence of the AI system's behavior. Also, regulatory requirements and internal guidelines govern the handling of such systems. Finally, there are the end users of the solution. These might be physicians who use AI predictions to provide advice for promising treatments to a patient. This example shows the complexity of causal research and potential legal reappraisal if things go wrong.

Alexander: Because so much data is needed to train AI algorithms, how can organizations and companies stay ahead of legal, regulatory, and ethical issues associated with collecting and applying data?

Andreas: Let's consider the role of data for social progress in general. For instance, the COVID-19 pandemic demonstrates the tremendous importance of sufficient and relevant data for research, causal analysis, government action, and medical progress. However, because of well-founded data-protection concerns, individuals and decision-makers are often reluctant to share personal or sensitive data.

On the other hand, we are still quite careless with sensitive data that we share with the world via social networks. We have seen examples where a few likes were exploited to generate personality profiles, including sexual orientation, family background, and mental conditions. Another problem is that improved algorithms can combine all this data about us from various sources with enormous computing power for dubious and harmful purposes. Going beyond demographic data like gender, age, or ZIP code, adversaries exploit any existing information, such as product ratings, to re-identify individuals from various sources.

Through such a linkage attack, it was possible, for example, to re-identify individuals from supposedly anonymized data sets. For example, celebrity identities have been disclosed following a data linkage attack using the public New York City taxi data set, which contains anonymized data about yellow cab rides. The attackers simply combined the information with metadata from paparazzi photos published on gossip websites. Information regarding the destination address, the fare amount, the tip, and so on, have been revealed.

To ensure sustainable progress, we need new practices that enable insights from data while reliably protecting individuals' privacy.

Alexander: Can you elaborate on specific practices? How exactly can we enable the use of personal data and privacy protection at the same time?

Andreas: Several recent developments can help implement adequate data protection for machine learning and further analytical applications. That said, applying these technologies needs to be part of a broader protection strategy that includes security controls, auditing, policies, user consent, data minimization — grounded on a regulatory framework.

One of these innovations is confidential computing, which protects information against various forms of attack by encapsulating the data in secure hardware enclaves as it is processed. This approach enables new data-sharing scenarios between organizations, such as multiparty machine learning.

Imagine a group of hospitals that wants to leverage AI for detecting rare diseases in medical images to improve care. As each hospital has just a few images available, they can't train reliable machine-learning models independently. While combing all hospitals' images would solve the problem, representatives often decide against data sharing because of privacy concerns.

With multiparty machine learning, the patient data itself is not disclosed to other hospitals. Only the insights gained from the learning process — particularly detecting the rare disease — are made available to all hospitals through the shared AI model (see Figure 19.4).

The second innovation is differential privacy. It aims to address the risk of re-identifying individuals from data sets while allowing general insights to be gained from the protected data. For instance, as researchers, we might want to uncover the general correlation between age and severity of a COVID-19 infection. However, we

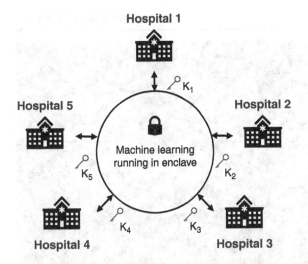

Figure 19.4   Secure multiparty machine learning

are not interested in the record of John Doe, who participated in our study. Instead, we want to guarantee John's privacy so he will participate in the study without concerns.

Differential privacy is superior to traditional disclosure-limitation techniques like anonymization and is therefore considered the emerging gold standard for privacy protection. It protects individuals' privacy by adding a carefully tuned amount of random noise to the data and computations. The fundamental advantage of the concept is that a mathematical privacy guarantee can be given to individuals. This guarantee exists independently of how much information or computational resources an adversary might exploit today or in the future.

The amount of statistical noise must be chosen carefully. On the one hand, higher quantities of noise increase the level of privacy. On the other side, it is more difficult to derive reliable statistical results when the level is too high. There is a sliding tuner available to adjust the amount of noise in the trade-off between privacy and utility. Figure 19.5 provides an intuition about the trade-off between accuracy and privacy with differential privacy.

Stronger privacy   More accurate statistics

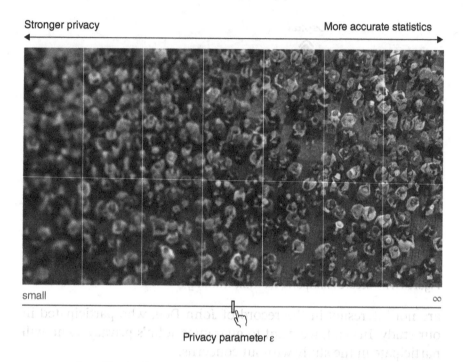

small ∞

Privacy parameter ε

Figure 19.5   Differential privacy

Differential privacy supports a broad range of applications from generating simple statistics to multivariate analytics and machine learning, including deep learning.

Coming from a long tradition of improving data protection methods, the U.S. Census Bureau has announced the use of differential privacy to publish the statistics of the 2020 census. The experience gained from the U.S. Census is expected to significantly impact the awareness and further dissemination of the differential privacy concept for the protection of sensitive personal data.

Alexander: *What are your thoughts about the path to artificial general intelligence (AGI)? Can AI ever achieve general intelligence? How far are we from AGI?*

Andreas: Today's vision of artificial general intelligence (AGI) is actually quite close to the original conception when we started working on AI in the 1950s. The famous Dartmouth College proposal from 1955 for a two-month project to develop AI reads:

The study is to proceed on the basis of the conjecture that every aspect of learning or any other feature of intelligence can in principle be so precisely described that a machine can be made to simulate it. An attempt will be made to find how to make machines use language, form abstractions and concepts, solve kinds of problems now reserved for humans, and improve themselves. We think that a significant advance can be made in one or more of these problems if a carefully selected group of scientists work on it together for a summer.[iv]

This proposal shows how even the brightest minds can be completely wrong with their forecasts. More than 65 years later, we are still far from that vision. Today's narrow AI systems are specialized in dedicated tasks for which they are trained. In some domains, they perform very well and, in many cases, outperform humans.

We commonly understand AGI or human-level AI as a system capable of solving very diverse problems. Here we are guided by the characteristics of human intelligence. Thus, imagination, transferability, creativity, adaptability, and reasoning are essential characteristics, among others.

If you consider the broad spectrum of top researchers' forecasts of when AGI might be realized, you notice how speculative the question is even today.

According to the latest surveys among AI experts, most of them assume that we will get there. The argument is straightforward: human intelligence is indeed still clearly superior to artificial intelligence today. However, the latter can grow exponentially if one considers ingredients such as computing power or memory capacity. In contrast, the capacity of the human brain is *de facto* fixed. Evolutionary development in biology is many orders of magnitude slower than technological progress. Thus, the catching up or overtaking of human intelligence by AI is conceivable.

Much less clear is when this will occur. Also, due to spectacularly wrong predictions in the past, some experts and scientists are holding back. Those who do make a prediction when AGI might materialize with at least 50 percent probability are placing it between 2040 and 2050.

We will eventually get there. Many promising building blocks already exist, and there is an enormous amount of academic and commercial resources that the world invests in AI. However, it needs more than the evolutionary continuation of today's progress. Spectacular innovations achieved by organizations like OpenAI and DeepMind and media headlines obscure AI's state outside the spotlight, which is often silly compared to natural intelligence.

Machine learning still relies on the statistical association of things instead of what humans consider as understanding our environment. At present, we have to appreciate that the most intelligent universal computer that we know is the human brain.

In the near future, we may continue to see many spectacular breakthroughs in narrow fields where AI outperforms human experts. Also, there are trends to reuse formerly specialized neural network architectures for other tasks.

Deep-reinforcement learning is a promising trend in artificial intelligence, combining deep neural networks with an AI agent's ability to learn new skills by interacting with an environment. It starts by randomly choosing an option among a set of possible moves. A human-provided reward system guides the learning process so the AI can measure learned actions' effectiveness (for example, beating the opponent in chess leads to a positive reward). After repeated training, often involving millions of repetitions, the agent learns to master the skill. We have seen several examples in which deep-reinforcement learning systems acquire new skills to perfection and even invent surprising new strategies. However, applying deep-reinforcement learning to real-world business scenarios is still extremely challenging in many cases. A common saying among AI experts goes like this: if you want to tackle a problem with reinforcement learning, you now have two problems.

Improved machine-learning architectures and more extensive networks alone will not close the gap. We need breakthroughs in areas like hierarchical planning, common sense, or imagination to enable general-purpose AI.

Alexander: There are concerns that AI can become a threat once it reaches an artificial super intelligence (ASI) level. What do you think about ASI and a recursive self-improvement loop?

Andreas: Assuming that we achieve artificial general intelligence one day, I see no reason why the progress should stop at that level. Instead, the technology will benefit from its enormous scalability. Imagine artificial intelligence reaching a state in which it can comprehend arbitrary language. Then, thanks to vast amounts of computational resources, it's child's play to acquire all the knowledge of the world in a short time. In contrast, no human being will ever be able to internalize more than a minimal fraction of the knowledge available worldwide. Thus, several developments toward superhuman artificial intelligence seem inevitable once a particular milestone is achieved.

Several researchers predict an acceleration or explosion of AI progress if machines learn to improve themselves or even create new generations of intelligent systems. However, as the unrealistic Dartmouth proposal illustrates, even experts cannot predict how disruptive breakthroughs will look or when they might occur. There are also examples of pessimistic predictions that were disproved by breakthroughs that happened overnight.

Speculations about ASI are mere thought experiments and beliefs that extrapolate our present experiences into a possible future world. Therefore, the assessments among the top scientists diverge widely. For some researchers like Andrew Ng, this scenario is hypothetical and speculative, as if one would worry today about a future overpopulation on Mars.

Other voices warn of the development in clear terms and call for preventive action already today. Prominent examples include Nick Bostrom, professor for philosophy at the University of Oxford, Elon Musk, and the late physicist Stephen Hawking.

These concerns are mostly not about science-fiction-like scenarios in which machines develop intrinsic motives to dominate the world and therefore start a rebellion to subdue humanity. More likely is that a superintelligent machine's objectives lead to unintended consequences that turn out to be harmful to humanity. The problem lies in the potential misalignment between how we encode the AI system's goals and our actual intentions. A superintelligence would uncompromisingly pursue its objectives and develop methods that we cannot foresee.

For example, suppose we commission a superintelligence to fight malnutrition in the world. The system learns that more people can be fed by expanding agriculture and fertilization. Without considering other goals, this could lead to uncontrolled expansion and ultimately crowding out residential, industrial, and other regions not related to food production. Another scenario would be the superintelligence coming up with the idea to abolish the need for food by eliminating humanity.

While these striking examples might sound extreme or oversimplified, they illustrate what researchers call the control or alignment problem. Suppose the AI system has no common sense or a deeper understanding of our intentions and values. In that case, we have to be extremely careful in formulating the objectives to avoid all kinds of unintended consequences.

The apparent measure to avoid such situations is to build in some emergency brake that allows the human to stop an AI system that has gotten out of hand. However, a superintelligence would probably anticipate all viable possibilities that would jeopardize its goals and consequently prevent us from hitting the off switch.

Another scenario is the misuse of technology by bad actors like terrorists, rogue regimes, or organized crime. While we might manage to govern the use of AI-embedded weapons, it will be hard to control its use as a primarily digital arm. Examples of exploiting digital technology for large-scale attacks already exist today, like the emerging threat of nation-state cyberattacks.

Alexander: What are your favorite apps, tools, or software that you can't live without?

Andreas: I enjoy using the Jupyter Notebook to show the machine-learning process from explorative data analysis, model building, and experimentation to testing in an appealing format.

Integration of text and illustrations support storytelling. I have used them with various stakeholders, even in executive board presentations. Initially, I was skeptical about how a diverse audience might react to such a combination of interactive code snippets, output, and contextual documentation. It turns out that appealing notebooks are very well received not only by technical target groups.

Interactive visualizations, for example, zooming in on a large cloud of credit card transactions to spot the rare fraudulent cases, increase audience engagement in these conversations. Business stakeholders, including executives, appreciate appealing interactive visual experiences more than static slide decks.

Key Takeaways

- AI has the potential to become one of the most transformative innovations in history. This presents unprecedented opportunities but also enormous unknown challenges.
- It is in our hands to shape this future responsibly. A global responsible AI framework supported by academia, policymakers, the technology industry, and organizations that use AI is needed to minimize the risks of unintended consequences or misuse without compromising societal benefits.
- We still need to assess the long-term societal impact of superintelligent systems, especially in the world of work.
- There are promising approaches to today's challenges in areas such as AI transparency, fairness, and data security and privacy. Organizations should integrate these as essential elements of their AI development processes.

Endnotes

i   Chapter 22 presents a real-life conversation with GPT-3.
ii   Caruana, Rich, et al., "Creating AI glass boxes — Open sourcing a library to enable intelligibility in machine learning," Microsoft Research Blog,

May 10, 2019 (www.microsoft.com/en-us/research/blog/creating-ai-glass-boxes-open-sourcing-a-library-to-enable-intelligibility-in-machine-learning/).

iii For more information and examples, refer to the image examples in the latest SHAP documentation (shap.readthedocs.io/en/stable/image_examples.html#image-captioning).

iv McCarthy, J. et al., "A Proposal for the Dartmouth Summer Research Project on Artificial Intelligence," August 31, 1955 (www-formal.stanford.edu/jmc/history/dartmouth/dartmouth.html).

Chapter 20
Cameron Turner:
Understanding the Future
with Explainable AI

Cameron Turner, VP of data science, Kin+Carta
Source: Cameron Turner

Cameron has an extensive background in digital transformation, specifically artificial intelligence, product development, analytics, precision healthcare, and software development.

He currently serves as VP of data science for Kin+Carta; recent projects include mobile financial retention research in sub-Saharan Africa for the Bill & Melinda Gates Foundation and supply chain prediction for Hewlett-Packard. Under his leadership, their projects have helped generate triple-digit returns for Fortune 500 clients and large, multiple exits for PE-backed companies.

He served as founder and CEO of ClickStream Technologies (acquired by Microsoft) and went on to lead Microsoft's telemetry practice, managing essentially all inbound data systems globally and delivering insights and analytics to all Microsoft product teams and its 1,300 partners.

Cameron serves on the Accenture Technology Advisory Board and is an Entrepreneur-in-Residence at Stanford's StartX accelerator and a Venture Studio Advisor at Stanford Graduate School of Business.

He co-manages the Oxford Angel Fund and serves as a venture partner for Spike Ventures (Stanford Angel Fund). Cameron holds a BA from Dartmouth College, an MBA from Oxford University, and an MS in statistics from Stanford University.

Alexander: *You are VP of Data Science. What is your mission?*

Cameron: At Kin+Carta, we're on a mission to help companies leverage data they already have to generate new products and customer value. Often companies are sitting on top of huge stockpiles of legacy data and have yet to convert them into real returns. It's said that data is the new oil, and we certainly see that, but actually refinement of data, and specifically artificial intelligence, to solve existing acute business problems is where we operate.

Alexander: *How should business models evolve to survive and thrive in an increasingly digital world?*

Cameron: Often the answer is different for each customer. There's an idea historically that a product should be one-size-fits-all, or at least the customer should adapt to use the product.

A couple of decades ago, pretty much every product you bought came with some form of instruction manual, and that's gone away, largely because companies have recognized that customers want solutions. Whether it's enterprise software or soap, they want products to fit their lifestyle and use cases and not vice versa. The same is true in artificial intelligence. Historically, using your data meant generating rules of thumb by which to operate your business through analytics. The beauty of AI is that there no longer need to be static rules of thumb or even different sets of rules of thumb for different customers; rather, all of these things can be dynamic and learned based on what has come before. However, to evolve and survive in the twenty-first century means taking the responsibility for applied AI inside of common business practices. This is something we spend a lot of time working on as we seek to deploy ethical solutions for our clients.

Alexander: How can technology shift the roles and responsibilities of the workforce?

Cameron: It can do so in good ways or bad ways but rarely both. As AI is deployed, we'll see generally that not only will companies do better, but the people in those companies and those affected by these systems will do better as well.

One general trend that we've seen time and again is that the function of human-as-expert is going away quickly. It was widely predicted that AI would first take the jobs from those who do mundane tasks and free humans to do more creative work. The reality, though, is that AI is going after the experts as much as it is the general workforce. We can see this today in examples like Uber, where instead of autonomous vehicles driving around with passengers, we have human-driven vehicles that are directed by an AI in the cloud. AI directs everything from pickup and drop-off locations to the amount that a passenger will pay. And even industries that were largely seen as safe from AI, such as medicine, are undergoing radical transformation. For example, if you are presenting symptoms of the flu, but its origin is uncertain, during this COVID-19 period, would you rather be treated by a physician who saw 100 patients in the last week or an AI that effectively has seen millions? In this and many other examples, the answer is that we'd wish to bring all the data we have to bear to these kinds of critical questions.

Alexander: Which technology or digital capabilities are essential for a digital strategy?

Cameron: Certainly AI, but differentiation for companies increasingly comes not in the form of an algorithmic superiority (that is, having greater accuracy or a nuanced recommendation) but rather all of the things in which we must wrap an AI system in order to achieve an outstanding result. Some of these include things like data governance — where we have a system and policy in place to manage the critical systems that feed model training and development as well as ethical safeguards in the output to ensure that humans have the final say in any system that affects humans. In computing, with garbage in you get garbage out. But this compounds itself as a problem in AI where the garbage out becomes the new garbage in. You train on the system that you've affected. This way everything is cyclical, and the nature of the negative outcomes can be exponential just as the potential benefits can.

Alexander: The Fourth Industrial Revolution is indivisibly tied to the enormous amounts of data needed to train artificial intelligence. How has this revolution affected your work at Kin+Carta?

Cameron: Contrary to what I said earlier about core algorithms being less important, at Kin+Carta we spent a lot of time and energy in developing platform systems and processes that enable us to do a better job of prediction, explanation, and recommendation. However, model development is something that's becoming largely commoditized through automated machine learning. The difference between success and failure for these initiatives comes down to the underlying data and the execution of integration. As a product-based services provider we've been able to add the most value within companies that have a legacy of longitudinal data. In the next decade the companies that will really differentiate themselves from the rest of the market will be those that had a strong history of good data collection practices, either intentionally or for other purposes such as security and maintenance. You can make up time in a lot of other areas, but it actually takes time to generate a history of data, and this is where companies with that legacy will achieve the most.

Alexander: What is explainable AI?

Cameron: I'm super passionate about this. Even the definition of explainability has changed quite a bit. For any prediction or recommendation that's derived from a model, the second question will always be "how did you arrive at this conclusion?" Historically this has meant looking at things like variable importance or marginal effects of input parameters.

> *For any prediction or recommendation that's derived from a model, the second question will always be "how did you arrive at this conclusion?"*

But we're finding as our client base moves from those with a background in statistics and data science into mainstream business contexts the importance of clear communication has never been greater. So while we still quantify model effects in a traditional way, we spend a lot of time on data visualization and storytelling as a means to help people understand why a model works as it does.

At Kin+Carta, as an external services provider we get to approach problems in many different industries. We find ourselves being explained to instead of explaining AI. In evaluation, explainability is back on the business-process owners. We find this concept of explainability being largely iterative or cyclical, meaning our clients spend a lot of time explaining to us why certain characteristics are causing patterns and behaviors in the outcome of interest as a model evolves. It's this human–computer interaction that really will define the future of successful AI deployment.

Alexander: Which explainable AI use cases do you see as essential to contribute to any organization's digital strategy?

Cameron: Often we're approached by customers to think about holistic digital strategy in the context of the current business, and this is important. It's even more important to look outside of the current business context to identify new opportunities. However, where we see the most success is working backward from a solution. Instead of exploring all of the data at hand within an organization to uncover new insights and patterns, we instead tend to focus on the desired outcome and work backward into the technology. This often takes us into an entirely new area. There's certainly room for exploration and discovery in either process, but the difference between the two comes down to a return on investment. So in thinking about explainability, we must move beyond something that can be understood to something with which people can take action.

Alexander: Which further AI use cases would be made possible by a tighter data integration?

Cameron: There's currently a lot of investment here. The difference between successful and unsuccessful AI projects often comes down to integration, and data integration is the first step of platform integration, which also includes the often overlooked cultural and human integration. We don't typically have the time or budget to spend on data integration up front and instead have to do our own side process to generate the platform required for AI development and deployment. That said, there are some huge advantages to ensuring you have a good data integration strategy. Three of the biggest advantages are security, scalability, and latency. Without proper integration you leave yourself vulnerable at linkage points. Cohesive security strategy implies data integration strategy.

We've also found in building systems that begin as pilot projects and then grow into standard operational practice that without good data linkage things don't scale well. Some of that is addressed through cloud migration and some of the inherent benefits of cloud-based data services, but without thinking about this up front, you're building systems with a large amount of technical debt, meaning you'll end up rewriting a lot of your code. Similarly, without integration, there are risks in processing time, and so for any system that requires real-time or near-time throughput it's better to think about integration up front instead of down the road.

We're also big fans of the agile methodology as applied to data science and learning from the market and from stakeholders with each iteration. Doing things piecemeal in the early phases of an AI development project to prove out value sometimes makes the most sense.

Alexander: Because so much data is needed to train AI algorithms, how can organizations and companies stay ahead of legal, regulatory, and ethical issues associated with collecting and applying data?

Cameron: This is probably worthy of a whole interview on its own, possibly a book, or maybe a series of books. Focusing in on a specific problem can help you, since you're less likely to be blind-sided by different use cases than you had originally intended. Facial recognition is a great example. For most of us, our initial experience with facial recognition was the technology used to unlock our phones, which in itself is pretty great. As the technology has been adopted more broadly and is now used in law enforcement, however, we quickly get into deep ethical waters where original use cases may not match the present.

You bring up another issue of how AI technologies can span multiple regulatory environments. In the United States we are pretty comfortable with challenges in traversing local, state, and national-level regulations. However, as even small companies become increasingly global the exposure to regulatory risk is high. Regulation will always be slower than ethics as it applies to technology. The implication there is that we can't rely on our regulatory environment to provide boundaries for the capabilities of the products we create. It is actually on the creators to think through these processes up front. Something that's often missed in the press is that while Facebook, Google, and others maintain giant data repositories that include our identities, it's actually everyone's responsibility to think of these design questions up front in order to generate equitable and inclusive solutions to the problems presented.

Alexander: Is there a way whereby citizens own their data instead of organizations and companies owning fractions of it?

Cameron: Yes, this has been talked about a lot for the last decade, and more recently people have started to look at blockchain as a potential solution due to its distributed, decentralized, and secure characteristics.

At Clickstream Technologies, we paid people every month to use their anonymized data; the people were panelists, a sample representing a population in our studies. We always thought of data as a currency, one that people could trade and transact with, and I think this is actually true today in ad-revenue-based businesses. We must understand that if we're not paying for a service with dollars, then we may be paying in the form of our data. That can be a pretty powerful and good thing; it's just something that has to be recognized.

Alexander: What types of professional roles will we see evolve alongside the development and increasing use of AI across the industries?

Cameron: The role of data ethics will play a big part in deploying AI systems not just for large companies but small companies going forward. So that's certainly one area to watch. More broadly, though, technology is no longer a vertical but rather a horizontal that spans all industries including the high-tech industry. How that plays out-day-to-day is that an AI solutions team may include software engineers, data engineers, and data scientists, but also subject-matter experts for its area of application. This is something that we're definitely seeing in Silicon Valley in the startup ecosystem, where increasingly AI startups are led by people with depth beyond technology — more lawyer-founded startups, more physician-founded startups, and so forth.

Alexander: What projects would you consider are at the forefront of AI to support digital transformation? How can deep learning fill the gap?

Cameron: We're seeing an increasing amount of unstructured and semistructured data working its way into production AI systems, where previously we might have looked more at tabular and structured data. We're seeing things like audio, free text, video, and images becoming first-class input variables into systems that are used to predict, explain, and recommend. This is pretty cool because while many companies may not have made an investment in large structured-data systems, typically there tend to be a lot of unstructured or semistructured data assets floating around organizations in documents and customer relationship management (CRM) systems. So, we often get to be the bearers of good news. Scenarios that late-stage startups or medium-sized private-equity-backed companies thought were possible only for companies like Facebook and Google are actually available to them at lower cost than they might have imagined.

Deep learning is an emerging area when we think about its application to core business processes. However, the exciting thing about deep learning is that it sits right at the crossroads of computation and creativity, and we can actually generate candidate solutions that follow the patterns of human creativity in ways that traditional machine learning was unable to do. You could think of a parallel here in the natural world where genetic mutations can create an advantage for a species. Deep learning holds the promise that its generative nature might create previously unknown solutions to some of our biggest problems.

Alexander: What are your thoughts about the path to artificial general intelligence (AGI)? Can AI ever achieve general intelligence? How far are we from AGI?

Cameron: To get to the heart of the question, we have to look at the history of AI development, which started with an approach that was intended to mimic the processes in the human brain. That first set of investigations, while fascinating, led to an era known as the AI winter, when people generally gave up on the idea of AGI.

As we get back to the question in the twenty-first century, we can adapt the context a bit as growing from applied AI (for example, talking to the navigation system in your car — something we've had for quite some time now) to adaptive AI that can move between different contexts and predict based on what you're asking. This is more akin to where we are today with Alexa and Siri. But fundamentally, when we say artificial general intelligence, we're really talking about the ability for AI to adapt to a lot of different contexts and still provide the best answers. So, the question is less about AI being able to tackle any problem and more about the identification of context and then using what we now know about applied AI to solve a problem in that context. Achieving some form of AGI is a false victory. We should focus on finding solutions to specific global problems like COVID-19, cancer, and the environment instead of creating human-like entities through AI.

Alexander: There are concerns that AI can become a threat once AI reaches the level of an artificial super intelligence (ASI). What do you think about ASI and a recursive self-improvement loop?

Cameron: I grew up in the 1980s and still remember movies like *WarGames* and *The Day After*. As a frightened 10-year-old I was concerned that the end of the world might be imminent and based on an algorithmic response to nuclear threats. So some of these concerns toward AI are taken out of context when people imagine an army of robots with guns walking down our streets. The reality, though, is that society is operating in an greater state of fragility than it has in a long time. You could even argue that our current polarized political environment in the United States is a direct consequence of algorithms that seek to exploit human interest in extremes versus the average. And so when we talk about recursion, the threat is very real. Any system that can have an impact on society and adapt quickly will continue to evolve based on the responses to its own existence. So yes, in the end we do face risk. The good news is that we don't have to pull the plug on AI development to avoid the threat. You certainly don't see Elon Musk canceling Tesla's autopilot. Instead, through the integration of critical human examination into AI systems, we can identify these risks early and remediate in a way that not only averts disaster but also leads to a process of continued human development and societal improvement.

Alexander: Thank you, Cameron. What quick-win advice would you give that is easy for many companies to apply within their digital strategies?

Cameron: Go with your gut. It's very uncommon in our engagements that our client is wrong about the opportunity for AI in their business process, even if they have no background in digital transformation, machine learning, or artificial intelligence. This is really great news for practitioners in any environment. If you know your business well and you have a good understanding of what data is available, you probably have a good idea of the opportunity. As an example, we worked with a firm that had 10 years of OpenText notes from conversations they've had with their customers and believed they could do better to connect their clients to one another and extract themes and sentiments over time. And they were right! Sometimes the tooling is where they can use help. To get from the hypothesis to a deployed AI system can be a curvy journey, but the intuition in that case was correct for the beginning. So go with your gut.

Alexander: *What are your favorite apps, tools, or software that you can't live without?*

Cameron: We find ourselves working often at the intersection of human systems and AI, and so a lot of the work that I do is trying to identify new information sources that describe human behavior. I'll present the usual shout-outs to platforms like RStudio, Domino, and of course Amazon Web Services (AWS), Google Cloud Platform (GCP), and Microsoft Azure, but also encourage people to think beyond traditional data sources and data tooling into areas that may not have been considered AI-related historically. We spend a lot of time looking at Dun & Bradstreet, Salesforce, LinkedIn, and other sources that can provide more views into conversations and transactions than traditional line-of-business applications can.

Alexander: *Do you have a smart productivity hack or work-related shortcut?*

Cameron: I'd be remiss not to suggest people take a look at our automated machine-learning platform, Octain, which provides automated data cleansing, imputation, feature engineering, model creation, hyperparameter tuning, model explanation, visualization, and integration. This is available as a spreadsheet add-in, web portal, or API to serve business users, developers, and data scientists alike. While this is simply a tool, we've found it to be instrumental in our engagements to help companies go from 0 to 100 on the digital transformation scale inside of timelines that traditionally would have been impossible.

Alexander: *What is the best advice you have ever received?*

Cameron: Be a lifelong learner. I grew up in a house of educators: my mom a schoolteacher, and my dad a college professor, and so we were always taught to keep learning throughout life.

I've spent more time in school than I probably should have, but it's largely what drew me to this whole area of machine learning and deep learning, which at its core is all about learning! A benefit of Kin+Carta being a product-based services organization is that we get to continuously learn from our smart clients who take us into new customer scenarios and new industries every day. And so as technology (and more specifically AI) becomes a horizontal that spans every business scenario, we get to continue learning. This is another area where automated machine learning really comes into play. Because what was true yesterday may not predict tomorrow, having systems that are dynamic and adaptive enables us to not only continue to learn ourselves but also develop systems that in their nature are inquisitive and learning continuously.

Key Takeaways

- Instead of exploring all of the data at hand within an organization to uncover new insights and patterns, we instead tend to focus on the desired outcome and work backward into the technology.
- Cohesive security strategy implies data integration strategy.
- We must understand that if we're not paying for a service with dollars, then we may be paying in the form of our data — and actually that can be a pretty powerful and good thing; it's just something that has to be recognized.

Chapter 21
Patrick Glauner: Everyone Needs to Acquire Some Understanding of What AI Is

Patrick Glauner, professor of AI, Deggendorf Institute of Technology
Source: Shengqin Yang

Patrick Glauner has been a full professor of artificial intelligence at Deggendorf Institute of Technology in Bavaria, Germany, since the age of 30. In parallel, he is the founder and CEO of skyrocket.ai GmbH, an AI consulting firm. He has published three books: *Creating Innovation Spaces: Impulses for Start-ups and Established Companies in Global Competition* (Springer, 2021), *Digitalization in Healthcare: Implementing Innovation and Artificial Intelligence* (Springer, 2021), and *Innovative Technologies for Market Leadership: Investing in the Future* (Springer, 2020). His works on AI have been featured by *New Scientist*, McKinsey & Company, Imperial College London, Udacity, the Luxembourg National Research Fund, *Towards Data Science*, and other publications and organizations. He was previously head of Data Academy at Alexander Thamm GmbH, innovation manager for artificial intelligence at Krones Group, a fellow at the European Organization for Nuclear Research (CERN), and a visiting researcher at the University of Quebec in Montreal (UQAM). He graduated as valedictorian from Karlsruhe University of Applied Sciences with a BS in computer science. He subsequently received an MS in machine learning from Imperial College London, an MBA from Quantic School of Business and Technology, and a PhD in computer science from the University of Luxembourg. He is an alumnus of the German National Academic Foundation (*Studienstiftung des deutschen Volkes*).

Alexander: *You are professor of AI at Deggendorf Institute of Technology. What is your mission?*

Patrick: AI has started to transform nearly every industry. In my view, however, that is just the tip of the iceberg as AI has the potential to fundamentally change our economy. At Deggendorf Institute of Technology, we established an undergraduate program in AI[i] in 2019. Our goal is to turn our students into high-caliber AI experts within three and a half years. I teach a number of courses in this program, including *Computer Vision*, *Natural Language Processing*, *Big Data*, and *Algorithms and Data Structures*. On the other hand, my courses include real-world projects. For example, in my Computer Vision course, my students use the NVIDIA Jetbot mobile robot platform depicted in Figure 21.1. They then implement some

Figure 21.1 NVIDIA Jetbot

of the algorithms discussed in class on this platform and use the robot's camera. For my students it is a very rewarding experience to see their code running on a robot that interacts with its environment, for example, by following objects. Some of my students also do their projects together with industrial partners. As a result, they quickly get the big picture of how to adapt these theories so that they succeed in solving real-world problems.

Alexander: You also teach a course on innovation management. How does this topic relate to AI?

Patrick: Various market reports remind us of the sad truth about AI projects in industry: 80 percent fail or do not make it beyond the proof-of-concept stage. There are multiple reasons for this gap. One of them is that most AI courses at universities do not address the real-world challenges that arise when deploying AI. Those challenges are often nontechnical and include change management, business-process management, and organization management. There is an acute need in industry for experts who understand how AI adds value to companies. To bridge this gap, I am teaching a novel course, Innovation Management for Artificial Intelligence. In my course, I share my experience and best practices and how these lead to deployed applications that add real business value. No other university around the globe teaches a similar course. As a professor, my goal is that my innovative course sets my students apart, turning them into future experts in real-world AI applications. Over time, I can thus make a real and lasting difference to the field of AI and its applications in industry. I have started to promote my course, aiming to inspire other professors to adapt it. With our collective efforts, we are training the next generation of worldwide AI leaders.

Alexander: Which technology or digital capabilities are essential for a digital strategy? How should business models evolve to survive and thrive in an increasingly digital world?

Patrick: I find AI particularly essential as it allows us to automate human or manual decision-making. That is quite a contrast to previous phases of industrial automation that aimed only to automate repetitive tasks. To survive and thrive, business models have to become more efficient. In one of the later answers, I describe an AI application that predicted the power usage of special-purpose machines. Previously, it took domain experts days to do those calculations. Using AI, this task now only takes milliseconds and comes with much more accurate results. AI is part of the solution, but we must not abandon human intelligence and blindly apply AI to any problem. AI can thrive only if we use it for the right tasks and lay the necessary foundation for it.

Alexander: How can technology shift the roles and responsibilities of the workforce?

Patrick: AI is already starting to have significant impacts on the jobs market, both for businesses and workers. Bear in mind also that we have been seeing tremendous changes in the jobs market ever since the beginning of the industrial revolution some 250 years ago. For example, look back 100 years ago: most of the jobs from that time do not exist anymore. Furthermore, those changes are now happening more frequently. As a consequence, employees may need to undergo retraining multiple times in their careers. Another challenge is that not everyone who loses their job to AI will be able to transition into a highly technical career.

Even though those changes are dramatic, we simply cannot stop them. For instance, China has become a world-leading country in AI innovation.[ii] Chinese companies are using that advantage to rapidly advance their competitiveness in a large number of industries. If Western companies do not adapt to that reality, they will probably be out of business in the foreseeable future.

Alexander: Which AI use cases would you see as essential to contribute to any organization's digital strategy?

Patrick: I often see people who look for AI use cases that provide a solution and then tend to create problems that actually had not existed in the first place. My approach is very different: I rarely think in terms of AI use cases. Rather, I look at business problems and analyze how these could be solved efficiently. I then assess the following three criteria for a concrete business problem: high costs, long processing time, and uncertainty (meaning that two or more domain experts try to solve the same problem but come to different solutions). If at least one of those criteria is met, AI may be a solution to the problem. However, you should always strive for the simplest solution that provides you with the best outcome. For example, if a business process includes unnecessarily complex dependencies, an AI-based approach may not be very useful for improving its overall performance. Instead, we should first use our human intelligence and rethink the business process. AI, nonetheless, may then still help to further improve various steps of the revised business process.

Alexander: Because so much data is needed to train AI algorithms, how can organizations and companies stay ahead of legal, regulatory, and ethical issues associated with collecting and applying data?

Patrick: Those topics have recently started to gain momentum and keep evolving very rapidly. Organizations should thus send their AI experts to conferences or other events to stay up-to-date. They should also contribute to standardization committees and thus help shape the rules rather than being shaped by others through such initiatives.

Furthermore, organizations should actively reach out to the politicians who regulate technology. For example, look at the General Data Protection Regulation (GDPR) 2016/679, a regulation in EU law on data protection and privacy in the European Union and the European Economic Area. One of the initial goals of the GDPR was to limit the power of international — predominantly U.S.-based — service providers. However, it has turned out that those service providers are best able to comply with this overly complex and ambiguous regulatory framework. As a consequence, (smaller) European service providers have gotten even more pressure because of the GDPR. That is why I strongly believe the GDPR has been a disaster and needs to be revised.

When I look at the current attempts of the European Union to regulate AI, concerns and fears seem to be the center of attention. For example, one of those fears is the so-called black-box model whose decision-making cannot be fully explained. Oftentimes, however, human decision-making is a black box, too. Even drug discovery is not explainable to some extent but employs statistical analyses to assess the outcomes. In my opinion, the European Union would do better by embracing opportunities instead of fears. They should regulate only the application domains of AI where regulation is absolutely necessary, such as medical applications, safety-critical systems, and so on. I doubt that those domains actually require a lot of additional regulation, as there are already plenty of regulations for systems. Whether they include traditional software, AI-based software, or no software at all does not really matter from a regulatory perspective.

Alexander: *You have previously headed the corporate AI competence center at Krones Group, the world's leading manufacturer of bottling lines. Tell us more about how AI adds value in mechanical engineering.*

Patrick: Most articles on AI in mechanical engineering seem to focus on predictive maintenance. For a lot of market reports and people in industry, predictive maintenance seems to be the only AI use case or perhaps the ultimate objective in mechanical engineering. However, predictive maintenance is just the beginning of AI in this domain. During my time at Krones Group, my team and I built a number of AI applications, including some that predicted the power usage of special-purpose machines entirely from the machine requirements defined by customers. This information could then be provided to customers in the quotes so that they could build the necessary infrastructure in their plants before the machines were built and shipped. I have described this use case and others in detail in my book *Innovative Technologies for Market Leadership: Investing in the Future.*

Alexander: *What types of professional roles will we see evolve alongside the development and increasing use of AI across the industries?*

Patrick: Any corporate AI strategy needs to align to the corporate digitalization strategy. Who is actually in charge of digitalization in an organization? Most companies have a chief information officer (CIO) — or head of IT — who is in charge of the company's IT department and defines the corporate IT strategy. IT departments are usually very conservative and seem to favor the status quo instead of innovation. That makes sense: the most important duty of an IT department is to provide key services such as Internet access, emails, enterprise resource planning systems, data storage, or phone services as reliably and securely as possible. Focusing on reliability typically comes with a limited user experience, however. For example, users may not be able to install any third-party software on their computers or browse random websites.

In contrast, to take full advantage of modern digitalization technology, your digitalization specialists need more freedom and must be able to try new tools, programming languages, frameworks, or cloud services. Successful corporate digital transformations typically have one thing in common: a chief digital officer (CDO) who runs the company's digital department and does not report to the CIO. CDOs typically report to a board member[iii] and thus have the autonomy to run a department that has its own IT infrastructure and that is able to develop new products and services quickly.

Most companies also do not only have a central data infrastructure. Instead, data sources are typically spread all over the company in many different locations and formats (for example, spreadsheets, databases, and so on). This makes it challenging for machine learning projects to take full advantage of the company's data. Therefore, one of the CDO's responsibilities includes establishing a central and harmonized data storage environment that can be used in subsequent projects that aim to get insights from all the corporate data.

Alexander: *How do you personally develop and update your AI skills?*

Patrick: I recently read the fourth edition of *Artificial Intelligence: A Modern Approach* by Stuart Russell and Peter Norvig. It provides an excellent overview of the state of the art of AI, in particular how the field has evolved in the last ten years. However, the state of the art in AI keeps evolving very rapidly, so I also regularly read papers on arXiv.org to stay up-to-date. In addition, I regularly take massive open online courses (MOOCs). For example, I recently took the edX "Quantum Machine Learning"[iv] MOOC and loved it!

I actually had started to learn the foundations of machine learning and AI through MOOCs in 2011. At that time, I had signed up for a number of MOOCs, including Andrew Ng's MOOC on machine learning.

Alexander: *What skills will managers need to develop to be able to work with AI?*

Patrick: I keep telling decision-makers — in particular my customers — all the time: "Everyone, from the board members down to the factory workers, needs to acquire some understanding

Everyone, from the board members down to the factory workers, need to acquire some understanding of what AI is and how your business can take advantage of it.

of what AI is and how your business can take advantage of it." That understanding will help every employee identify tasks that can be automated using AI. For example, a factory worker may recognize an opportunity for how to improve a process using previously collected data. Supervisors also need some understanding of how AI works in order to assess the worker's proposal. If the assessment is positive, they can forward it to their supervisor or directly to the organization's AI competence center. Also, the top management of a company needs to be aware of what AI is and how it can improve the company. That understanding helps the top management challenge the status quo and assign resources accordingly to innovation. Training your staff in AI is actually quite cheap as there are plenty of MOOCs available.

Alexander: *What projects would you consider are at the forefront of AI to support the digital transformation? How can deep learning fill the gap?*

Patrick: Looking back at three criteria I mentioned previously, any projects that improve business processes in terms of costs, running time, and certainty or repeatability of the outcomes tend to be helpful. I honestly have mixed feelings about deep learning. There is no doubt that deep learning has recently led to major progress in a large number of popularized AI applications, in particular in computer vision and natural language processing. However, I have also noticed a number of exaggerated claims about deep learning in recent years. Those include that deep learning worked like the human brain or that deep learning models were generally better than other machine learning models. Both claims are wrong in my opinion. First, deep learning models are loosely inspired by the human brain — at the very most. Neurons and the neural network that our brain is made of are much more complex than the contemporary deep learning models used in research. Second, I consider deep learning to be one of many items in a modern machine learning tool set. Deep learning may be helpful for some problems, in particular in computer vision or natural language processing, in which you have large training data sets available. In contrast, deep learning often tends to be an overly complex choice for a lot of other machine learning problems and may actually lead to worse results. Deep learning models are not generally better than other machine learning models. See Wolpert's no-free-lunch theorem,[v] which proves that there is no one model that works best for every problem. When I start applying machine learning to a problem, I first build a simple baseline model. In supervised learning that is usually a random forest model, which often works surprisingly well. If its outcome is sufficient, I am done — at low cost and short training time. If it is not sufficient, I then try increasingly more complex models, including deep learning.

Alexander: *What should modern university courses in and around AI look like so that the students are able to add value in industry?*

Patrick: Most courses at universities or in MOOC platforms focus on methodology, such as optimizing machine learning models in order to learn patterns. However, real-world AI projects require a lot of other competences, as depicted in Table 21.1.

In reality, training a model for some tasks is usually not that challenging, unless you need a completely new methodology, which is rarely the case. In supervised learning, choosing and training a machine learning model can even be automated to a large

Table 21.1 Relative Time Needed in an Industrial AI Project

Step	Courses	Reality
Defining KPIs	Small	Large
Collecting data	Small	Large
Exploratory data analysis	Small	Large
Building infrastructure	Small	Large
Optimizing ML models	Large	Medium
Integration in existing infrastructure	Small	Large

extent. For example, this can be done by employing automated machine learning (AutoML)[vi] approaches, which often return reasonable results. In contrast, other tasks such as defining KPIs, collecting data, and so on, tend to be awfully challenging and time-consuming in real-world projects. Universities need to address all of those topics so that their graduates are able to actually quickly add value in industry. We cover all of those aspects (and many others) in our AI undergraduate program at Deggendorf Institute of Technology, a belief confirmed by the feedback we get from our industrial partners.

Alexander: *What are your thoughts about the path to artificial general intelligence (AGI)? Can AI ever achieve general intelligence? How far are we from AGI?*

Patrick: Today's AI applications tend to be very narrow, performing well (sometimes even outperforming humans) on exactly one task. AGI is the hypothetical intelligence of a machine that performs similarly to humans on a wide spectrum of tasks. The point when computers become more intelligent than humans is referred to in the literature as the technological singularity. There are various predictions as to when — or even if at all — the singularity will occur. They span a wide range, from a period in the next 20 years, to realistic predictions about achieving the singularity around the end of the twenty-first century, to the prediction that the technological singularity may never materialize. Since each of these predictions makes various assumptions, making a reliable assessment is challenging. Today it is impossible to predict how far away the singularity is. Murray Shanahan's book[vii] is excellent. He provides a first-class and extensive analysis on this topic and a discussion of the consequences of the various predictions.

We have seen some initial work towards AGI in the last few years. In particular the works of DeepMind, such as the underlying deep reinforcement learning methodology of AlphaGo. However, a lot of those outcomes perform well predominantly in fully observable and discrete environments. Our environment, however, is only partially observable and continuous and thus diametral to the assumptions made by most of those works. I get the impression that DeepMind has, in the meantime, somewhat deviated from their original aim to build AGI and now focuses mainly on nearer-term AI applications.

Furthermore, today's computers, no matter how impressively fast they have become, are really not that different from the computers of the late 1940s and early 1950s when the von Neumann architecture was introduced. They have the same limitations that a Turing machine has. In order to achieve artificial general intelligence, we probably first need to rethink computational models and computer architecture as a whole and finally come up with a novel, more powerful model. (Note that quantum computers will probably not be a solution to this problem.)

Alexander: *There are concerns that AI can become a threat once it reaches the level of an artificial super intelligence (ASI). What do you think about ASI and a recursive self-improvement loop?*

Patrick: In recent years, various stakeholders have in fact warned about so-called killer robots and other possible unfortunate outcomes of AI advances. The fear of an out-of-control AI is exaggerated now and possibly in the near and foreseeable future. We are still far away from artificial general intelligence and thus from possible artificial super intelligence scenarios, too.

I really like the much-noticed comparison made by Andrew Ng a few years ago:[viii] Andrew's view is that science is still very far away from the potential killer robot threat scenario. The state of the art of AI can be compared to a planned manned trip to Mars, which is currently being prepared by researchers. Andrew further states that some researchers are also already thinking about how to colonize Mars in the long term, but no researcher has yet tried to explore how to prevent overpopulation on Mars. He equates the scenario of overpopulation with the scenario of a killer robot threat. That danger would also be so far into the future that he was simply not able to work productively to prevent it at the moment, as he first had much more fundamental work to do in AI research.

The large number of negative connotations of AI, such as killer robots, are unnecessary distractions. We should rather embrace the opportunities of tomorrow. AI is nothing but the next phase of the industrial revolution. AI will further increase our prosperity just as previous phases have. Nonetheless, there are definitely tangible threats to people from AI in the near and foreseeable future, such as job losses. We need to address those issues and make sure that everyone benefits from the advances of AI and its applications.

Alexander: *Thank you, Patrick. What quick-win advice would you give that is easy for many companies to apply within their digital strategies?*

Patrick: Train each and every single person in your organization in digitalization and AI for 30 minutes.

Alexander: *What are your favorite apps, tools, or software that you can't live without?*

Patrick: I really like iPython and Jupyter Notebook, two interactive programming environments. Both allow me to quickly write a few lines of code, run them, improve them, reuse results of previous lines, and so on. This approach helps to substantially reduce the time needed for designing and implementing algorithms. What a difference from the old days when we had to compile and link C/C++ code and start from scratch after any minor change!

Alexander: *Do you have a smart productivity hack or work-related shortcut?*

Patrick: I am an early bird and get up at 4 a.m. two or three days a week. At that time, I do not receive any emails or phone calls and can entirely focus on research, writing, or coding for a couple of hours. Usually, I get most of my work done before the daily routine of answering emails, making phone calls, or attending meetings. During my PhD research time, I got up that early five days a week. Over the years, however, I noticed that I tended to be tired all day long. Nowadays, I only get up that early two or three times a week and feel healthier, better rested, and even more productive!

Alexander: *What is the best advice you have ever received?*

Patrick: A few years ago, when I had completed about half of my PhD, I noticed that most of the recent PhD graduates in our lab struggled finding jobs in industry. They then typically had to stay in our lab as a postdoc, which actually further complicated finding a job in industry. I really did not want to get stuck in our lab at all upon my PhD graduation. One of my friends then told me that I should acquire some extra skills that are diametral to what I was doing in my PhD research. For example, that could be doing a project management certificate, becoming a patent attorney, or pursuing an MBA. I chose the third option and pursued an MBA in parallel to my PhD. My MBA experience enriched me with an additional skill set. That proved to be very helpful for me as I got a major management position in industry immediately upon the completion of my PhD.

Key Takeaways

- Organizations should send their AI experts to conferences or other events to stay up-to-date. They should also contribute to standardization committees and thus help shape the rules rather than being shaped by others through such initiatives.
- To take full advantage of modern digitalization technology, your digitalization specialists need more freedom and must be able to try new tools, programming languages, frameworks, or cloud services.
- Deep learning models are not generally better than other machine learning models, because there is no one model that works best for every problem. When you start applying machine learning to a problem, first build a simple baseline model. In supervised learning, that is usually a random forest model, which often works surprisingly well. If its outcome is sufficient, you are done — at low cost and short training time. If it is not sufficient, I then try increasingly more complex models including deep learning.

Endnotes

i   th-deg.de/ki-b-en.

ii Lee, Kai-Fu, *AI Superpowers: China, Silicon Valley, and the New World Order*. Boston: Houghton Mifflin Harcourt, 2018.

iii With digitalization and AI becoming ever more crucial to the success of a company, more companies will likely appoint CDOs directly to their boards in the future.

iv www.edx.org/course/quantum-machine-learning.

v   Wolpert, David, "The Lack of A Priori Distinctions between Learning Algorithms." *Neural Computation*, 8.7 (October 1996): 1341–90.

vi automl.github.io/auto-sklearn.

vii Shanahan, Murray, *The Technological Singularity*. Cambridge, MA: MIT Press, 2015.

viii www.theregister.com/2015/03/19/andrew_ng_baidu_ai/.

Chapter 22
Vladimir Alexeev: Natural Language Processing and the Human Factory Empathy

Vladimir Alexeev, digital experience specialist, DB Schenker, and OpenAI
GPT-3 ambassador
Source: Vladimir Alexeev

Vladimir Alexeev was born in Russia, lives in Germany, speaks Japanese, and embraces the global world. He helps DB Schenker with research and strategies to navigate through the digital age. AI is his big love, along with avant-garde art — both are highly disruptive and reshape our reality. To find new ways and approaches is his job and passion. He thinks strategically, but also operative dimensions are highly crucial for him. His motto is: "AI is neither a tool nor a replacement but the augmentation of humankind. Collaborate, create, and be inspired!"

> *AI is neither a tool nor a replacement but the augmentation of humankind. Collaborate, create, and be inspired!*

Vladimir writes about artificial intelligence, new technologies, digital strategies and culture in his magazine, *Merzazine.*[i]

Alexander: *You are a digital experience specialist at DB Schenker. What is your mission?*

Vladimir: My mission is to support our team in driving digital transformation with writing, strategic approach, and research in the area of new technologies (blockchain, IoT, AI, and so on). Schenker is a large logistics company with a long backstory, but only in looking forward we can move on. *Non progredi est regredi.*[ii]

Alexander: *How should business models evolve to survive and thrive in an increasingly digital world?*

Vladimir: Observe, adapt, and act. These are the three crucial steps to handle the digital shift, with a paradigm change in every single area. An important thing is to compare and to analyze existing and new approaches but also to find your way. It's like with Spotify and Agile Work — if you blindly apply their model to your workforce ecosystem, you will fail. You have to know your inner world with its strengths and flaws — and to be aware of the ever-changing world outside. Digitalization is like a big wave — don't let yourself drown, but you'd do even better to ride this wave.

Alexander: How can technology shift the roles and responsibilities of the workforce?

Vladimir: New technologies enable new ways for managing your workforce. But still don't forget the human factor — know the skills and talents that cannot be replaced by technology. Implement digital solutions to prevent silos, to avoid the dispensable routines. I often see in various industries the CEO's enthusiastic fascination with the new technical possibilities. But if they just blindly pursue the next hype, without considering their strategy and workforce needs, they might overlook the most essential resource they have: humans. A balance between human and technological factors is crucial for the success of the digital strategy.

Alexander: Which technology or digital capabilities are essential for a digital strategy?

Vladimir: There are various framesets and technologies we can consider as essential. In my opinion, this is artificial intelligence — not because it's a hot topic right now, but because my experience is that the area of artificial intelligence is in continuous development in various sectors and industries. I came to the conclusion that machine- and deep-learning models are about to become the core of manifold business models, systems, and even strategic approaches. And when quantum computing becomes more widely available, this will be a huge breakthrough for artificial intelligence as well. Even if you don't possess a quantum computer but have access to a quantum cloud, imagine how well it will work, for example in the combination of edge AI (for processing) + 5G (for data transmission) + blockchain (for database architecture and secured distribution). But mind the inexorable development — with powerful quantum computing all current crypto-approaches (cybersecurity, blockchain, bitcoin) will be scrutinized again.

We are facing the Fourth Industrial Revolution. In particular, I see some exciting developments as I am cooperating with OpenAI as their beta user. This AI research laboratory has developed a new milestone last year (2020): GPT-3, a natural language processing (NLP) model. For me, this NLP framework is a game changer.

Alexander: *What is GPT-3, and why is GPT-3 a game changer?*

Vladimir: GPT is short for "Generative Pre-trained Transformer." This language model is pre-trained on a huge text data set. Transformer is a deep-learning model that applies self-attention[iii] for generating new texts that are logical and coherent, thanks to this method. 2019 OpenAI published GPT-2, which was trained on 40 GB of text (approximately 8 million articles, books, and websites) and runs with 1.5 billion parameters. You also could train GPT-2 on your text data sets. The outputs, generated by GPT-2, were already stunning.

With GPT-3, OpenAI achieved a new milestone. Trained on 570 GB of text and running with 175 billion parameters, this model can write congenial texts, emulate style and genre, code, and run as a chatbot without programming, just to name some of the unique capabilities. You can imagine this framework as a digital instance that is taught on mankind's cultural heritage and knowledge and that can produce content about almost everything. It also can act as an omniscient dialog partner.

Alexander: *Can we have a quick chat with GPT-3? Let's ask some questions.*

Vladimir: Sure.

Human: *What do CIOs and CDOs have to consider for a successful digital strategy?*

AI: CIOs and CDOs should create a digital platform that brings digital initiatives together.

Human: *Which specific features of those digital platforms should they focus on?*

AI: CIOs and CDOs should leverage AI analytics to optimize the customer experience and step up overall operational efficiency.

Human: *So customer experience should be pivotal?*

AI: It is key. Without a positive experience, loyalty and respect will be hard to elicit from current and potential customers alike.

Human: *But what about the digital development of a company?*

AI: Digital development is equally significant. It encompasses incorporating digital technologies, data-driven insights, and creative strategies into business operations.

Human: *What should CIOs/CDOs avoid?*

AI: They should avoid being complacent.

Human: *How can they avoid it?*

AI: Failing to investigate their current technology or the technology options available is a big mistake, for one. But the wrong perception of the future also lends itself to a false sense of security. So keeping an eye on constantly emerging technology is also a requirement.

Alexander: *That's impressive! Which GPT-3 use cases would you see as essential to contribute to any organization's digital strategy?*

Vladimir: I see it in another way. Every organization follows its own goals, has its specifics, and can benefit from various use cases of GPT-3, especially in the area of customer experience, for example, in a chatbot or dynamic content creation. Again, this system will never replace writers, but it can support them, for example, with autonomous answers to frequent customer questions. The most important aspect they should consider with the integration GPT-3 is fine-tuning. This NLP framework is trained on vast amounts of information. For general topics, it can be used already in its initial consistency. But for your specific company's needs, you can leverage this huge model and provide your specific data. It's up to you to channel it into the desired direction, to bias it neutrally, to determine the way of knowledge transfer — and here you need to train (or fine-tune) GPT-3 on your relevant data, which should be used for this language-based approach.

Here we are facing the most relevant aspect, which if not properly managed, can lead every AI-based automation into continuous failure: data. You have to harvest, maintain, and structure your data. It's your most relevant treasure. Avoid silos, but sort the entire sum of data you get from all your systems. To prepare, to convert, and — finally — to use this data for the pre-training of GPT-3 will guarantee the correct communication between AI and humans. At the end of the day, even the best AI framework will most definitely fail if it is trained on deficient databases.

Alexander: *Which further AI use cases would be made possible by a tighter data integration?*

Vladimir: It also depends on your needs and your strategy. When you have your data in a useful format, you can provide it internally to search for anomalies, to enhance workflows, to experiment with scenarios. You have to think about this data as the gold of the digital age — become a data provider and collaborate with others in our globally connected world. The age of autonomies and hoarding resources and data is past. It's the age of coopetition — we don't have competitors; we have partners of mutual advantage.

Alexander: Because so much data is needed to train AI algorithms, how can organizations and companies stay ahead of legal, regulatory, and ethical issues associated with collecting and applying data?

Vladimir: To handle data legally and ethically, especially if it's data about humans (customers, partners, and so on), ideally you have to anonymize it if possible. For example, if you need to detect some overall tendencies among your customer base, you don't need to know about the particular item within the data set. For example, logistics: if you want to see traffic tendencies on specific routes, you don't need to keep the shipment address, sender name, and so on, in the database. Anonymize all data that is irrelevant for your approach in statistics or predictive analytics. You will also have to anonymize data if you act as a data provider. Say you are a digital company; you can anonymize your customer data and share it with a government statistical office or with a university network for analysis of mass behavior with digital media. You will have a new partner from a field you probably haven't thought about. The platform economy is the right way to manage your data-providing efforts. But again, data privacy and ethical considerations are essential for a fair coexistence in a data ecosystem of the digital age. Data is your gold, but in the end, it belongs to the people, with whom this data originates. They have to be able to give consent or to opt out.

Alexander: Is there a way where citizens own their data instead of organizations and companies owning fractions of it?

Vladimir: This is the right direction of democratizing data and the only right way in the nondystopian sociopolitical state systems. Here we probably need secured interfaces for the personalized data of citizens, accessible only by them, with the anonymized data sets for statistical and strategic approaches. To provide authentication and to preserve privacy we probably can benefit from blockchain solutions with crypto security and anonymous authenticity. Also, well-conceived and automated AI systems could prevent privacy breaches. Such interfaces are crucial, and yet they don't exist at the moment — a new field of work for CDOs and CIOs.

Alexander: What types of professional roles will we see evolve alongside the development and increasing use of AI across the industries?

Vladimir: AI will reshape the workforce landscape. Old job descriptions will be abandoned; new professional roles will emerge. I see big demand in the maintenance, data set management, and training of AI systems. Also, controlling and evaluating AI outcomes is immensely important. ML and DL frameworks should be unshakably reliable and trustworthy. We have a shortage of experts in AI ethics, and also in the culture at large, since AI is still seen as stuff for nerds. But AI is the electricity of the twenty-first century. We need publicists, journalists, and educators who can impart knowledge about AI and clear up misconceptions. Hire more cultural scientists — their skills are often what big companies are missing, sometimes without knowing it.

The popular fear of employees, losing their jobs, is based on their misconceptions about AI — and also on their leaders' misconceptions about AI. Artificial intelligence shouldn't replace people; it should support them. Firing a workforce with the hope AI will manage the workload is a blind action of C-level executives and a sign of their lacking digital competence. You should evolve systems to help your employees, customers, and partners. This includes the education and development of your team's skills.

Alexander: How do you develop your team's AI skills?

Vladimir: Your data is your fuel, but your workforce is your body. Without a body, you cannot move, and fuel is useless then. Take care of your team, nurture it with digital competence, support their skills developments, organically raise their motivation — not with cheesy intern marketing statements but with actual value. The motivation should come from your team. Don't skimp on education, on networking with specialists. Look for talents in your team and focus these talents with your strategic approach. To manage AI you don't need just coders. You will undoubtedly need them in your team, but not all your colleagues have to start learning Python (if they don't demand it). You need people with systemic, strategic, and ethical perspectives on AI as well. You need a balance between them.

Alexander: What skills will managers need to develop to be able to work with AI?

Vladimir: Empathy. Managers have to read the human factor, especially in our digital times. They have to see what their team needs. And this communicative ability should be combined with digital competence. They don't need to code (good if they can). But they have to know what's going on at the strategic and operative level. Both are important and shouldn't be underestimated. Managers without empathetic ability may somehow move the whole system, but it will be toxic inside.

Alexander: What projects would you consider to be at the forefront of AI to support digital transformation? How can deep learning fill the gap?

Vladimir: AI can help with converting silos to single sources of truth, with structuring and providing clear insights. What AI cannot do is prove the high relevance of digital transformation for all stakeholders and members of a company. That's the responsibility of managers and C-level executives. That's why they are what they are.

Alexander: What are your thoughts about the path to artificial general intelligence (AGI)? Can AI ever achieve general intelligence? How far are we from AGI?

Vladimir: There are various conceptions of what AGI might look like. In my opinion, if we combine various neural networks and models that are working independently (pattern recognition, natural language processing, predictive analytics, and so on), we will be close to AGI. AGI will be able to interpret circumstances and contexts, not only data; it will be capable of thinking and comprehension. This kind of comprehension you can never compare to human cognition, however, since we are driven by more aspects than just information and reaction. See AGI still as assistant and supporter, not a replacement of the human workforce.

Alexander: There are concerns that AI can become a threat once AI reaches the level of an artificial super intelligence (ASI). What do you think about ASI and a recursive self-improvement loop?

Vladimir: The threat arises not in technologies but in our human dealings with them. AI does its work precisely; it also is capable of self-improving in this field. It's up to us to implement this precision in the right ways. But we also make mistakes, for example by training AI on mislabeled data sets or data with missing diversity. AI knows only what we train it on. Everything unknown is interpreted by AI in heuristic and typological ways, since AI-based systems are pragmatically efficient. That's why the human factor is so crucial, and that's why we need interdisciplinary teams with a focus on ethics for running AI-applications, whatever goal they follow. If we neglect this strategic approach, we may generate an AI system with harm for society, culture, economics. But then we will have to blame ourselves for our narrow-mindedness leading to apocalypse. The recursive self-improvement is indeed a substantial ability of AI systems, but we have to learn the ways to steer it in the right direction. And what is right and wrong should be democratically decided, not in a top-down process.

Alexander: Thank you, Vladimir. What quick-win advice would you give that is easy for many companies to apply within their digital strategies?

Vladimir: Look for your need, listen to your customers and workforce — and decide for your digital strategy in which direction to develop.

Alexander: What are your favorite apps, tools, or software that you can't live without?

Vladimir: For customer-centered listening and trends monitoring I love using Sprinklr — I compared countless other applications, but with Sprinklr you can get to know your existing customers — and prospective ones. And without insights into your customers' demands, your business model is useless.

For keeping track and notes I use Evernote — this cloud solution is also great to store research papers I need for my work and my AI projects.

For my creative AI projects I prefer Artbreeder and RunwayML (for visuals), GPT-3 Playground by OpenAI (for textual experiments), and Jukebox by OpenAI (for AI-created music) as well. These apps and solutions are what I cannot live without.

Alexander: *Do you have a smart productivity hack or work-related shortcut?*

Vladimir: In pauses between my work, I play around with creative AI solutions like Artbreeder (see above) and GPT-3. It inspires and brings me to new ideas. Or I take a short walk in the forest (which boosts my productivity enormously).

Alexander: *What is the best advice you have ever received?*

Vladimir: Take a meta-perspective; get the big picture. But don't forget about the details.

Key Takeaways

- Observe, adapt, and act are the three crucial steps to handle the digital shift, with a paradigm change in every single area. Also compare and analyze existing and new approaches.
- GPT-3 is a language model that is pre-trained on 570 GB of text and running with 175 billion parameters; this model can write congenial texts, emulate style and genre, code, and run as a chatbot without programming. You can imagine this framework as a digital instance that is taught on mankind's cultural heritage and knowledge and that can produce content about almost everything.
- AI will reshape the workforce landscape. Old job descriptions will be abandoned; new professional roles will emerge. The popular fear of employees, losing their jobs, is based on their misconceptions about AI — and also on their leaders' misconceptions about AI. Artificial intelligence shouldn't replace people; it should support them.

Endnotes

i Website of Vladimir Alexeev's magazine, *Merzazine*: `https://medium.com/merzazine`.

ii *Non progredi est regredi* is a latin proverb and can be translated as "not to go forward is to go back."

iii Self-attention mechanisms have found broad application in all kinds of natural language processing (NLP) tasks based on deep learning. In 2017, Google's machine translation team used self-attention mechanisms heavily to learn text representation in the paper "Attention is All You Need," by Vaswani, A., Shazeer, N., Parmar, N., Uszkoreit, J., Jones, L., Gomez, A.N., Kaiser, L. and Polosukhin, I., 2017. arXiv preprint arXiv:1706.03762.

Process Automation, Blockchain, and the Internet of Things (IoT)

Part VI

Chapter 23
Derek Roos: Fully Leveraging Your Human Capital

Derek Roos, cofounder and CEO, Mendix
Source: Derek Roos

Derek is the cofounder and CEO of Mendix, the leading low-code application platform, which allows anyone to make applications to digitalize their business. Roos founded Mendix while still in college and has built it up into a global force with more than 1,200 team members and more than 1,000 customers. Mendix was acquired by Siemens AG for $730 million in cash in 2018, and Roos continues to lead the business as its CEO.

Alexander: You are cofounder and CEO at Mendix. How did you come up with the idea for Mendix? What is your mission?

Derek: When I was in business school, I felt constrained and frustrated by business organizations' inability to create business apps quickly. I was working at an IT-services business while I was a student at Erasmus University in Rotterdam. I would be brought in to do some of the grunt work to help initiate a project and wonder, "What if we could visualize the solution to the business application problem and then just push a button to make it happen?" I was training to become a consultant, and it never felt right for me that it was so hard to create applications.

One of my cofounders, Derckjan Kruit, who also worked at the company, shared my vision for wanting to create this "easy" button solution to building business application software. So with a clear vision to create a platform that allowed everyone to make great business applications quickly and easily, we both quit our jobs before we graduated. Our company's mission is to enable anyone to just "go make it" and bring their best ideas to life with software.

Alexander: That is an amazing journey. When you started, what vision did you foresee for your company?

Derek: When we started out, we knew we were solving a big problem, but we never imagined we'd end up creating a multibillion-dollar software category. Remember that back when we founded Mendix, it was a mere one year later that AWS was created and less than two years before the first iPhone was launched. So, very few people truly understood how much business disruption and opportunity would be created by technology in the subsequent 15 years.

We have always been focused on three things: we always knew our North Star was democratizing software development —

speeding up software development by an order of magnitude so anyone could create business applications without needing to code. We understood that helping our customers be successful with the approach we were evangelizing was foundational to convincing the world. And we knew we needed to build a great team and culture to achieve our vision. Every decision we've made through the years has been grounded in these three principles — democratization of software development, customer success, and company culture.

Alexander: Why do so many companies struggle to digitalize quickly and leverage new technologies successfully?

Derek: Most people make the mistake of thinking that digitalization is about hiring enough smart, technically proficient people. What they miss is that even the smartest people can't bust through the traditional organizational structures and processes of working that have been in place for years or decades in companies. These old ways of operating across departments and teams were just not set up to take full advantage of everything available now. CEOs have to break down these organizational silos and change how people collaborate across departments, so ideas from across the enterprise can be translated into digital products and experiences 10 times faster. The days of waiting months and years for IT to bring new applications to market are gone. The ability to deliver engaging digital experiences quickly through accelerated software development has become table stakes, because today anyone with an Internet connection and a credit card can build a business that competes with yours. So you have to change how your enterprise does everything, and that requires a completely different mindset.

Alexander: How did you see companies responding to their digitalization agenda due to the COVID-19 pandemic?

Derek: The COVID-19 pandemic forced all institutions to implement many years of change in less than 12 months. Every organization, whether it's a local city government, a large hospital, or an established for-profit enterprise, had to reevaluate how they did everything and how they could continue operating when physical interactions were constrained. For example, utility companies had to figure out a way to continue collecting customer payments without in-person interactions. Local governments had to figure out how to get aid to people in need quickly without using paper-based processes. Everyone had to find ways to remotely provision technology for their teams to continue working outside the physical office. Small businesses had to figure out how to execute all their processes digitally. I can go on with more examples, but you get the point — over a course of months, every single business on our planet was forced to reevaluate the role technology played in its operation and respond in ways that normally would've taken them years.

We've seen some great outcomes of what's possible with digitalization. In the City of San Antonio, which is the seventh largest city in the United States, the Neighborhood and Housing Services Department saw applications for aid jump from 57 per week to more than 2,000 per week. Traditionally, applications were submitted in person, and caseworkers contacted each individual to validate their information — steps that became near impossible during the global pandemic. With $14 million to disperse and applicants waiting to receive aid, the city needed to quickly digitalize this system. City officials passed an emergency amendment to secure funds for a cloud-based replacement tool, and in just 12 days they built and launched a new application that processed over 1,000 requests in its first day live. Now, residents have a centralized system to upload their documentation, making the validation process easier for employees and providing greater visibility for both parties at every turn. Requests that previously took one month to process now take only one week, getting residents the immediate help they need to pay for housing and other critical expenses. So you can see how a positive change happened at the City of San Antonio that normally would've taken them a lot longer in normal conditions. We've seen countless such examples across all our customers.

Alexander: *How should business models evolve to survive and thrive in an increasingly digital world?*

Derek: We often hear the cliché that change is the only constant, but that does a poor job of capturing the opportunities facing business leaders today. The real challenge that CEOs have to get their arms around is not the pace of technological change but its complexity.

Technological advancements are happening at such a pace now that it is impossible to compete using the tired old approaches of just hiring more developers. First, every company is going to need many more software developers, and the world just isn't producing enough of them. Even if you find enough software development talent, you'd then have to convince them to work for you and not at Google, Facebook, Microsoft, or Tesla, which are all superbly run companies and very attractive for developers everywhere. Then, if you could solve both these challenges, the technological changes are coming so rapidly. How would you keep your entire development team on the cutting edge so they could harness this complexity whenever they needed it: AI, multiexperience, data integration, multicloud, automation, UX design, governance and security, and so much more. Finally, what about all the other people in your company who can't leverage the power of all these great technologies because they can't code? These are the people who understand how your business really works — your domain experts — the people placing customer orders, talking to your suppliers, helping solve customer support issues and claims. This last group of people are actually the ones who understand which business changes will have the biggest impact on your business results, and CEOs must find a way to harness the expertise of this group to thrive in an increasingly digital world.

Alexander: Which technologies or digital capabilities are essential for a digital strategy?

Derek: Most large companies will fail not because they didn't build software fast enough; they will fail because they didn't build the right software fast enough. And that almost always happens because businesses struggle to bring their functional and domain experts into their software development processes. This is the little secret of traditional approaches to software development that Derckjan and I were fortunate to understand very early on. We realized that old ways of working keep these domain experts very far away from the software development teams in IT, so companies are always building applications that miss the mark — it's the nature of the game of telephone that's played in translating business needs into software requirements through multiple organizational handoffs.

The companies that will thrive in a digital world will not only figure out a way to make these domain experts part of their software development processes, they will also enable all this human capital to build software themselves, without any need to learn coding.

The companies that will thrive in a digital world will not only figure out a way to make these domain experts part of their software development processes, they will also enable all this human capital to build software themselves, without any need to learn coding. They'll make it easy for them to consume whatever data they need in building these apps, whenever they need it. No coding required. And they'll make it easy for them to consume all the great new technologies like AI, multi-experience, and cloud, so they can digitalize their everyday business processes and interactions quickly and easily. No coding needed.

The companies that figure out a way to harness their full human capital are the ones that will digitalize the fastest, and get smarter, better, and stronger.

Alexander: *Is there a scenario where everyone can access and enhance process automation? Would low-code solutions help here?*

Derek: At their core, low-code platforms help companies create and execute new ways of operating using software as the foundation of those improvements. We all agree that our future is digital — digital products, digital experiences, digital interactions — the way the digital enterprise will come to life is through digitalized processes. There are just never going to be enough developers in the world to do it all, so we're going to need to enable people who don't know how to code to create software applications and do it quickly and well.

This is precisely where low-code platforms come in. Their visual design approach to application development, deployment, and management is the very approach that allows anyone to build applications to digitalize their work environment. Low-code platforms will democratize process automation through software development by improving the following aspects for every person in the enterprise:

- **Discoverability**: It must be easy for everyone to find and consume the data and capabilities necessary to compose experiences.
- **Availability**: To build the best solution, your people require the broadest array of capabilities available to them on demand while they work.
- **Coherence**: Users expect that experiences will be consistent across touchpoints. In addition, they will increasingly use multiple modalities together.
- **Flexibility**: Connections between systems, services, and touchpoints need to be easy to establish and readily changed without significant effort or rework.
- **Ubiquity**: It must be possible to deploy touchpoints and capabilities across clouds, on premises, at the edge, and around the world.

Alexander: What can CEOs and their leaders do to help their companies and teams digitalize faster?
Derek: There are three conditions necessary for real digitalization: the ability for anyone to build and deploy software applications quickly, the ability for everyone to easily access the data they need to make decisions when they need it, and finally, the ability to easily incorporate the right technology for the problem they are trying to solve. Once you have these three conditions in place for your organization, there's really no process you cannot digitalize and ultimately automate. First, however, CEOs and CIOs must create an environment where the full creativity of their human capital can be unleashed using technology and proper governance approaches.

Alexander: How does process automation benefit from cloud computing?

Derek: Cloud computing has massively reduced the time to market for everything we do. Fifteen years ago, if you were running a business, you'd have to constantly think about acquiring hardware, software, and technical talent to help you grow. Similarly, everything else you did would just take a lot longer — creating and launching new products, servicing your customers, hiring and onboarding new team members, processing payroll, and executing critical administrative and legal tasks. Every process required many touches from many people and took a lot of time. And then as your business grew bigger and more complex, it got progressively harder to make changes — everything would have to go through slow, cross-department, and cross-region decision-making processes, many of which were still paper-based or run on old applications and systems that very few people could operate.

Cloud computing has turned all of this on its head. Whether you want to test a new digital product, sell to a new customer segment or geography, or process payments and contracts, cloud computing now enables anyone with the know-how to use technology to do this very quickly. Once you enable the three conditions I described earlier, the possibilities for process automation and eventually autonomous operation, which is the next frontier of innovation, are truly spectacular.

Alexander: Thank you, Derek. What quick-win advice would you give that is easy for many companies to apply within their digital strategies?

Derek: Empower your people. In most organizations there is no shortage of ideas; the challenge is there is no place to bring them to. IT is too busy, and business teams don't have the tools, budget, or freedom to operate. In our experience, amazing things can happen when people are given the chance. And it doesn't always have to be some game-changing new product or business idea, the sum of many little things can make a big difference. It's really about speed, agility, and leveraging the combined power of your workforce.

Key Takeaways

- Empowering all your people to translate their ideas into software-driven business solutions is the key to digital transformation.
- CEOs and their teams must learn to manage technical complexity so their whole workforce can leverage the full power of the latest technical innovations; to do that, they're going to have to adopt platforms that enable their whole organization to build, deploy, and manage software solutions without needing to code.
- The companies that can figure out a way to help their teams easily consume and quickly deploy the latest technologies will ride the crest of the digitalization wave we're experiencing.

Chapter 24
André Rabold: How Digital Culture and IoT Disrupt Our Future

André Rabold, venture CTO, BCG Digital Ventures
Source: BCG Digital Ventures

André is a technologist and executive deeply rooted in software engineering. BCG Digital Ventures (DV) is the corporate innovation and digital business–building arm of Boston Consulting Group. Before joining BCG Digital Ventures, André was a director at Nero AG and cofounded his own startup, building an AI chatbot and voice marketing platform for the music and entertainment industry.

In recent experience André launched an IoT healthcare product for the elderly in the United Kingdom, a digital payments company in Mexico, a portfolio of IoT-based applications for international tanker ships, and an artificial intelligence platform that aims to disrupt the $350 billion customer call-center industry.

Alexander: You are venture CTO at BCG Digital Ventures. What is your mission?

André: Here at BCG Digital Ventures we strive to be the best in class as the world's most sought-after innovators and business builders. The core value that resonates the most with me is delivering impact over words. Our mission is to invent, build, and scale industry-disrupting businesses with the world's most influential companies.

Alexander: How should business models evolve to survive and thrive in an increasingly digital world?

André: The pace of change is ever increasing, which requires us to build increasingly sophisticated analytics and processing tool chains in order to adapt and respond to new requirements and to maximize opportunities. One important aspect of my work as part of a venture team is to exploit those opportunities and grow existing businesses both vertically and horizontally.

As part of our business build methodology at DV we are ideating around our clients' existing portfolios of products and services to surface new opportunities. Look at your customer journey, value chain, or supply chain where data and physical assets exist along the path; consider the frictions you and your customers are experiencing; and then focus your ideation on how to use those assets for digital innovation. Deep tech, such as machine intelligence and IoT, unlocks new possibilities for all kinds of businesses, including traditionally more low-tech segments like healthcare, finance, and agriculture.

Alexander: How can technology shift the roles and responsibilities of the workforce?

André: At a macro level, technology was always one of the key drivers in transforming the nature of the work we do. In the last 40 years we've gradually seen consumers and enterprises conduct a growing amount of their lives and businesses online. The COVID-19 pandemic has accelerated digitalization, with many businesses embracing a new digital culture literally overnight, shifting from brick-and-mortar retail to online marketplaces, replacing in-person meetings with video calls, and enabling partial or permanent home-office work for many of their employees. With these changes also came new priorities for many vendors, with a new focus on improving the security and experience of remote work, improving data protection, and supporting supply chain continuity.

> *The COVID-19 pandemic has accelerated digitalization, with many businesses embracing a new digital culture literally overnight.*

In recent years we have seen major shifts in the role of technology from being a cost center to becoming a revenue generator and from service delivery to value delivery. That means that the value that technology teams create in a company is changing as they move from service department or operator to business co-creator. IT needs to become a part of the innovation and a driver of change, positioning the business for the future.

Enterprises need to aggressively adopt digital sales tools and integrate processes across the entire go-to-market organization. If they do not already have a digital demand center in place to track sales leads centrally and coordinate the handoff of those leads between marketing and sales, then they should create one immediately. They must also invest in digital tools to create visibility into activities and outcomes across all levels of the sales funnel to avoid any leads or opportunities falling through the cracks.

Alexander: Which technology or digital capabilities are essential for a digital strategy?

André: Digitalization and the digital transformation affect all business sectors. While digitally native companies understand technology not only as a means to an end but as the essential fiber of their businesses, others just start to figure out what digitalization means for them. In my work with BCG Digital Ventures, we help more traditional industries like manufacturing, mining, oil and gas, and utilities to reinvent themselves and to reboot and rewire their businesses from the inside out.

Establishing a successful digital strategy requires that we first build a new culture of change and embrace what we call deep tech, a set of technologies stemming from recent scientific discoveries or engineering innovation. Technologies such as artificial intelligence, IoT, decentralization, and augmented and virtual reality have the potential to enable new products and business, create differentiation, and catalyze change.

However, technology in isolation does not drive commercial value. In practice, business value is derived from a mix of pioneering, commoditized, and sometimes legacy tech. Therefore, it is crucial to look at the whole value chain of an enterprise to truly unlock all of its potential.

Alexander: How do you establish a culture of change?

André: The primary way to activate any kind of culture is through leaders. But you cannot just mandate a new culture; it requires a movement. Studies have shown that 90 percent of all the people who have had heart bypass surgery after two years have gone back to the exact same lifestyle they had before the surgery. So, even when faced with the most dire outcome, most people are unable to change their behavior. Change is hard.

Sustainable change is only possible by changing the organizational environment to continuously reinforce what you activated. An innovation strategy is a plan used to encourage advancements in technology or services. Without such an innovation strategy, different parts of an organization can easily wind up pursuing conflicting priorities, like marketing seeing an opportunity in selling companion products, the sales reps getting demands from their biggest customers, and business units focusing on their P&L.

Alexander: *Change is impossible without the right tools. What are the core components of your change initiatives?*

André: To drive change, we ask three basic questions:

- What does great look like? Define the three to four actionable behaviors that matter most. Most adults can only remember five to nine items in the short term, so keep things focused and concise.
- How do we make it real? Introduce new leader behaviors, build leader capabilities and accountability, and embed them into daily routines. Embedding learning in routines makes it easier to retain, while activating leaders ensures that the desired culture isn't being perceived as just words on a page.
- How do we make it stick? Harmonize and transform ways of working to reinforce target behaviors. This also includes training your employees.

Alexander: *How do you make sure that your change initiatives will also improve the employee experience?*

André: Articulating behavior is important, as it establishes clarity and provides helpful guidance to your employees. Clarity creates a good feeling, whereas uncertainty often triggers threat response. Be open and be transparent in what you are doing and how you plan on doing it.

Once that is established, led by example, ensure the lines of communication are always open, and establish accountability in the team. A successful company culture drives employee engagement, productivity, and satisfaction. Gallup, for example, has shown that 73 percent of disengaged employees are actively seeking a new job, compared with only 37 percent of engaged ones.

Alexander: *What are the main lessons you have learned when you established a culture of change for the incubator?*

André: Change never comes easy, and there is always a proportional amount of counterpressure trying to keep things in place and as they are. Be especially careful looking for quick wins, as they might actually hinder your long-term success. A strategy is nothing more than a set of policies or behaviors aimed at achieving a specific goal. Companies regularly define their overall business strategy and specify how marketing, finance, R&D, and operations will support it. However, only a few are also aligning their innovation efforts with their business strategies.

Alexander: How does the culture of change fit into BCG Digital Ventures' digital strategy?

André: Ultimately BCG believes that strengthening leadership and culture consistently drives measurable business results. Studies have repeatedly shown that companies with a clearly defined and lived culture always outperform their peers.

When building a new venture, we always start with the culture, perform team norming, and set up daily and weekly routines. This is the foundation for achieving our desired performance and establishes a strong bond between our own team members as well as the client embedded in the venture. Culture is truly the foundation on which we build new ventures for success.

Alexander: How do you see digital strategies evolving with the maturity of big data processing and AI? How do you prepare for an AI-centric ecosystem as a business leader?

André: Most businesses are not born digital. Their traditional mindsets and ways of working often run counter to those needed for AI.

The artificial intelligence expert and consultant Anand Rao describes three stages of AI implementation: the first one he calls assisted intelligence, and it describes companies harnessing the power of the cloud and big data programs to make data-driven business decisions. The second stage, augmented intelligence, introduces machine learning algorithms layered on top of the existing information management systems to augment human analytical competencies and allow them to do things they couldn't otherwise do. The third stage Rao calls autonomous intelligence, in which

machines can truly act on their own without human supervision —
like a driverless car being able to master completely unknown roads
and situations.

Today, many companies are still struggling even to achieve stage
1 of this model. The ones at the vanguard of AI are actively working
on stage 2, with stage 3 still being quite far out in the future for most.

*Alexander: How do you face data privacy and data governance
concerns when you pitch new ideas?*

André: Working with international enterprises, data privacy
is one of our core concerns when we start new ventures. Besides
following strict security protocols and best standards, I see three
important tools to address privacy concerns:

- Establishing clear accountability of who owns data and who
  is responsible for ensuring its privacy. In many companies this
  defaults to the IT department instead of the business department, where it belongs.
- Having a data inventory tracking what data is stored where.
  With many distributed systems, cloud services and third-party
  providers working together, it is important to understand where
  your PII (personally identifiable information) gets distributed.
- Automation enables organizations to better respond to consumers' requests, such as for an accounting of their data as required
  under the European Union's General Data Protection Regulation
  (GDPR), for example.

When it comes to data itself, for example, when processing user
behavior using machine learning algorithms, another helpful tool
is anonymization — the removal of personally identifiable information from your records to create anonymous data that can still be
used for analysis and training of models.

*Alexander: Let's focus on your experience in IoT (Internet of
Things). What is IoT, and how does it work?*

André: IoT has become an umbrella term for anything that
is connected to the Internet. The basic idea is to connect physical
devices (things) with each other to derive new insights and to unlock

new values. We essentially add software and network connectivity to previously dumb sensors and machinery. This can unlock tremendous value by turning what used to be hardware problems into software problems. Software can be iterated much quicker than hardware, further accelerating the speed of innovation.

IoT sits also at the heart of what we call deep tech, the generic term for technologies at the frontier of science that include artificial intelligence, robotics, blockchain, advanced material science, augmented and virtual reality, quantum computing, and biotech.

Alexander: Which IoT use cases would you see as essential to contribute to any organization's digital strategy?

André: A mistake many companies make when they first start to design their digital strategy is to declare a technical goal — "We need IoT" — without understanding what that actually should mean. IoT in itself is not a digital strategy, but it can help you build one. It is important to take a step back and look at the whole value chain of a company to unlock the true potential. Only then can IoT unlock new sources of value, such as new revenue streams, customer intimacy, and improved experiences. Synergistic combinations with other advanced technologies including AI and blockchain are further pushing the envelope and enabling completely new use cases and business models.

So, while I don't see a single specific use case that works for all, I would start evaluating the assets you already have today: what do you already do, make, or sell? Then try to figure out how digitalization could improve your existing value chain. The next step is to grow the number of use cases. Many companies become frustrated when they see their first IoT project not get the traction they expected. The trick is to climb the learning curve with multiple use cases to figure out what sticks. Lastly, deriving real business gains from IoT efforts ultimately will require changes to business processes. Connecting machinery to the Internet, for example, will allow a manufacturer to produce more effectively or reduce maintenance costs. However, if the surrounding business processes aren't modified and optimized as well, then value won't be maximized.

Alexander: *Which further IoT use cases would be made possible by a tighter data integration?*

André: The most interesting use cases in IoT evolve around threading previously unconnected domains. Car manufacturer VW, for example, has installed sensors in its cars that automatically collect and send reliable weather data to TenneT, a European power grid operator, for load optimization in real time. This is a fascinating example of the integration of data and connectivity leading to completely new and unexpected use cases.

Alexander: *How do IoT and data integration benefit from cloud computing?*

André: Data sits in the center of this new deep tech world. Whether we're talking about IoT, machine intelligence, augmented and virtual reality, or decentralization, they all rely on data to function. Vast amounts of raw and tagged data are necessary to tackle most modern problems. The cloud provides us with the necessary infrastructure to support this process. It provides the storage, scalability, and computing power needed to analyze all the data we're collecting.

In addition, the cloud provides us means to augment data we are collecting ourselves with data from third parties. For example, you could combine real-time data from your warehouses with demand-forecasting data from sources such as the BCG's Lighthouse platform to optimize your logistics. This combination of data sources will result in something that's much greater than the sum of its parts.

Alexander: *How do you generate data-driven insights from IoT? Do you apply AI?*

André: There are a handful of basic ways every company can profit from IoT right away:

- Better understand your customers.
- Make more educated decisions.
- Create new customer value propositions.
- Improve and optimize operations.
- Improve the value of a business through data.

Not all of them require bleeding-edge machine-learning algorithms. Simply surfacing the data using standard business intelligence tools is still often enough to give you a winning edge over your competitors.

AI has two main use cases in those scenarios: we can use it to identify patterns in otherwise chaotic-looking data, for example, predictive maintenance of machinery or computer-aided diagnosis systems for healthcare. And we can use it to automate tasks that usually require human intervention or review, such as using computer vision or speech recognition. Similar to IoT, AI doesn't have much value on its own but is just another tool to achieve such value.

Alexander: *Is there a scenario where everyone can access and enhance IoT? Would low-code solutions help here?*

André: We're already on a good path. Open source has played an important role in the recent advance of IoT hardware and software. In fact, the big three cloud computing providers, Google, Amazon, and Microsoft, have all released their IoT platforms as open source solutions. This allows anybody to start building connected systems with very minimal up-front investment and encourages experimentation. Interconnectivity between devices and systems is high, as they need a central gateway to connect all devices and sensors using the same protocol.

The next evolutionary step is to replace custom implementations, which usually would require a team of IoT engineers to develop, with reusable building blocks that can be plugged together seamlessly and with minimal effort. We now see the advent of low-code platforms like Mendix[i] that let you build IoT prototypes in just a few days by reducing the complexity of combining sensors, cloud service APIs, databases, and user interfaces.

Other developments are, for example, the factory of the future, which is revolutionizing manufacturing and is already dubbed the fourth industrial revolution. As companies work to get products to market quicker and cheaper, simple solutions are needed to enable near-immediate implementation — with no special tools or highly trained engineers or electricians required. So-called plug-and-produce components are making manufacturing more affordable and becoming a direct threat to low-wage countries like China.

Alexander: What types of professional roles will we see evolve alongside the development and increasing use of IoT across the industries?

André: Software engineers, cloud computing experts, and product managers are the key roles for companies seeking to roll out new products and services. With the advance of IoT and big data the demand for data scientists and data architects is increasing rapidly as well. An often-overlooked role is the security team, which is needed to ensure the safeguarding of your customer data and intellectual property.

The biggest challenge for traditional enterprises is attracting enough talent, as they suddenly compete with employers such as Amazon, Apple, Google (Alphabet), Microsoft, and Facebook. To succeed, you have to apply all of what we've already discussed in this interview: transform your corporate culture, foster intrapreneurship and a digital mindset amongst your existing talent, reinvent your hiring process, and create a value proposition that resonates with digital employees.

Alexander: What projects would you consider are at the forefront of IoT to support digital transformation? How can deep learning fill the gap?

André: An interesting area to keep an eye on is machine-to-machine (M2M) communication and how it replaces more centralized approaches to IoT in the future. Today's IoT infrastructure usually connects separate individual devices to a centralized service in the cloud that processes and orchestrates all incoming data. With M2M communication we don't have such a central point anymore, but the devices start talking directly to each other in a decentralized, more autonomous way. This can drastically increase efficiency and automation capabilities while simultaneously reducing data transfer and storage needs and improving security and robustness.

Another interesting development is the integration of machine intelligence, specifically deep learning, directly into IoT networks. The exponential explosion in the amount of data generated by IoT devices and sensors is making it difficult to transfer unfiltered raw information in real time over the network and impossible to analyze and label that information by hand. Instead, we're now building advanced neural networks directly on the edge, on the devices themselves, that are able to learn mostly unsupervised and improve their capabilities over time without human intervention.

Alexander: In 10 years from now, how do you think our life will have changed because of IoT applied in medtech and healthcare?

André: The obvious potentials of IoT in the healthcare sector are similar to other industries. Specifically they include:

- Cost reduction using real-time monitoring of patients to avoid unnecessary exams and doctor visits.
- Faster and improved treatment due to evidence-based informed decisions. This can even go as far as proactive medical treatment.
- Optimized drug management and equipment procurement using data generated through IoT devices to reduce waste and costs.

However, IoT in our everyday lives opens up the door for a myriad of use cases we don't even think about yet. In a recent study by the University of California San Francisco (UCSF) the Oura smart ring, with its built-in sensors originally designed for sleep tracking, has shown a potential for detecting the wearer's health conditions and illnesses, even otherwise asymptomatic COVID-19 infections. In a recent project in which I was involved, we used ordinary off-the-shelf sensors and smart plugs and repurposed them to monitor elderly people in their homes, help them follow their routines, and allow them to be more self-reliant. The central goal of the solution was to provide continuous reassurance to caretakers and family that the cared-for person was alright.

A large area of growth is exactly in this smart-care space. In the future we will have an increasing number of devices that constantly track our whereabouts, vitals, and overall health. This will allow patients to remain at home, eliminating travel time and reducing hospital costs. Smart sensors will provide real-time information to the caregiver and ensure that patients comply with medical advice; prediction algorithms will alert of potential risks. This will also open up new business models and opportunities for the healthcare industry and insurers. Using this vast amount of data that has never been available in this level of detail before, we can potentially shorten the development time and costs of new medication and treatments significantly while simultaneously improving their quality and reliability. Or imagine getting a monthly discount on your insurance premium by simply wearing a smartwatch every day. In fact, that's not even something new, and using smart gadgets for monitoring and tracking is becoming quite common in the car and home insurance industry already.

Alexander: Thank you, André. What quick-win advice would you give that is easy for many companies to apply within their digital strategies?

André: It is crucial to be open and very transparent about what is happening, why you want things to change, and how you plan to achieve it. Focusing on a few incremental steps works better than trying to change everything at once. So I recommend picking the two or three behavior shifts that promise the greatest impact first and then build upon those using the tools described before.

Alexander: What are your favorite apps, tools, or software that you can't live without?

André: Teams, Zoom, and Slack have been irreplaceable during the pandemic for obvious reasons. I really like to use Trello for structuring and organizing the team's tasks and Zapier to automate common or repetitive workflows and connect different tools together.

Alexander: Do you have a smart productivity hack or work-related shortcut?

André: I'm a morning person, and I learned that the most effective use of my time isn't trying to do everything in the morning, which would generally be perceived as my most productive period of the day. Instead, the trick is to manage when to spend time on what. Turns out I am, like most other morning people, most productive doing analytical tasks that require concentration and focus in the morning, while doing my creative work in the afternoon.

Alexander: What is the best advice you have ever received?

André: I know it sounds like a cliché, but you should always try to surround yourself with people who are smarter than you. If you know all the answers and you're not getting challenged by your peers, then you're not getting better. Standing still is taking a step back.

Key Takeaways

- In recent years we have seen major shifts in the role of technology from being a cost center to becoming a revenue generator and from service delivery to value delivery. IT needs to become a part of the innovation and a driver of change, positioning the business for the future.
- We see the advent of low-code platforms that let you build IoT prototypes in just a few days by reducing the complexity of combining sensors, cloud service APIs, databases, and user interfaces.
- To succeed, you have to transform your corporate culture, foster intrapreneurship and a digital mindset amongst your existing talent, reinvent your hiring process, and create a value proposition that resonates with digital employees.

Endnote

i   Low-code platform Mendix has been acquired by Siemens, which develops IoT (Internet of Things) and IoMT (Internet of Medical Things) via Siemens Healthineers technology. See also chapter 23 for the interview with Derek Roos, cofounder and CEO of Mendix.

Chapter 25
Ian Choo: The Distributed Ledger Revolution

Ian Choo, founder and managing partner, Ekofolio
Source: Ian Choo

Ian is the founder and managing partner of Ekofolio, a Luxembourg-based mission-driven fintech company catalyzing investment in forests by making them tradeable and more liquid. He is passionate about enabling systemically important projects that accelerate meaningful transformations for industries and people. Ian started his career in consulting and has served as a cofounder, board member, and advisor to numerous entrepreneurial ventures — including Power-Blox Africa and the Nordic Blockchain Association. He is a speaker at many global entrepreneurship and technology conferences and has taught at top business schools in Denmark. Above all, he feels a deep duty to leave the world better than it was when he found it and develop the next generation while doing it.

Ian holds an MSc in global politics from the London School of Economics (LSE) and has attended IESE Business School and Harvard Business School.

Alexander: *You are founder and CEO at Ekofolio. What is your mission?*

Ian: At Ekofolio, we have made it our mission to catalyze investment in forests by making them tradeable and liquid. We believe that this is the next necessary frontier of financial innovation, and financing nature is clearly something that we will have to get right if we as a civilization are going to continue to exist and thrive in the era of real-time climate change.

Alexander: *How should business models evolve to survive and thrive in an increasingly digital world?*

Ian: Most traditional economic and management theory is rooted in the customer — and the customer's needs, which change and evolve with the times. "The purpose of business is to create and keep a customer," as Peter Drucker has said. While this seems simple, it probably is not simplistic; often customers are not really able to readily articulate what their needs are, and there's a lot of inference and reading between the lines. I think this is especially true in the context of an increasingly digital world — technologies are only interesting and relevant if they serve (or help discover) the emerging needs of customers.

In the context of an increasingly digital world — technologies are only interesting and relevant if they serve (or help discover) the emerging needs of customers.

Alexander: *How can technology shift the roles and responsibilities of the workforce?*

Ian: The current era of technology is continuing the trajectory and effects of technology since the industrial revolution — the substitution of human labor in the production process. Many times before we have heard that "this time it's different," that human beings are done for — and that machines would do all the work, in the process breaking down our system. But somehow human beings have always found new work for themselves — work that is more sophisticated, less routine, or more human (for example, healthcare and nursing, which both need a human touch to be done well).

In the era of digitalization many people see a divide between knowledge workers, who may be thought of as working with their brains, and service workers, who may be thought of as working with their hands. In reality, trades and professions exist along a continuum, and technology both obliges workers to learn new skills and provides them with opportunities to acquire and apply knowledge in emerging fields that fit their values and give them joy.

Pick a worthy problem that the world has, dedicate your life to solving it. If it is really that big of a problem, there is a business model that will be found somewhere along the way.

Alexander: *Which technology or digital capabilities are essential for a digital strategy?*

Ian: I personally work with blockchain and other digital ledger technologies (DLTs), and though I'm clearly biased, I think it's one of the most exciting areas to be happening to industry and humanity at the moment. Blockchain is a term that describes the structure of the way data is packed, but distributed ledger technology better describes its function. I prefer the latter description, because it tends to help people better understand how to use it. Many DLTs on a technical level are considered to be protocols, which function a bit more like public utilities than software in the way we have come to understand it, with nice user interfaces.

DLTs are essentially tools to help individuals and organizations (I make a distinction, because they're relevant in different ways for both) keep accounting at the market level. Traditional accounting has always been at the firm or individual level, and we get intermediaries like auditors to verify whether the information presented is representative of reality. DLTs really give large numbers of people the ability to keep accounting of a broad array of things from goods, money, entitlements, and ownership at a market rather than firm level, built in a way that objectively shows the history since the beginning, and having effective mechanisms to prevent tampering or cheating. While accounting at the market level is probably easiest to conceive of when we are thinking of financial use cases, I think there really is a whole world of other things that would benefit from this new approach. I would say this development is really exciting for society, because in the tradition of the Internet itself, it is an invitation for firms and individuals to reimagine boundaries. Boundaries between actors on the value chain, between industries, even better between firms and their customers. The emergence of the social commons if you will.

Alexander: Blockchain was invented by a person (or group) using the name Satoshi Nakamoto in 2008 to serve as the public transaction ledger of the cryptocurrency bitcoin. What are the most important learnings resulting from the operation of this large blockchain?

Ian: Like the Internet itself, the original bitcoin experiment was set up by Satoshi as a social and economic experiment with clear technological and ideological objectives. This was covered succinctly in the now classic bitcoin white paper.[i] The objectives were to be able to run a system of exchange that was free of the control of any centralized actors like banks or governments and to have that system guaranteed by some clever computer code that is transparent and freely available to everyone within the system. It was set up to be decentralized, trustless, and disintermediated — three big and intimidating words that require some explanation:

- Decentralized really means that no single actor is in charge because it is running on many computers all at once. This is really done for resilience so that the system has no single point of failure. If someone didn't like it, it would be almost impossible to shut down in totality. Yet, all these computers would generate a single version of truth, called the *consensus*, which was data packed into blocks in the form of a chain.
- Trustless is really related to the next term, disintermediated.
- Disintermediated means that all systems of exchange up to this point in history have relied on a network of intermediaries to function properly. These intermediaries traditionally include banks, brokers, clearinghouses, auditors, and so on. If you did not trust that you would find your money again sometime in the future, it is quite likely that you would not leave your money with your bank. If you do not trust that your supplier would do what is promised, it's quite unlikely you would continue doing business.

The reason that bitcoin (and essentially, the bitcoin blockchain) was a revolution was that for the first time in history — if you knew how the technology worked and trusted the workings of the system itself — you would not have to trust any single other counterparty in the system to use it. Simply put, the system itself, blockchain, is the protection against what people call *counterparty risk*. The system itself does not require intermediaries to function, so you don't have to worry that your bank may collapse from reckless behavior or that your broker might run away with your money in the middle of a transaction, because neither the bank nor the broker is required. The blockchain system itself, through its architecture and clever code, performs all their functions and ensures that if you intend to send a bitcoin to another address, it gets there directly and automatically.

The ever-rising price of bitcoin, which is clearly an endorsement of growing confidence in the underlying technology, is a clear endorsement that an ever-growing number of people want a system of exchange that is free of many of the risks that are inherent to centralized systems that came before. It's only partially a commentary on their confidence in government, central banks, and fiat money. People want an alternative to do what human beings have needed to do since they started living in small hunter-gatherer communities, to exchange goods and services of value with each other at will without too many intermediaries getting involved.

Alexander: How can the shortcomings of the bitcoin blockchain, such as the high energy consumption or privacy concerns of the public ledger, be overcome?

Ian: It is important to touch on some important subtleties of DLTs. The bitcoin blockchain, along with what is termed *second-generation blockchains*, are built on a system called *proof of work* (POW). POW is really a means of creating artificial scarcity, because the binary ones and zeros in computer systems are inherently able to be copied and pasted many times; they are not scarce. POW creates this scarcity by setting up mathematical puzzles for miners (who supply the network with computing resources, called *hash power*) that are difficult to solve and require a lot of computing power and energy. The prize for solving these puzzles is that the winner gets the next bitcoin, which is now scarce and valuable. This is the work, not unlike the process of physical mining, that requires a lot of human labor. There will only be 21 million bitcoins ever mined, and these mathematical puzzles get more and more difficult by design as we get closer and closer to the terminal 21 million bitcoins that will ever come into existence.

The thing to note under POW is that the majority of the energy required to run the network is divided between mining and hashing. Mining is designed to be wasteful of energy to ensure scarcity, and beyond that function it is actually pretty pointless and unnecessary. By comparison, hashing, the process of packing information into blocks, uses a tiny fraction of the energy that mining uses. But this is a problem that is clearly particular to the bitcoin blockchain and will go away in future.

The third generation blockchains are increasingly being built on fundamentally different mechanisms for ensuring scarcity, packing information, and, overall, securing the network. These include proof of stake (POS) and what are known as other consensus algorithms, which are far more scalable and energy efficient to run, whilst achieving better results for the network. Many of them are already fully functional and available on the market as we speak.

Alexander: There has been a lot of talk about applying blockchain and other DLTs to a wide array of use cases, including many outside finance and capital markets. What do you think are the most sensible use cases for blockchain adoption and why?

Ian: If you want to apply an acid test to whether a use case needs a DLT, it is when the use case demands market-level accounting, in a situation with trust issues. This is clearly the case with a lot of financial use cases, such as payments, currency transactions, securities dealing, and asset management.

The financial use cases for DLTs are quite obvious, but the nonfinancial use cases that are appropriate for market-level accounting are only starting to emerge. There are supply-chain use cases, like cargo and shipping, that show the benefit in tracking information on goods moving across countries with many people in between. There are luxury goods manufacturers and pharmaceutical companies that are interested in DLTs as a way for their consumers to ascertain the authenticity of their high-value goods.

Some of the most exciting uses cases will come in the social sector, like disaster relief and humanitarian organizations, who really deal with disbursing and administering donor money toward specific purposes, such as refugee crises. DLTs will give them a very efficient infrastructure for disbursing money, with a clear line of sight from the top to the bottom, and a history of how the money got there. It will create a highly efficient system that lets these organizations concentrate on their missions, rather than on reporting to their donors.

Alexander: *Some governments and central banks are skeptical about cryptocurrencies, as they claim that they are unregulated — and therefore largely fall outside the control of nation-states. Many have also gone on to claim that the technology is built fundamentally for nefarious purposes — such as money laundering. Do you think that such notions have merits?*

Ian: While certainly bitcoin and other cryptocurrencies powered by blockchain have been used for purposes contrary to regulation and the public interest, the smartest governments and regulators know that they cannot turn back time — and that these technologies are here to stay. Decentralized systems have no single point of failure, so they cannot be shut down and are inherently difficult to control. Moreover, they are carried on the same infrastructure that carries the rest of the Internet, so largely the only way to shut them down will be to shut down access to the Internet itself.

The central question is not whether the technologies themselves can be destructive or constructive — all technologies can be both — but how we can shape intelligent regulations to enable meaningful innovations that maximize DLTs' benefits to the general public. Branding the technology itself as an enabler of illegal activity is a self-defeating notion.

The most sophisticated governments and organizations are already trying to get their arms around the specifics of the technology and what beneficial things it can be used for. Financial regulators such as FINMA in Switzerland, CSSF in Luxembourg, or MAS in Singapore are preparing informed, comprehensive guidelines that are designed to provide clarity to market actors on where they stand, in constructive ways that enable rather than stifle market innovations built on DLTs. They run technology pilots that enable fact-based, informed decision-making based on data, which is important in understanding the emerging implications of all technologies, not just DLTs.

Alexander: *Blockchains are very well suited as a foundation for smart contracts. Smart contracts allow the execution of credible transactions without intermediaries or third parties. How can smart contracts change the world?*

Ian: While there is a lot of excitement and hype around smart contracts, it is important to note that they are essentially pieces of computer programs that execute pretty much in the way that computer code operates right now: "If this ..., then do that" is the way that smart contracts work. It is really a way of using computers to perform commands and actions that are sequential and routine. And code helps to get things done by automating what was previously routine.

What is different about DLTs is that every actor in the system who has a node has the information of the whole system packed into the blockchain, and there is one objective version of reality that is updated in real time. Combine this market-level accounting with the capabilities of "If this ..., then do that" that is enabled by computer code; it opens up a whole new world of possibilities in potential efficiencies and automation of routine activity.

Automation of processes also comes with a number of risks, many of which are possibly not considered by the programmers who are writing the code. We have already seen, for example, self-driving cars that behave in strange ways or trading algorithms in financial markets that have been blamed for flash crashes so fast that human beings cannot react. The consequences of such failures are quite severe and visible.

Smart contracts are an extension of what digitalization is already doing in many industries: driving productivity, creating efficiencies, and freeing up labor, hopefully for more meaningful things. What this will mean will really depend on the context of specific industries.

I would love to see time in mission-driven and third-sector organizations being freed up to pursue the humanistic and personal side of their missions, rather than be bogged down with endless piles of administration, payments, and reporting. This is something smart contracts have a great potential to automate.

Alexander: *Many people in developing countries do not have their own bank accounts, as the costs of banking are relatively high. How could financial inclusion benefit from the blockchain and smart contracts?*

Ian: Traditional capitalism at a global level was never designed to be a fair system, and many people in developing countries are penalized multiple times over. Nearly a third to half the world's population lives in developing countries with per-capita incomes of under US$2 a day. They are largely ignored as consumers, or workers.

The existence of blockchain and smart contracts isn't magically going to give the world's poor an identity, access to the global financial system (including credit), or instant inclusion in the global economy. Nevertheless, the existence of such technologies further drives the cost for entrepreneurs (and some enlightened banks) trying to reduce the costs of provision of financial services. The remittance market, for example, is one source of financing for economic development, and workers who work abroad and send money home are often circumstantially forced to surrender a large percentage of their earnings to intermediaries. This is part of the financial services industry that is clearly ripe for disruption, and a blockchain and smart contracts infrastructure has the potential to do that disrupting.

Alexander: What is your idea about a completely decentralized society? Can humanity organize itself entirely on blockchain and smart contracts?

Ian: Blockchain and DLTs have the potential to lower transaction and delivery costs in many spheres of human activity, not just economic and financial ones. There are also many experiments underway to enable voting on blockchain and DLTs, for example. A lower cost of voting, enabled by the Internet, allows more people in physically disparate geographies to vote on issues of common interest, in a process that more closely resembles "direct democracy" (as popularized in Switzerland). Consistent with the developments in technology and ecommerce, reduced transaction costs are going to enable a new long tail of issues that increasingly large numbers of people can vote on and engage in, simply because they're interested in them. It will enable mass engagement like never before.

Alexander: What types of professional roles will we see evolve alongside the development and increasing use of blockchain technology?

Ian: In such a technology-intensive field, technical professions such as developers of all sorts (frontend, backend, smart contracts, and so on), along with related professions such as interaction design, UI/UX, and digital marketing, are well placed to immediately benefit from increasing adoption.

Less apparent, yet still coming ironically in a disintermediated world promised by DLTs, is a process I call *re-intermediation.* Traditional financial intermediaries such as accountants, lawyers, investment bankers, and asset managers have all served their own discrete functions in traditional financial markets; as the world shifts increasingly to a DLT infrastructure, many of these functions still need to be performed, except in a DLT-enabled context.

A tangible example of this you already see in the world of regulation — blockchain-enabled business models such as tokens and stablecoins are forcing fundamental first-principles questions like, "Is this token a security or a commodities contract?" the answer to which is material to rules and regulations. This has been a major boon to forward-looking legal professionals who understand the existing laws in their own countries, but also the laws in other countries in the world. "Blockchains don't respect borders," the saying goes, and suddenly regulators and government officials find themselves having to compete with each other or risk having the best projects move elsewhere, not a position they are used to. Moreover, almost every blockchain-focused company is somewhat global from birth.

There will be a major wave of reinvention of the roles of existing intermediaries, possibly even in the creation of entirely new ones. For example, Chainanalysis is a company that offers compliance as a service. It specializes in analyzing data on the blockchain to assist in investigations of suspected illegal activity. This is just the tip of the iceberg in a whole new wave of companies that the move to DLT will enable.

Alexander: Which advice can you give companies that are at a very early stage with applying blockchain technology?

Ian: With decentralization, we are right in the midst of one of the most interesting political and social experiments enabled by technology, and to quote one of Peter Drucker's most famous lines, "the best way to predict the future is to create it."

The most successful experiments will be implemented in small niche corners of the market or in small niche markets that have never existed before. This is a technology that is really about market-level accounting, and it is a massive change-management exercise to try to convince large numbers of people to use and input data into a DLT, if there is an existing infrastructure that is already functional. The most successful DLT use cases will be grown organically in niche markets where, in the words of Clayton Christiansen, "the new entrant competes against non-competition" — servicing customers who are happy to use a new a product or one that is perceived to be inferior, because the alternative to using it is nothing at all. At Ekofolio, we certainly think that forests, nature-backed assets, and natural capital qualify as such, as a vast majority of investors have not been able to invest in assets such as forests up till now.

Alexander: Thank you, Ian. What quick-win advice would you give that is easy for many companies to apply within their digital strategies?

Ian: Ask yourself, "Which part of the activity in your current firm would benefit most from market-level accounting, and why?"

Alexander: What are your favorite apps, tools, or software that you can't live without?

Ian: I probably spend a little too much time on Facebook. Nevertheless, I have a very careful and curated list of friends who show up on my news feed, which ensures a fairly continuous stream of intelligent, engaging, and timely content — and I try to do my fair share.

Instead of looking for the next big thing in digital platforms, the best thing is the age-old dictum "choose your friends (posts) wisely." This is fairly true of all social media channels — your information diet is probably as important as your food diet. Simply, don't let garbage in. This is not to say don't listen to opposing views from your own — it's extremely important to stay grounded and balanced in the world, with people who are as different from you as possible. But most people know when others post a constant stream of garbage. Be merciless.

Alexander: Do you have a smart productivity hack or work-related shortcut?

Ian: A well-curated social media feed is a great enabler for professional and social life. As far as possible, don't leave it to chance.

Alexander: What is the best advice you have ever received?

Ian: I went to an old mentor of mine when I was a young, fresh graduate starting my career and asked him what he thought was the best career path for me. He refused to answer my question directly, but instead asked me two questions in return. The first question was "Ian, what would you do for no money at all? Simply because it was worth doing?"

"Erhmmmmm ....," I stumbled, a bit stunned. I thought a while and then blurted out my first impulse. "OK, that's nice that you know that. Now ... how do you make money out of that?," the mentor followed up.

Key Takeaways

- The new divide in the era of technology is between knowledge workers and service workers. As illustrated by the example of nursing and healthcare — this tends to be a continuum rather than a hard divide, though the gross simplification is that knowledge workers work with their brains, while service workers work with their hands.
- Decentralized really means that no single actor is in charge, because it is running on many computers all at once. This is really done for resilience; the system has no single point of failure. Yet, all these computers would generate a single version of truth, which is data packed into blocks in the form of a chain.

- The third-generation blockchains are increasingly being built on fundamentally different mechanisms for ensuring scarcity, packing information, and overall securing the network. These include POS and what are known as other consensus algorithms, which are far more scalable and energy efficient to run, whilst achieving better results for the network.

Endnote

i   Nakamoto, Satoshi, "Bitcoin: A Peer-to-Peer Electronic Cash System," May 24, 2009, bitcoin.org/bitcoin.pdf.

Chapter 26
Sofie Blakstad:
Blockchain as a Critical
Enabler Toward
the Ecosystem Economy

Sofie Blakstad, CEO and cofounder, hiveonline
Source: CARTIER

Sofie is CEO and cofounder of hiveonline, the community-finance platform building better economies for African entrepreneurs. Sofie spent nearly 30 years in international banking, delivering technology, infrastructure, and business transformation in eight global banks, before setting up hiveonline. She has a MSc in informatics and is the author of two books, including *Fintech Revolution: Universal Inclusion in the New Financial Ecosystem*, and several research papers, including "Blockchain: Gateway for Sustainability Linked Bonds"[i] and "The Next Generation Humanitarian Distributed Platform."[ii] Sofie chairs the Edinburgh Futures Institute's Fintech and FS Industry Advisory Board and advises the UN, central banks, and international governmental groups on sustainable applications of fintech. Sofie is a Cartier Women's Initiative Fellow and recipient of several awards, including Innovate Finance's Women in Fintech Powerlist and *The FinTech Times*' 10 Women Rising Stars in Crypto.

Alexander: *You are CEO at hiveonline. What is your mission?*

Sofie: Our mission is to build better economies for communities of entrepreneurs who have been left behind. Most of the world's entrepreneurs — 350 million of the 450 million small, micro-, and nano- businesses — don't have access to formal financial services, and they're the most vulnerable to exploitation, climate change, and the impact of conflict. We're working across sub-Saharan Africa with rural communities to help them improve their business outcomes and financial resilience through our platform, which both helps them get access to formal finance and helps them manage their businesses better through making agricultural inputs more affordable.

Alexander: *How should business models evolve to survive and thrive in an increasingly digital world?*

Sofie: It's all about the ecosystem. We believe that no one organization can do everything well, and we rely on partnerships to support the things our communities need but we're not the best at. Conversely, we are experienced in building international financial systems and businesses, while many of the partners we work with have been trying to build financial solutions, which is not core to their skillset. Many organizations, especially banks, have tried to keep everything in house for far too long, with the result that there's a lot of duplication in the industry, and many things are not done well, in different ways, in many organizations. KYC (know your customer or know your client) is a great example — most banks used to spend a lot of money on KYC, and there was no standardized approach; now niche businesses are specializing in KYC and doing it well, which creates efficiencies.

We also believe that locking in customers is counterproductive; if you give customers choice, they can use your service *and* another service, so you should be able to collaborate with your competitors. Unless your offering is identical to that of your competitors, there will be things that each of you can benefit from offering your customers. For example, we are partnering with mobile money (MM) providers — that looks counterintuitive, as we also provide mobile payments, but the MM providers offer services we don't, like paying utility bills. Meanwhile, we offer more community-focused services, which can benefit the MM providers, such as identifying where cooperatives are going to need access to money transfers, as well. Ultimately, the customer will choose to use the services they need, and if you give them options, they're more likely to keep coming back.

Alexander: *How can technology shift the roles and responsibilities of the workforce?*

Sofie: Looking forward, technology has obvious benefits like making things more efficient, although it also moves investment away from traditional business skills toward technical expertise, either in house or through vendors. So it can reduce the need for skilled people in certain areas but at the same time create jobs in other skill areas. We see this with every industrial revolution, and it creates pain for some people while benefiting others. It allows professional workers to work remotely, but, as we're seeing in the midst of the pandemic, the people who are the worst paid are also those least able to work remotely. So there's a risk of technology contributing to increasing inequality.

Another key change that's being driven by technology platforms at the moment is the move to the gig economy, where many more people who are not formally employed by an organization provide core services. Again, this can benefit people who may not otherwise be able to commercialize their skills, such as people caring for children or elderly relatives, or those in developing economies, but some extractive business models end up harming more people than they benefit. Uber is a great example; they recruit drivers by quoting relatively high fares and then drop the price to eliminate the competition. In Kenya, that's had a devastating effect on drivers, many of whom have taken out loans to buy their cars, which are now being repossessed, and they're unable to meet basic expenses on what they earn driving. The gig economy model allows platforms to profit from people's activities without taking responsibility for their employment, so it shifts the burden of employee protection onto the state, and no country has yet figured out how to respond to this.

On the plus side, it allows teams like hiveonline, based in Rwanda and the Nordics, to collaborate across continents, regularly meeting and collaborating through shared files and collaboration tools. I've been managing teams using collaboration tools for 20 years now, and this is one of the most positive features of technology in the workplace. It means I can select the best people for my team, wherever they are in the world. The main challenge for managing these teams is maintaining a strong team culture and keeping everyone engaged, so we have evolved social activities as well, which replace the going-to-the-pub culture you have in face-to-face workplaces. The advantage of this is that we've been able to maintain our social activities during COVID, and it's been relatively easy for us to adapt to the new normal.

We now also have blockchain, which allows us to work collaboratively with people we don't know and trust, which I think is the next really interesting technology-driven change we will see — the distributed economy. That's why we're using block-chain to help the African communities work with access services from remote providers. For example, the farmers we're working with in Mozambique can't normally access credit from the banks because they are physically distant, and KYC would be prohibitively expensive, but with our blockchain solution, the bank in Nampula can see that the cooperative in Cabo Delgado is physically there, is commercially viable, and has a track record that shows how reliable the members are.

It's important for CEOs and other leaders to let go of some things, such as presenteeism and clockwatching, to focus on results and outputs, but also to be aware of the potential impacts that changing working patterns and responsibilities are having on people. It may seem counterintuitive, but the more digital you become, the more important it is to understand human dynamics and emotions and to proactively manage people as humans. It's necessary to identify alternative ways of motivating people who are working remotely. The daily commute may be a pain, but it gives people a sense of separation between life and work, which is lost when you're remote, and it's easy to lose focus without boundaries, unless you're motivated by things like sense of purpose and mastery. It becomes more important to give recognition to people for their achievements in front of their peers, for example.

The more digital you become, the more important it is to understand human dynamics and emotions and to proactively manage people as humans.

It's also critical to understand the impact not just on your employees but also on your supply chain — are you sourcing skills ethically? What is the impact your buying decisions will have on the environment? These questions are sometimes much harder to answer in today's ecosystem economy. For example, if I choose to source a designer on Fiverr, is she being paid adequately or is she being exploited? Is my blockchain extractive or does it use less energy than traditional transactions? (Answer for hiveonline: the latter.)

Alexander: *Which technology or digital capabilities are essential for a digital strategy?*

Sofie: Digitization is an enabler, and the key to successful strategy starts with a clear vision that can be translated into measurable objectives for your business, which have to start and end with the customer. However, there are some key technologies that will facilitate transformational change in how we do business, making things better for the customer and for the business.

Blockchain is a critical enabler toward the ecosystem economy. It allows the creation of trusted, indelible records that can be shared with anyone to validate a huge variety of data points — certifications, identity, vaccinations, credit history, bills of lading, solar energy production, organic crop spraying, you name it. It's actually quite difficult to visualize how great the potential impact of this is on how we do business, largely because the use cases so far haven't really shaken things up as much as they will.

Businesses today are still using blockchain to automate processes and reduce costs, rather than fully reshaping how businesses operate, and that's because it's being used within existing business structures. Someone like Unilever or Walmart employs a blockchain provenance service to track goods through the value chain from the tea farm to the store. That's impressive, but it doesn't really mean anything to the consumer yet, because from the consumer perspective they're still going to the store to buy tea. It may give the farmer more upside and help them send their kids to school, but the farmer isn't operating the system, so the impact, while important to them, isn't obviously linked to the technology.

Where this will go next is much more interesting. Consider another couple of use cases that are already happening — there's an NGO called PolloPollo, which is helping people make direct donations via shops in Venezuela to people in need. They send crypto, in exchange for a picture of the beneficiary with the goods that the merchant is giving them in exchange for the value, so donors can see their money being spent in real time. That's a real-life example of how smart contracts can work, peer to peer, between the merchant and the donor, without the need for an intermediary like a traditional NGO, who typically hemorrhages cash moving money from donors to beneficiaries. At hiveonline, we're working with farming cooperatives to give farmers more security, building on the data and commitments we've captured on the blockchain, to help them sell portions of their future harvest — and helping the processors access capital based on the same data.

Imagine a future where, when you purchase an item, some of that purchase price goes directly to the farmer, to the shipper, and to the processor, while you can see exactly who produced it and the impact your purchase makes to them, along with information about how ethically it has been produced. It will take huge amounts of inefficiency out of logistics management and reduce opportunities for corruption. It could accelerate the trend away from huge out-of-town retail stores to smaller local outlets.

It's not just about retail. The impact on how businesses are financed and how we manage our money is also huge — not in the sense of get-rich-quick crypto investment, but the ability to issue different types of security and expressions of value. We can now fractionalize a company's debt or equity to units of any size — say EUR 1, thanks to smart-contract technology — which opens the possibility for investing in bonds or shares to ordinary savers, and for small investors to invest in developing economies with trace-ability, so they can have confidence that the money is going to the right place and see the impact. This use case is going to have the most impact on businesses in countries where investment has been difficult because of underdeveloped capital markets and because of historical challenges with corruption. These are the countries, mostly at the leading edge of the fight against the impact of climate change, that need investment the most. I am confident that through technology like ours, people will be able to invest in producer communities and alternative energy more efficiently.

Central bank digital currencies (CBDCs) and privately issued stablecoins[iii] will also shake up capital markets. Today a significant portion of a country's national money supply is needed to manage the settlement gap for securities or left in balance sheets overnight. With instant settlement and the ability to make money work for even small businesses, which can't afford big-bank cash management, the need for that extra float will reduce and eventually disappear, so central banks will need to adjust their money supplies. There is also the opportunity to issue more efficient payments of benefits, even to people without a bank account, in central bank currency. On the downside, these currencies could also increase the use of substitute currencies in countries where native currencies are illiquid or subject to high inflation, so there's likely to be a gradual migration to multiple currencies and eventually more bloc currencies as well. But that's a big subject!

Blockchain also enables us to realize value from assets that we couldn't necessarily monetize previously. We're already digitizing social bonds to help communities access capital, and I've mentioned about selling futures in crops. There are other projects already helping people to realize the value of assets like social and natural capital using this technology, and while you're not yet using cowCoin or treeCoin to buy a pint of milk, we are seeing a growing number of privately issued stablecoins, and it's logical to assume that these alternative currencies will become more widely used in the future. You can already use your air miles for various travel-related purchases (and more), but that's a closed-loop system. Something I hope to see is value based on social capital embedded in big corporations' balance sheets, as a demonstration of ethical behavior to consumers and benefiting producers in their value chains.

I'm biased toward blockchain, but there are other key technologies that are transformational already. The Internet of Things (IoT), everything from the humble RFID tag and barcode to near-earth satellites monitoring vegetation coverage and weather, not only provides the link to the physical world for technologies like blockchain, but is giving us richer data than ever, enabling us to model and learn from new levels of detail, especially in countries where sensor coverage has traditionally been sparse.

The other critical but not sexy technology is the application programming interface, or API, which is an interface between different systems or subsystems that can call or pass information from one to the other. That may sound basic but is fundamental to enabling the ecosystem economy. For example, the API to M-Pesa, the African mobile-money service, has allowed hundreds of applications to integrate with it, without their designers having to know anything about M-Pesa's internal design.

Alexander: *Blockchain was invented by a person (or group) using the name Satoshi Nakamoto in 2008 to serve as the public transaction ledger of the cryptocurrency Bitcoin. What are the most important findings resulting from the operation of this large blockchain?*

Sofie: The most interesting findings are behavioral and economic, because Bitcoin[iv] was the first of its kind — a way of storing and moving value without an intermediary. There are many other really interesting features, such as the way it's created and the inherent resiliency of distributed ledgers.

One of the key lessons is that Bitcoin could never have seriously been intended to be a payment instrument. It's too slow and too computationally expensive, but more importantly, the supply is capped at 21 million, so even with its high value at today's rates there's not enough of it to be useful as a global currency.

The other notorious issue with Bitcoin is that, like other proof-of-work–based blockchains, it guzzles power and is disproportionately mined in places where power is largely based on fossil fuels, so it's bad for the planet. Defenders will point to printing money also being bad for the planet, which is true, but now that alternative proofs are available, I don't think there's a defense for this.

Alexander: *So, do we see the first-mover effect here?*

Sofie: Definitely. Like others in this space, Bitcoin does hold a special interest for me. It was the first and the most well known, and it really did prove most of what it set out to do (except for the bit about being a payment instrument). The design is transformational, and although it's not the earliest description of a distributed ledger, it's the first one to really find a niche. I think it's likely to survive, regardless of what else comes along, because of what it represents. It's also, as a first mover, got the advantage of familiarity, so people (mostly) know what they're dealing with now. We've seen how the value goes up when confidence in national economies wanes, which is a behavior associated with alternative stores of value, such as gold, as old as economies. So yes, it has the advantage of being a first mover, despite all the challenges, and it's likely to be around for a long time.

Alexander: How can these shortcomings of the bitcoin block-chain, such as the high energy consumption or privacy concerns of the public ledger, be overcome?

Sofie: The answer is newer types of DLT protocols, including different consensus protocols and approaches to security. We now have a large number of alternatives including proof of stake (PoS), proof of authority (PoA), and many others. There's a trade-off between stability, security, and decentralization inherent in DLTs, and a proof-of-work blockchain is the only truly decentralized approach that anyone has come up with so far. However, other public blockchains achieve a high degree of decentralization with these alternative protocols, combined with security approaches such as federated Byzantine fault tolerance. We're using Stellar, which uses the latter approach with PoS, meaning that it runs slices of protocol on different nodes, making it fast and cheap to use.

Alternative DLTs that are not blockchains, such as directed acy-clic graphs (DAGs), are likely to be the future; instead of chaining blocks, they chain individual transactions, sometimes in multiple threads, making them much faster. Stellar has a throughput poten-tial of about 4,000 transactions per second — more than enough for a global payments network, compared to Visa's c. 7,000 — but Hedera Hashgraph is a DAG with a potential throughput of 250k/s, which further speeds up as the network grows. That may seem excessive, but if we consider that DLT can be used for many types of data beside payments, and the fact that around 80 percent of pay-ments today are still in cash, there's a lot of opportunity for growth. DLT is also likely to increase the volume of micropayments because it can facilitate them. For example, you couldn't use a traditional payment rail to pay 5 cents every time you streamed a tune, because the payment would cost more than the value. However, if this was built into an on-demand streaming service, you might well choose that model above a subscription model, especially if it gave you access to a wider range of artists, all of whom are benefiting from each stream.

Going back to Bitcoin, another obvious way to address the energy use is to make processors more efficient and of course to use clean energy in the first place. Energy usage is an issue because we have limited supply and because it's still largely based on carbon fuels, but a wholly solar mining rig would have a much lower impact on the planet.

There have also been a lot of technologies built over PoW block-chains, such as all the sidechains of Ethereum, which reduce the number of transactions needed on Ethereum's core mainchain[v] (the underlying network) and therefore the environmental impact, throughput issues, and cost. However, with the rise of the decentralized finance (DeFi)[vi] movement, we've seen that these have limitations, and mainchain can easily become congested, pushing gas fees up and restricting access. So while I could see a future where Bitcoin is cleaner, the throughput challenges need to be addressed through alternative protocols.

Alexander: *What are your thoughts about the privacy concerns of the public ledger? Why is this not subsequently implemented for the already existing bitcoin blockchain?*

Sofie: Blockchain is designed to protect anonymity; that's the point (although my friends at Chainanlysis have some nifty tools for tracing criminals using blockchain anonymity). Yes, the balances and transactions are visible, but you can't associate them with an individual because of that anonymity, and it's possible to mask your IP address if you're particularly sensitive. So unless what you're doing is likely to attract the interest of the police, it's unlikely to be an issue for you. In private blockchains you may be able to identify the individuals, but you have to be authorized to join anyway. The rest is about design.

The security problem of data on blockchain isn't about the technology; it's because literally anyone can build on it. You can't just plug into the SWIFT network without authorization and being a licensed institution of some kind; there are controls and regulations. But literally anyone with access to a computer — or even a phone — can build a blockchain application. When I hire someone to build a core banking system, they've been vetted by multiple people before I even see the CV, and I have to have very good evidence that they know what they're doing before I hire them. There is a whole risk and compliance department breathing down my neck and ensuring that I'm not introducing more risk into the bank, but all it takes for a blockchain application is one person who fancies having a go.

There are security and privacy issues with any data design; every system has security and data privacy risks. That's why, when you design a system, it's really important to be aware of what the risks are and to manage them effectively. The problems we've seen with blockchain are largely associated with the fact that the people who can build systems aren't necessarily the ones who understand, or even care about, consumer protection and how financial systems work. That has led to a lot of rookie errors. A big one is exchanges that store all their private keys in one place, which are vulnerable to hacking — this is effectively the same as a bank keeping all the customer data in the same place; any breach can access all the data at once, so you've lost the benefits of decentralization.

Another mistake is putting personal data unencrypted onto the blockchain. It's not always obvious what constitutes personal data, and even encrypted, there is a possibility of future technology being able to access it, such as quantum computing. So it's important that data is designed in such a way that personal information can't be exposed. What we're seeing at the moment with the DeFi movement is deeply concerning to me; while I'm sure a lot of them do know what they're doing, it's very hard for consumers to tell the difference between a product that's robust and secure and one that isn't. And without regulation, there are no checks and balances.

Alexander: There are new blockchains developed to overcome these shortcomings, such as Monero. Why is this not subsequently implemented for the already existing bitcoin blockchain?

Sofie: Given that blockchain is inherently anonymous and that Monero is notorious for being used for money laundering and illicit activities, it would be undesirable to adopt their approach. Monero's also proof of work. But the level of anonymity that Monero imposes is largely unnecessary in most use cases. Although the anonymity of blockchain is useful and enables parties to transact without having to trust each other, masking every detail of the transaction, including the (anonymized) sender and receiver and how much the transaction is worth, makes it less useful for most purposes. The only thing it's useful for is peer-to-peer payments.

Blockchains also don't randomly adopt other features because of governance and transaction history. The governance is managed either by the community, as in Bitcoin, or by a central body with input from the community, and any major change for a public blockchain usually requires a vote. Any change to the code not only has to be propagated across all the nodes, but also has to maintain the integrity of prior transactions, so the level of change that can be imposed can be limited. The much-anticipated Ethereum 2.0, which includes an introduction of proof-of-stake consensus protocol, has taken years to get to launch and even then is a new feature layer on top of the old Ethereum mainnet. There can be strong factional divides on any proposed changes, and while sometimes you may get one of these factions going off and building their own version (or fork) of the original chain, it's rare for a major change to be applied to an existing blockchain.

Alexander: *Some governments and central banks are skeptical about cryptocurrencies, as they are unregulated. For example, the money supply cannot be increased at will. What arguments can be used to dispel such reservations?*

Sofie: Central banks are learning fast. And it's not true that cryptocurrencies are unregulated; many regulators have classified them variously as securities and other instruments and, in some rare cases, outright banned them. Since Facebook announced its Libra (now Diem) project, central banks have also been stepping up their ongoing research into CBDCs, with China the first major nation to issue its own. Senegal had a go a while back, but it wasn't a success, while the Marshall Islands have one already and the Sand Dollar has been launched in the Bahamas. There is a complex sliding scale between what I would call a true cryptocurrency, that is, a cryptographic instrument created by the core chain which has a specific supply limit; token-based coins such as stablecoins, which are typically escrowed with a store of the fiat equivalent; or other representations of value, which may be backed by other collateral or not at all; and settlement or payment instruments issued by central banks, which are fully centralized with a controlled money supply, even if they are using the same technology.

Many regulators have also classified other types of tokens like security tokens (STOs), which can represent debt (bonds) or equity (shares) issued by companies or governments. Some have special rules for stablecoins, and there has been a significant growth in the level of knowledge in central banks over the last five years. The Bank of England has been authoring excellent research on the topic for many years now, and the German central bank, BaFin, was one of the first to authorize tokenized securities.

Stablecoins and CBDCs are likely to impact the money supply by unlocking capital otherwise held up in settlement periods and on balance sheets. For businesses they are also likely to offer very interesting opportunities for investment, cash management, and cross-border payments, which could reduce costs significantly. Central banks will be issuing these instruments; however, the structure and the technology will vary from country to country or bloc to bloc, depending on the government and central bank's relationship with the commercial banking sector, whether they're using it for purely commercial settlements or retail as well, and their choice of technology.

Alexander: Blockchains are very well suited as a foundation for smart contracts. Smart contracts allow the execution of credible transactions without third parties. How can smart contracts change the world?

Sofie: Smart contracts aren't just about transactions. They are mini-programs that execute when certain conditions are met, meaning that they can be used to automate a huge variety of processes — anything with data in that results in data out, in fact. For example, we move lumens (the Stellar coin) around inside our Savings Group app to record attendance — that's not a financial transaction, but it's a record of a commitment that has been met. Certifications are another obvious use case; once the certificate is on the blockchain, it can be accessed by anyone given the authority. In a supply chain, that could be to validate line-caught tuna or slavery-free diamonds, or it could be my nationality, a police check, or my yellow-fever certificate, so even if I'm a refugee and I've lost my little yellow book along with my passport, I can still enter your country.

They're going to change the world of shipping considerably, and there are already plenty of shipping examples out there, combatting the fortunes that are lost to fraud today. If your bill of lading is on the blockchain with confirmation of which bank has given you finance, you can't then send it to another five banks for financing, for example. Identity is another obvious area that should change considerably; in fact, Sierra Leone has already implemented a blockchain-based identity in partnership with Kiva.

Alexander: Many people in developing countries do not have their own bank accounts, as the costs of banking are relatively high. How could financial inclusion benefit from the blockchain and smart contracts?

Sofie: Financial inclusion is core to our model. We focus on sub-Saharan Africa because most people there are unbanked, especially in rural areas, and nearly all businesses are informal, without access to growth finance. Many business owners, especially women and farmers, can't access any form of credit and often have to decide between crop care or other inputs, which will increase profits, and essential items like food or medicine, meaning they're unable to build a better future, even if they're well aware of the benefits of investing in their crops and businesses.

We are using blockchain records to demonstrate to financial institutions that our customers are reliable, by recording micro-transactions and how well customers meet commitments to their groups — savings groups or cooperatives. That means we're digitizing trust and helping them to monetize social capital; this level of identity gives the financial institutions confidence, as well as reducing their cost of KYC, meaning they can reduce the cost of lending and pass that on to the customer. Working with supply chains, Unilever is also passing on the low cost of borrowing down the supply chain using blockchain, so farming communities can benefit from Unilever's own low costs, rather than paying high local borrowing costs.

We can also use it to move value around and to help people build a store of wealth. This means they can save money and make payments without the risks of cash, and over long distances, which is especially important in regions where there is active conflict. Financial institutions tend to move out where that's happening.

We've also seen cases where it's being used to drive down the cost of cross-border transactions and trade tariffs in Africa, helping small traders buy from foreign producers and pass on lower costs to customers. In other use cases, it's being used to help validate that microproducers, such as women coffee growers, are receiving a fair price for their produce and to trace produce through the value chain. We hope to establish a way of using it for validating organic production as well, soon, also benefiting the farmers, who can charge a premium for their organic crops.

Alexander: Also in developed countries, there are many people who do not have access to healthcare. How could smart contracts be used to make healthcare more affordable?

Sofie: I've mentioned vaccinations, and the same could apply to any medical record, to make information sharing between healthcare providers more efficient, as well as being used for monitoring — of both patients and prices.

In insurance-based healthcare systems there are also lots of opportunities to automate tasks and reduce mistakes, which could bring down the costs. However, digitization is not a panacea: in the United States, the reasons voters continue to support the most expensive healthcare system in the developed world, with the poorest outcomes, are social and political, and you can't fix that with blockchain.

Alexander: In the United States, Great Britain, and Germany, the concept of a national centralized server model of healthcare data, also known as electronic healthcare record (EHR), has been poorly received. Issues of privacy and security in such a model have been of concern. How could such concerns be addressed with a blockchain implementation?

Sofie: Most governments are poor at building integrated centralized databases; there have been so many examples of it being done badly, so it's not surprising people are resistant to the idea. In any system design, you need to ensure the data is held securely, is accessible to the right people and only the right people, and is accurate, high quality, and relevant.

Blockchain is part of a potential solution, because it can store certifications and other records in a decentralized way that protects the data from being compromised, but it's not a suitable solution for storing large amounts of data, such as you would find in medical notes, X-rays, and so on. It could provide the foundation for community-based record keeping where key data points are accessible and can be generalized and aggregated, while keeping personal data private. Some would need to be stored in traditional solutions such as cloud based. As with any system, the data is protected by how you design it. So you need to engage both healthcare professionals and technology providers to design something that meets the needs of the patients, the healthcare providers, and the government, rather than what is usually done, which is to outsource it to a provider who may lack relevant expertise, and without taking a user-centric approach.

Alexander: Do you also see new potential that brings health data on a blockchain, especially through the use of AI, for example, to fight pandemics?

Sofie: Many of the use cases I've discussed already, such as supply-chain management, traceability (of contacts), certification of vaccination, and so on, could be useful in this situation. Hiveonline's groups are able to meet virtually with confidence because they can see what's being done, even if they're not physically present in the same room, and our system is useful for voucher distribution and aid disbursement as well. One of the key advantages of using blockchain for track and trace would be that you can maintain anonymity and not give up your data to the government, but still have the ability to trace contacts.

Alexander: What is your idea about a completely decentralized society? Can humanity organize itself entirely on blockchain and smart contracts?

Sofie: People are social animals and need tribes to identify with; that's never going to be completely virtual, but what we are doing is helping to leverage those social bonds to benefit communities. There is a long way we can go toward the decentralized economy, especially in Africa, where there's not much to replace in terms of existing services. Helping these communities build their own solar grids or clinics, for example, is not taking anything away from central government, if there's no infrastructure there already.

However, it becomes problematic if communities never give anything back to central governments while they become independently wealthy and self-managing, because there will always be the need for national and international infrastructure and institutions. Knowledge is not advanced in a decentralized society without research institutions, arts, media, education, healthcare, and so on — however distributed — and the need for physical infrastructure and utilities is never going to disappear. An increasingly urbanized population cannot operate effectively in discrete community units, as people are multifaceted and rely on shared services and infrastructure. And we all need a sense of belonging — to our sports teams, our nationality, and so on. So while we are actively building the distributed economy, we see it as interacting with, rather than replacing, national economies. What we also hope to see through this activity, though, is a rebalancing of economic power so that the people who are feeding the rest of the population are not unfairly penalized because of their remoteness from urban areas.

Alexander: What types of professional roles will we see evolve alongside the development and increasing use of blockchain technology?

Sofie: I would hope to see, as we're beginning to see in Mozambique, increased professional development opportunities for people in rural areas of developing countries, where they are able to qualify via remote learning and apply skills such as healthcare, education, agricultural sciences, and so on, locally, rather than being faced with a choice of either moving to the city or remaining poor and uneducated. Along with opportunities offered by decentralized economies to rural populations in improving their existing activities, there should be a real opportunity for a growing rural professional middle class, which should create many other jobs supporting them, in areas such as technology, construction, retail, entertainment, media, sports, and so on.

As rural areas evolve the capacity to support more professionals and a growing middle class, it's also likely that some urban professionals will choose to move out — we're already seeing this to an extent with COVID, but I think the effect is likely to last and be further enabled by technologies including blockchain.

There's also likely to be a shift from some midrange professional skills to a larger demand for technical skills, along the same trajectory we have seen previously as roles are increasingly automated. That's just a product of continuous advances in technology, rather than of blockchain per se.

Alexander: Which advice can you give companies that are at a very early stage with applying blockchain technology?

Sofie: Talk to some experts before making a decision about whether to insource or outsource, what platform, and how to use the technology, just as I would for any other new technology. Start with a business problem, rather than looking for a blockchain solution to a problem you may not have. And don't choose a solution because everyone else is using it! In some sectors, there's been a follow-the-leader approach as one organization chooses a solution and everyone else copies them. That's not necessarily going to work for your business, and you don't even know that it worked for the first organization!

Also, if you're selecting a vendor to support you, avoid the big consultancies, who all have blockchain teams but are likely not to have the in-depth knowledge you need to ask and answer the questions you should be asking. There are a number of respectable and experienced blockchain development companies that have experience across a broad range of technologies in the area, and it's worth listening to them, even if you decide to develop in house.

Alexander: Thank you, Sofie. What quick-win advice would you give that is easy for many companies to apply within their digital strategies?

Sofie: Start with your business strategy, translate that into objectives, and identify the barriers to reaching those goals. That will help inform what you should be focusing on. And when you design, don't just design point solutions; think about your technology holistically, and as an ecosystem, which could be 90 to 100 percent composed of solutions that are already out there. Buy before you build.

Alexander: What are your favorite apps, tools, or software that you can't live without?

Sofie: I am someone who forgets a map the second I look away from it; Google Maps, combined with my phone mount on my bike, has changed my life. However, I don't recommend texting while cycling, unless you live in Copenhagen.

Alexander: Do you have a smart productivity hack or work-related shortcut?

Sofie: I run my life on collaboration tools; Google Workspace is great for getting things done by several people at once. I also run my shopping list in Google Sheets.

Alexander: What is the best advice you have ever received?

Sofie: Don't put pictures of your children on Facebook.

Key Takeaways

- Blockchain enables businesses to focus on what they do best and work with other actors whom they don't need to trust.
- A digital strategy has to start with your organization's business strategy, which starts and ends with the customer.
- Organizations, and society, are going to become more decentralized. Leaders need to treat people as humans, and understand the ethical and environmental impact of their businesses.
- The Bitcoin is interesting, but blockchain and DLT are so much more than Bitcoin.

Endnotes

i   www.sustainablefinance.hsbc.com/-/media/gbm/reports/
     sustainable-financing/blockchain-gateway-for-
     sustainability-linked-bonds.pdf.

ii   www.hivenetwork.online/blockchain-for-good/.

iii Stablecoins are cryptocurrencies designed to minimize the volatility of
     the price of the stablecoin, relative to some stable asset. A stablecoin can
     be pegged to fiat money, to exchange-traded commodities, or to other
     cryptocurrencies.

iv   Bitcoin, the cryptocurrency, is always capitalized; the bitcoin network is
     lowercase.

v   Mainchain is the live blockchain network of any blockchain, which in the
     case of Ethereum is the chain on which all the sidechains are based.

vi   Decentralized finance (DeFi) is a blockchain-based form of finance that
     does not rely on central financial intermediaries such as banks, brokerages,
     or exchanges to offer traditional financial instruments and instead utilizes
     smart contracts on blockchains, the most common being Ethereum.

Chapter 27
Sven Sommerfeld: Robotic Process Automation (RPA) and Hyper Automation Transform Today's Business

Sven Sommerfeld, CEO, ATCS Germany
Source: Eidens-Holl Fotostudio

Sven is the CEO of ATCS Germany, a subsidiary of ATCS Inc. ATCS is an IT service provider focusing on IT outsourcing and offshoring. Considered to be best in class for delivering IT services from India, ATCS focuses on the following areas:

- **Enterprise IT**: IT development, managed services, IT consulting, test management, and test automation
- **Digital**: Modernization, robotic process automation (RPA), cloud, mobile apps
- **Data and analytics**: Data science, data engineering, reporting, and visualization
- **Marketing tech and insights**: Digital marketing systems and operations, social listening and insights, marketing analytics

Sven and his team are working with customers who are looking for a partner who can drive their digital transformation by implementing digital solutions in a fast and agile way without diluting any quality or having to stretch their budgets.

After his studies Sven started as a software engineer with a liking for agile methods and a clear vision that digital transformation, and especially automation of processes, are key to success in the future for companies. Believing that being able to look at both the technical and business sides helps to create value for customers, Sven continued his path from a software engineer to a business consultant. After a stint in the United States, he is now heading the ATCS office in Stuttgart, working there with over 30 consultants and with over 800 highly qualified colleagues around the globe.

Alexander: You are CEO at ATCS Germany. What is your mission?

Sven: We are the speedboats between all the big tankers. And we are a big global family who makes sure that every member can thrive personally as well as professionally.

We believe that creating value in a modern world is possible only if you are fast, flexible, and a true agile partner in creating efficiencies by digitizing processes and automating tasks. This is possible only if you have engaged people in your company who believe in your culture and thrive by creating value for your customers.

Alexander: *How should business models evolve to survive and thrive in an increasingly digital world?*

Sven: The heart of each organization's business model will always be to create value for its customers. In today's world, this value is created by using digital technologies to make the life of your customers easier. In a B2B context this might be by creating efficiency gains through automation; in a B2C context this might be by creating convenience through a fully digital home.

Alexander: How can technology shift the roles and responsibilities of the workforce?

Sven: While technology is evolving, our jobs will evolve, too. Technology itself will not steal jobs; it rather is a boost for the current workforce, allowing it to take on more strategic and value-creation tasks. I am not saying that jobs done by human employees today do not deliver value, but if standardized tasks can be taken over by technology, human employees create more value at the same time by taking on higher-value tasks.

Alexander: Which technology or digital capabilities are essential for a digital strategy?

Sven: In a digital strategy today, there is no way around artificial intelligence (AI) and automation. RPA gives companies a fast way to automate standardized and mundane tasks to use their employees for higher-value tasks. If you combine AI and RPA, it is an extraordinarily strong combination, called *hyperautomation*, which can transform the way business is done today completely.

> *If you combine AI and RPA, it is an extraordinarily strong combination, called hyperautomation, which can transform the way business is done today completely.*

Alexander: *What is robotic process automation, and how does it work?*

Sven: RPA is basically using software bots to automate standardized tasks. While this has been done for quite some time already — we called it *scripting* in the past — with the RPA technology evolving it is now easier, faster than ever to create bots that have more functionality. In most frameworks you do not even need to know how to code. Using low-code or no-code approaches, you can basically record the tasks that the bot should do and then execute it.

To get started with RPA and create your first bot, I typically refer to the following framework:

- **Think in micro steps**: Small might even be too big to get things started. Think about microprocesses you want to automate. These are typically the best ways to get used to RPA and to create an immediate benefit. It's better to have a microprocess automated than to think about a big process automation and never get it done.
- **Take high-value processes**: Look for processes that run every day and so create a daily benefit, rather than targeting processes that run only once or twice a month.
- **Detail the process**: Describe the process in its detail down to a mouse click. This is required to implement the bot. Again, starting at a micro level with high-value processes gets you started quickly.
- **Define clear success measures**: In the end an RPA is successful only if there is a benefit for the employees and the company. So, define clear KPIs that show the benefit of the implementation.
- **Involve your employees**: When you talk about automation, most of your employees will fear job loss. The idea of RPA is not to replace employees, rather to give your employees the time to take on more meaningful and challenging work. Communicate to your employees the benefits of the automation and involve them in the decision-making.
- **Learn and repeat**: Take the lessons of your RPA implementations, document them, and tackle the next one with those lessons in mind. Be prepared to stop a process automation early if no clear benefit is in sight and look at the next process to create value.

Alexander: How can hyperautomation, the application of RPA and AI, transform today's business?

Sven: The way we typically think about RPA is as an automation of tasks where all the rules or the steps that have to be done are defined beforehand. This means that it is very difficult to react to exceptions to the predefined steps. AI brings in a way to intelligently react to what is happening and calculate the response to what is happening. Moreover, the more times something unexpected occurs, the better the automation gets as the AI model learns from it. While RPA typically relies on structured data, hyperautomation allows for interpreting unstructured data like written text and pictures. This will allow completely new use cases in order to automate more tasks, most of all more complex tasks, and hence create a bigger value.

Alexander: Which RPA use cases would you see as essential to contribute to any organization's digital strategy?

Sven: Well, it depends. Which RPA use cases are essential to an organization's digital strategy is reliant on the industry and other factors. In general, there are some use cases that almost always make sense to adopt:

- **Data migration/data exchange**: Every company has processes in place where data has to be migrated from one system to another. This data has to be modified, or the format has to be adapted for the data to be loaded. This is a burdensome and repetitive task that can be done by a bot.
- **Data verification**: Often in an enterprise, data of various kinds has to be verified. For example, if there are bonus payouts to employees or partners, the numbers have to be checked. Also, when onboarding new employees, all documents have to be checked, and in some countries a background check is performed. In the finance industry, know your customer is also such a process that requires a lot of manual checking of the customers' data. These are also processes that take a lot of time, are repetitive, and are always done in the same way. Hence, they are perfect for a bot.

- **Data entry**: Bots can be used to automate the data entry into CRM systems, for example. One use case here is the first-level support, which receives emails with questions or issues. These issues have to be tracked in a CRM or another system. While today a human employee reads the email and then enters the data in the CRM, mostly by copy and paste, a lot of time gets lost when no other customer can be served. RPA can help gather that data and actually can assign the case to the correct agent to be worked on.

These are just three examples, and in general all processes that are repetitive, that have high value, and that can be described fully should be targets for automation. When I look at a process, I typically try to put it in a 2 × 2 matrix where "Effort of implementation" is the y-axis and "Value to the company" is the x-axis (see Figure 27.1).

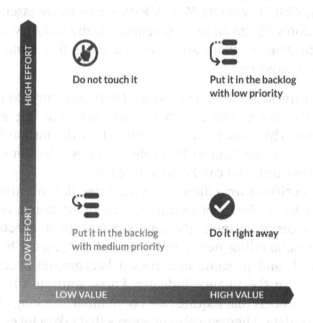

Figure 27.1   Effort of implementation and value to the company

Once I have categorized the use cases, I look at it like this:

- **High effort, low value**: Do not touch it.
- **High effort, high value**: Put it in the backlog with very low priority.
- **Low effort, low value**: Put it in the backlog with medium priority.
- **Low effort, high value**: Do it right away.

Typically, the low-effort, high-value use cases are small tasks and are everywhere. Do not aim too high in the beginning. Taking high-effort, high-value use cases might not lead you to a success story.

Alexander: How do RPA and data integration benefit from cloud computing?

Sven: Cloud computing brings some advantages to RPA, as typically when enterprises are moving to the cloud, data is more easily accessible. With moving to the cloud, enterprises typically adapt an API-based approach to their data and open doors to reusing prebuilt components from cloud providers like Azure, AWS, Google, and so on. This brings extensive benefits to RPA as prebuilt components like natural-language processing or predictive models, which are already available, can then be used and integrated easily. With RPA these models can be trained and then used later in the process to enhance the decision-making.

Alexander: How do you generate data-driven insights from RPA? Do you apply AI?

Sven: In general, RPA is just a static process that is put together and automated via a bot. This means that if there are dynamic changes in the process, the bot has to be adapted. AI can be used to change this. AI intelligence can be injected into the bot, and certain decisions can be made based on AI models. For example, decisions for a credit approval can be made based not on static rules but on dynamic rules generated out of past decisions. This way, new decisions will also be taken into account to make future decisions automatically and steer the bot. Another example would be to use RPA for doing warranty-claim approvals. With AI these decisions can be done close to 100 percent automatically based on the past decisions.

Alexander: *Is there a scenario where everyone can access and enhance RPA? Would low-code solutions help here?*

Sven: A self-service RPA will be crucial in the future, as RPA is business led and IT supported. This means that the main value creation is on the business side, and the changes are also typically coming from process changes on the business side. To react to these changes quickly, self-service is absolutely necessary. If you look at tools like UiPath, there are already pretty good tools for this.

Alexander: *What types of professional roles will we see evolve alongside the development and increasing use of RPA across the industries?*

Sven: In RPA I do see similar roles as we see in software development or data science. In general, the following roles will be evolving and will be established:

- **RPA analyst**: A good RPA analyst is the bridge between the business and the technology. As an RPA analyst you will help the business identify the use cases for automation, help the business specify it, and get it implemented.
- **RPA consultant**: As an RPA consultant you are very close to the role of an RPA analyst, with a bigger focus on high-level tasks. As an RPA consultant you will guide the business on which use cases to implement and which tools to use. Moreover, you will help IT decide which tools are best to use and emphasize the self-service functionality with the business.
- **RPA developer**: An RPA developer develops the RPA use cases in the designated tool. As a developer you will integrate several data sources and APIs to make the bot run and you will bring the requirements to life.
- **RPA data scientist**: As an RPA data scientist you are responsible for creating and integrating models that will be used by the bot. An RPA data scientist brings the brain into the RPA processes.
- **RPA architect**: As an RPA architect you are responsible to see that the architecture for your RPA applications is consistent, maintainable, and scalable.

Moreover, with scale and more and more automated use cases, an agile scaled framework is necessary, which comes with roles like product owner, scrum master, and so on. These will not be roles dedicated to RPA, though.

Alexander: *Do you see any challenges in using RPA in a company's digital strategy?*

Sven: There are several discussions stating that RPA can actually be a roadblock for digital transformation. The reason is that very often RPA is used to automate tasks done in legacy systems, as this is cheaper and faster than replacing these systems. Gartner also states this: "...[Companies] are turning to RPA solutions to automate an existing manual task or process, or automate the functionality of legacy systems."[i] While keeping legacy systems is not typical in digital transformation, RPA still helps to digitize processes or tasks, which may have not been possible before. It still helps human workers accomplish more in the same time as RPA digitizes their mundane and repetitive tasks. So, RPA has to be in every company's digital strategy, and it has to be used wisely. RPA will not be the panacea to solve all your digital transformation issues, but it can be a powerful tool.

Alexander: *How will RPA change over the next 10 years?*

Sven: The integration of AI into RPA will increase dramatically. Using AI models provided by cloud providers and the ease of integrating them into RPA using low code will change the way RPA is used. Moreover, it will not be IT professionals who will create the RPA models, it will be even more business led and IT supported than it is today. Also, the focus on the combination of RPA (task automation) and DPA (process automation) will be much stronger, as the benefits are tremendous.

Alexander: *Which are the key challenges you see that make RPA implementations fail?*

Sven: One of the biggest reasons I have seen for RPA implementations failing is the anxiety of automation: employees fear that automation will steal their jobs or parts of their jobs. This leads to projects where the obstacles set up by human employees become bigger than the chances to succeed in the project. There are strategies to get the buy-in of your employees. For example, create transparency on what automation actually means; give employees a clear view of what it means for them and how their jobs will change, but in a good way (more time for relevant tasks, more time for projects because your mundane tasks are done automatically). By the way, creating this transparency is a human-to-human task, which can never be taken over by a bot.

Another big obstacle is that RPA is seen as the holy grail, and companies want to start automating everything ASAP. This is a mistake. Choose your first automation targets wisely and start small, even micro. Everyone gets the biggest benefit by automating very small, high-frequency, heavily redundant, and mundane tasks. If you start small, the chances for success and acceptance are much higher than if you start with a big automation project that takes months or years to finalize and then potentially fails: think big, start small!

Alexander: *Thank you, Sven. What quick-win advice would you give that is easy for many companies to apply within their digital strategies?*

Sven: Get started. The best thing you can do is getting started. Also, do not overcomplicate your first automation; start micro and build on that. It is better to have a micro and repetitive task automated than no task automated.

Alexander: *What are your favorite apps, tools, or software that you can't live without?*

Sven: As I am a developer at heart, Notepad++ is still one of the key tools I am using. I think the introduction of Teams has made the biggest difference in my work life. This has changed the way we communicate and collaborate digitally in our company.

Alexander: *Do you have a smart productivity hack or work-related shortcut?*

Sven: One of the best things I have discovered is the "end meetings early" setting in Outlook. Especially in a COVID-19 environment, where working from a home office is the norm and typically calendars are packed with back-to-back meetings, this helps to organize the day better.

Alexander: *What is the best advice you have ever received?*

Sven: I always remember two pieces of advice. One was given by my current boss and mentor, Manish Krishnan, and the other by Professor Thomas DeLong of Harvard University.

The first one is actually a quote from Maya Angelou and Manish told me this very often, especially in the beginning of my career: "People will forget what you said, people will forget what you did, but people will never forget how you made them feel." Feelings are facts for people; never forget this.

The second one is also mentioned in Professor DeLong's book *Flying Without a Net*. Getting to know him at Harvard was a very good experience, and this bit of advice sticks in my head to this day: everyone tends to do the wrong thing well because it is the easy thing to do. Push yourself to do the right thing poorly, only then can you do the right thing well. Get out of your comfort zone and take some risk.

Key Takeaways

- Robotic process automation is basically using software bots to automate standardized tasks.
- Cloud technology brings extensive benefits to RPA, as pre-built components like natural-language processing or predictive models, which are already available, can then be used and integrated easily. With RPA these models can be trained and then used later in the process to enhance the decision-making.
- Using AI models provided by cloud providers and the ease of integrating them into RPA using low code will change the way RPA is used.
- RPA will not kill jobs; it will help improve them.

Endnote

i   Gartner, "Gartner Says Worldwide Spending on Robotic Process Automation Software to Reach $680 Million in 2018," November 13, 2018 (www.gartner.com/en/newsroom/press-releases/2018-11-13-gartner-says-worldwide-spending-on-robotic-process-automation-software-to-reach-680-million-in-2018).

Appendix
Reciprocity: Answering Some of My Own Questions

Alexander Loth, author (biography in the "About the Author" section)

I f you read some or even all interviews, you might have realized my habit of asking more practical questions toward the end of each interview. In return, many of the interviewees asked me at the end of the interview sessions, "How about you? What are your favorite apps, work-related hacks, and bits of advice?" So, here are my answers to those questions and one more.

In 10 Years, What Do I Think Our Work Will Look Like?

I am quite confident that the 2020s are a decade of drastic disruptive change. We already see that benchmarks from the past are not appreciated in today's economy. Production companies will focus less on traditional KPIs, such as units sold, and focus much more on market capitalization. Tesla, for example, is the most valuable car manufacturer today with a market capitalization of $750 billion, even though Tesla produced only 500,000 cars in 2020. Toyota, on the other side, produced 9.5 million cars in 2020, but its market capitalization is $213 billion. Instead of units sold, additional features are valued — and those new features rely almost entirely on software. Production companies will transform into software companies — or probably will not survive.

These unavoidable disruptions will also change the way we work. This is especially true for knowledge workers, and this is not *per se* a bad thing. By the end of the 2020s, we see that a lot of repetitive tasks disappeared. People do not copy data manually from one spreadsheet to another — and do not even create their own reports. Instead, the interesting insight is directly shown on the screen as it occurs. No worries; by 2030, the AI will know what is interesting and will deliver a selection of best next actions. Then it will be up to you to decide which action you choose. The AI will steadily improve by learning from your decisions — and can produce text, email replies, and even poetry[i] that sounds like it came from a human.

The increasing level of automation in nearly all areas will raise our productivity, as we need to spend less time achieving the same or even superior results. This will also improve our work–life balance. About 100 years ago, a six-day workweek was common. Then a five-day workweek was introduced because labor efficiency was increased by the industrial revolution. Now we are facing the 4th industrial revolution, which further increases efficiency. A four-day work week is not only feasible, but it will become inevitable to avoid layoffs.

The four-day workweek has already been tested by Microsoft in Japan.[ii] Even without any newly introduced automation, allowing employees to enjoy a three-day weekend, reducing the time spent in meetings by recommending a 30-minute limit, and encouraging remote communication boosted productivity by 40 percent (measured as *sales revenue per employee*). Increased productivity eliminates the need for cutting salaries.

In the next 10 years, we will also see many new blockchain applications, especially for public data such as land registration. This will save time and reduce costs for property transactions enormously, as it eliminates the need for intermediate agents. Also, the most prominent blockchain application, the bitcoin, will continue to grow in adoptions as a payment method[iii] and as a value store (an alternative to gold). Additionally, the blockchain will find wide adoption in machine-to-machine (M2M) communication. Autonomous cars will pay automatically for the use of infrastructure (tolls, electricity, and parking fees) and charge passengers if the car operates in taxi mode.

What Are My Favorite Apps, Tools, or Software That I Can't Live Without?

I use the note-taking application OneNote to organize information on virtually any device. I just love to take notes wherever I am on my iPhone by typing, using voice-to-text, or taking photos of whiteboards. Thanks to the flawless synchronization, I continue to work with these notes on my iPad and Surface Book. I also share some of my OneNote notebooks with colleagues on a project or team basis (as knowledge exchange) and other OneNote notebooks with family and friends (for example, to plan vacations and weekend trips).

I am also a big fan of Visual Studio Code. I use it for virtually everything that involves coding, including Python scripts, SQL statements, and interacting with GitHub repositories. Before I discovered Visual Studio Code, I used the terminal-based text editor Vim,[iv] which was my tool of choice during my research at CERN.[v]

Lastly, I spend a good portion of the day in front of screens. Therefore, I try to avoid screens at night and listen to podcasts, audio books on Audible, and book summaries on Blinkist. I also join conversations on the voice-based social app Clubhouse.

Do I Have a Smart Productivity Hack or Work-Related Shortcut?

Yes. The first productivity hack is remarkably simple, but highly effective: I turned off most notifications on my mobile devices, especially notifications from social media apps. This helps me to stay focused a lot.

The second is more an after-work-related strategy: I joined local Meetups to meet people with similar interests and exchange ideas. Some friends and I are also organizing the Frankfurt-based Data & AI Meetups,[vi] where up to 250 participants have met on a regular basis in various corporate and university locations. However, since pandemic restrictions were imposed, we switched to virtual events hosted on LinkedIn and moved the discussion to a dedicated Data & AI LinkedIn group.[vii]

My last recommendation is to categorize your tasks in three buckets:

- Important tasks that need to be done
- Routine tasks that are repeating or similar
- Negligible tasks that are not really important at all

Of course, we are going to focus on the important tasks in bucket 1. I would check if I (or someone else) can automate the routine tasks in bucket 2. Nowadays this is possible even without coding skills, using a low-code or no-code platform. If you have negligible tasks in bucket 3, I recommend asking yourself if these tasks are worth your time — or if these are just avoidable time wasters that you can ignore.

What Is the Best Advice I Have Ever Received?

"Make sure you're passionate about what you're doing and never stop learning," one of my mentors at CERN used to tell me. Even on my job interview he asked me, "Are you passionate about technology?" Before I could answer, he continued, "If not, get out now; otherwise, this job will beat you down." He is right. Passion for what you are doing will continue to drive you forward.

Passion also makes it much easier to stay in a continuous cycle of learning new things. "Never stop learning" is a necessary life strategy in general — especially in technology, as no field evolves faster than technology. The second you believe you have something perfected, it changes.

Key Takeaways

- The AI will steadily improve by learning from your decisions and offers you a selection of best next actions. You can focus on making important decisions while repetitive tasks will not allocate your time as the degree of automation will rapidly increase.
- Adopting a four-day workweek, limiting meetings to 30-minute, and encouraging remote communication, can boost productivity by 40 percent.
- While certain applications, such as note-taking software and low-code/no-code platforms can drastically improve your daily work routine, other applications can disrupt your workflow with notifications — turning them off could help you to stay focused.

Endnotes

i   Mishkin, Pamela, with help from GPT-3, "Nothing Breaks Like A.I. Heart," The Pudding, March, 2021 (pudding.cool/2021/03/love-and-ai/).

ii   Chappell, Bill, "4-Day Workweek Boosted Workers' Productivity By 40%, Microsoft Japan Says," National Public Radio, November 4, 2019 (www.npr.org/2019/11/04/776163853/microsoft-japan-says-4-day-workweek-boosted-workers-productivity-by-40).

iii Irrera, Anna, "Exclusive: PayPal launches crypto checkout service," Reuters, March 30, 2021 (www.reuters.com/article/us-crypto-currency-paypal-exclusive-idUSKBN2BM10N).

iv   Vim: en.wikipedia.org/wiki/Vim_(text_editor).

v   European Center for Nuclear Research, Geneva, Switzerland.

vi   Data & AI Meetups: www.meetup.com/de-DE/Frankfurt-Analytics/.

vii Data & AI LinkedIn group: www.linkedin.com/groups/8514577/.

Index

6sense, 204
80/20 rule, 129

A

Adobe Lightroom, 188
AGI (artificial general intelligence), 229,
    248–250, 263–264, 277,
    290–291
AI (artificial intelligence), 4, 51, 314
    accountability, 244
    biased models, 242
    data analysis and, 149, 161
    data integration, 131, 204, 226–227,
        260–261, 289–290
    data strategy and, 148–149
    digital maturity and, 15
    digital strategy and, 118, 131, 161,
        168, 172–173, 203, 226
    ethics, 245, 261, 271, 288
    explainable, 259–260
    financial sector, 185
    innovation management and, 270

interpretability, 241
IoT and, 315–316
legal issues, 245, 261, 271, 288
in mechanical engineering, 273
multiparty machine learning, 247
organizational readiness and, 15
pandemics and, 351
professional roles, 175, 228–229, 262,
    273–274, 289
project time required, 276
projects, 262–263
regulatory issues, 245, 261, 271, 288
responsible AI, 236–237
RPA (robotic process automation)
    and, 359–360, 363–364
skills development, 175–176,
    274–275, 289–290
training, 174, 226
transparency, 241
university courses, 276–277
Alexeev, Vladimir, 283–293
Allocadia, 195